# Chilly Billy

## The Evolution of a Circus Millionaire

By
William L. Slout

An Emeritus Enterprise Book
San Bernardino, California
2002

Copyright © 2002 by William L. Slout

All rights reserved.
No part of this book may be reproduced in any form
without the expressed written consent of the author.
Printed in the United States of America by Van Volumes, Ltd.

An Emeritus Enterprise Book
2995 Ladera Road
San Bernardino, California 92405

# INTRODUCTION

This is a story about William Washington Cole, a circus man from birth. It is not a complete biography by any means, but included are aspects of his heritage, his character and his style of management. Our study is confined to his sixteen years as proprietor of his solely owned circus, that grew from a modest beginning into one of the leading arenic organizations in the United States and earned for him the reputation of an astute and fearless tactician and a prudent financial manager. He never had a losing season during those years, which allowed him to accumulate a sizable amount of real estate, and which appears to have been acquired through cash, because there is nothing in the records of R. G. Dun & Co. to verify the use of credit. We terminate our study at the end of the 1886 season when he was barely forty years old. At this time he auctioned off his show property to replace James A. Bailey in the Barnum, Bailey & Hutchinson organization. This later phase of his professional career is being scrutinized by Judy Griffin and Stuart Hicks for inclusion in a book about James Hutchinson, inspired by the discovery of an invaluable cache of his correspondence with P. T. Barnum.

We are indebted to many people and groups of people who have been generously cooperative in assisting us in our research of Cole's activities. Our time spent in the Robert L. Parkinson Library and Research Center at the Circus World Museum in Baraboo, Wisconsin, was particularly fruitful. In addition to benefiting from its extensive collections, many of the illustrations herewith were reproduced from the bills, route books, and other advertising materials there. Fred Dahlinger, Jr., and his assistant Erin Foley extended their customary brand of hospitality and outstanding guidance that has become a hallmark of professionalism to circus researchers from the day Dahlinger took over the directorship of that institution.

The bulk of information about the Cole circus came from newspapers across the country contemporary to the visits made by the show. These were acquired through the interlibrary loan department at California State University, San Bernardino, and were made possible through the unselfish efforts of two lovely ladies, Lee Bayer and Annie Hopkins, to whom I bestow the greatest of thanks.

There were of course others who freely gave assistance, not the least being Stuart Thayer, Stuart Hicks and Judy Griffin, Michael D. Sporrer, Orin King, Steve Gossard, Greg Renoff, my wife Martha (who puts up with my eccentricities), and the many early explorers of the nineteenth century American circus, living and dead. To one and all I am very grateful.

William L. Slout

# I

William Washington Cole died of pneumonia at his winter residence in the Biltmore Hotel, Madison Avenue and Forty-third Street, New York City, at 9:00 p.m. Wednesday, March 10, 1915. His affliction was contracted during a recent visit to his summer home at White Stone, Long Island, and was followed by a ten-day illness. He passed away as quietly as he had lived.

"In the departure of this great soul the world has lost one of its grandest noblemen. A gentleman of wise foresight and mature conclusion. A fellow of infinite wisdom and most kindly discernment. A man always cool and calculating under the most trying circumstances, and to whom the accumulation of a fortune, which came liberally, made no difference in his manly character. Having known him intimately for more than one-third of a century, I can never recall a moment when I have seen him angry or excited, and, even though his patience might be taxed to the verge of distraction, he would remain as stoical as the sphinx and as positive as the Pole itself. A man of few words but endless thought, cradled in hardship but never spoiled by luxuries which he was later amply able to enjoy. Always turning a silent ear to evil reports and weighing every proposition like a philosopher. Often planning a campaign with well studied precision, and always on the safe side of defense with no retreat or compromise when once business war was waged."[1] These were the words of Louis E. Cooke, eulogizing a friend and employer of many years.

William Washington Cole

Cole's will was admitted to probate on March 19, 1915, in the Surrogate's Court of New York City. It revealed an estate that conservatively totaled around $5,000,000, which did not include his valuable New York real estate holdings. Such an amount made him the richest man the circus had produced up to that time. His widow, Margaret C. Cole, received the amount of $200,000, plus all of the household and personal effects—books, pictures, furniture, jewelry—and one-fourth of the large residuary estate.

Nor were charitable institutions neglected by him. A sum of $5,000 each was bequeathed to Actors' Fund of America, Charity Organization Society, New York Opthalmic Institute, and the Trinity Church of Paterson, New Jersey where his mother worshipped. The Presbyterian Hospital received the sum of $20,000, and $10,000 went to each of the following: the New York Association for the Improving the Condition of the Poor, the Madison Avenue Reformed Church, St. Vincent's Hospital, the Hospital Guild of the New York Medical College, and Bellevue Hospital. In addition, a host of relatives and friends was remembered.

Cole was born in 1847 on Houston Street, New York City, the son of contortionist William Cole and high school rider and wire-walker Mary Ann Cooke. He grew up in the close-knit world of the circus; and, although never a performer, represented a fourth generation of circus family.

His awareness of the business began at an early age, growing up as he did on various shows. In 1860, when he was a bare thirteen years of age, his mother joined the Orton Bros.' Circus; and it was there, while maturing into manhood, he encountered every phase of the company's activity—as ticket seller for the concert, spieler, layer-out, ringmaster, billposter, advance agent, and sideshow proprietor. He even ran a gambling device for himself called a "spindle and eight-die case," with which, George Conklin claims, he made a good deal of money.[2] From this classroom of experience, as a youthful circus proprietor he would at first emulate the Orton pattern of operation, then quickly adapt it to a model of his own and eventually become one of the leaders of his contemporaries.

Press agent Louis E. Cooke

To those who were not close, Cole was a man of unfathomable character. He retreated from public view, while denying personal glorification, even declining to have his portrait published. One year when his agent inserted his likeness in the advance courier, Cole immediately wrote the printers to have it replaced with other material. Indeed, at the time of his death the only photograph of him that could be found was one taken in New Orleans some forty years earlier.

George Conklin, who worked as Cole's animal trainer for several years, wrote that his employer looked the least like a showman of anyone in the business. He described him as "a tall, sad, scholarly-looking man," one who could be taken for a minister, but one desirous to remain unnoticed by the public. Unlike Adam Forepaugh, he never tended the front door, but left that to his mother and his uncle Henry. He gave orders to his men that if anyone asked for him they were to say they didn't know where he was.

He had a reputation of being close with his money, causing some of his employees to call him "the man with the brass collar." Yet his circus was known for having a democratic policy, viewed in the business as a "home show." Cole ate in the cook tent with the company, sitting at tables served alike for laborers and performers.

He was uncompromising in business, a man of deeds, not words. "He is a particularly closed-mouth man, not at all given to wind, brag, or bunkum," was the observation of press agent Charles H. Day.[3] This demeanor created a mystique of insensitivity and coldness, hence the appellation of "Chilly Billy." But to those who knew him intimately he was pictured as a man of quiet charm. Louis Cooke called him a showman with the blood of showmen, yet "the most modest and retiring of gentlemen."[4]

In 1883 the Des Moines *Iowa State Register* described him as a "smooth-shaven, slight-built man of about thirty-five years." It went on to say: "Very retiring in manner, Mr. Cole has shown the capacity for invention of W. W. Coup, as well as a facility for making money and keeping most of it hardly rivaled by generations of circus men. Des Moines people will recall that he had a large sum on deposit in Allen's bank when that institution closed its doors. Mr. Cole received a telegram announcing its loss [the] next day while he was eating dinner. He read it, tossed it to his chief of staff, and said, 'We'll have to work hard for awhile,' and finished his dinner with the utmost composure."[5]

Press agent Charles H. Day

"W. W. Cole possesses many of the qualities that made James A. Bailey a success," Charles Day wrote. "Mr. Cole is both a router and an advertiser."[6] As such he was illusive in his movements, always keeping his rivals guessing. "As a soldier, Cole would have been a Phil Sheridan or a Stonewall Jackson," J. M. Traber observed, "so difficult was it to put your finger on him or conjecture his plan of action."[7]

It was Cole's policy to constantly seek new territory. To be successful in this, he studied maps and acquainted himself with conditions of the areas and the progress of the new railroad construction within them. Louis Cooke has claimed that on more than one occasion a town would be contracted and billed before rails were fully laid so that the Cole circus could be the headmost in and reap the benefits of the novelty. It was the first show to travel over the Southern Pacific from Los Angeles to El Paso, and the first to use the Northern Pacific before it was even completed. The circus was moved to the West Coast four times, was routed across Canada as far as Halifax, Nova Scotia, and was transported to Australia and New Zealand.

Cole was a pioneer in the art of using great quantities of printer's ink in advertising a show. Circuses spent more for promotion than other items in their budget. Newspaper advertising was mandatory and the most inexpensive. Although at the start of the 1870s there were only 574 dailies in the country with a total circulation of 2.8 million, every community had a weekly paper of varying size that was adequate in preparing, even exciting, the citizenry for the troupe's arrival.

The use of illustrated posters was the most costly element and the most effective for creating an audience on show day. The billposters daubed the outside of buildings, fences, and other exterior structures. The lithographers hung panels and other sizes of paper in store windows and public places at vital locations. Because billboards as we know them did not exist in all but the largest cities, circuses had them constructed prior to each visitation.

Circus paper was measured by "sheets." A standard one-sheet was 28 by 42 inches, a half-sheet 28 by 21 inches. The size was based on the capacity of the machines that printed them. Any number of sheets were hung together at a single stand, depending on its available area for daubing.

Cole led his competitors in the use of paper, putting up as much as 100-sheet spreads to announce his attractions.

Although he was lavish in his billing practices and extravagant in the posting of large stands of paper, he was much more deliberate and closefisted in the use of news print. A general practice was to enter a single, modest advertisement several days in advance of arrival in a town, and perhaps another on circus day. Of course, this changed if he was facing opposition from a competing show; at such a time he would go all out, toe to toe, with his rival.

Like all good managers Cole was alert to the happenings in the competitive market. When he saw what was an outstanding attraction for others, he was quick to adopt it for his own use. Every year he had some feature to boom and, as a great believer in the use of circus paper, made the most of it. His pair of giants, the great elephant Samson, bicycle artists, a two ring format, electric lighting, and hippodrome races, all were hyped with immense spreads of lithos and gallons of ink. Surprisingly, he was frequently lauded by the press for exhibiting everything he advertised; yet in true circus tradition, common among all, there was unabashed exaggeration in the bills and press releases.[8]

His philosophy of management as revealed in a rare interview, was simple. When a reporter suggested that the circus business seemed risky, Cole's reply was: "Well, in one sense of the word it is, and yet should anyone be possessed of tact, good judgment and energy, there is no reason why he should not make a handsome fortune at the business. To do this everything must work like clockwork, for, as in a watch, should the slightest cog get out of order, there is a jar throughout the whole system. As in a good factory, every department must have its proper head, and then there is not likely to be any trouble.

"I used to think it was a good thing to drink occasionally, but, like Barnum, the Prince of Showmen, I have become a prohibitionist on a small scale. A man cannot drink whiskey and attend to his business, too; so I prohibit liquor drinking as far as possible among my employees, and drunkenness is punished by dismissal.

"The secret of success in the circus business, like that in most others, is, after gaining the knowledge of what you want to accomplish, to proceed economically, but fearlessly, and to work yourself, trusting as little as possible to subordinates."[9]

These precepts become clear as one follows Cole's career as an independent proprietor from 1871 through 1886. He continuously surrounded himself with able people with whom he had lengthy relationships. Al Richards, working in various assignments, was with him this entire time, as was Anson Van Zandt, gymnist and rider, and Young Leon and Miss Jessie Orton, former Orton Bros.' apprentices who grew into capable performers. Animal trainer George Conklin joined in 1873 and was an important member of the staff, and even followed Cole to the Barnum show in 1887. Clown Tom McIntyre arrived the same year and became a dependable equestrian director for the rest of Cole's management. And members of the advertising department were no exceptions. Along with Louis Cooke, one of the greatest agents of his day, were such stellar men as J. B. Gaylord, R. C. Campbell, William R. Hayden, and Alf Riel. Cole maintained the loyalty of them all.

He was careful in his selection of high-class performers but did not overload the program with them. By retaining a cadre of devoted people year after year, individuals took on responsibilities that otherwise would have required hiring extra help. In short, Cole was a prudent, thoughtful manager, not burdened by ambition nor susceptible to an over-active ego. He held his show to a manageable size, barely falling victim to the "enlargement craze." Unlike some of his competitors, he was content to remain a "one-train" operation. Through the use of short cages, allowing more to be carried by loading them crosswise on the flat cars, he sustained an adequate menagerie, yet limited transportation costs.

Two other concepts were useful in accumulating his wealth. By going into areas where few circuses had ventured—Texas, the far West, Canada and the South Seas—he was able to double his prices to $1.00 for general admission and 50¢ for reserved seats, concert and annex. Add to this, staying on the road from April to December for several of the seasons, his yearly income was increased accordingly.

Much of his success as a manager can be credited to his mother, to whom he had an unwavering devotion. One of his earliest memories dates to when the then Prince of Wales visited the United States, and while in New York City stayed at the Fifth Avenue Hotel at Broadway and Twenty-third Street. Mary Ann, a loyal Englishwoman, joined the crowd in front of the place and held her son aloft so he might see the future king of England as Prince Edward stood on the balcony of his residential suite. This gesture of dedication to her son would remain constant throughout her life and be of immeasurable influence for creating in him the special qualities that his successful career has shown him to possess.

Mary Ann was a strong-willed women who was well educated to the requirements of show life and the craft of surviving in it. She was born into a special circus family and carried the genes of its tradition. She braved the many pitfalls of working in a new country, where she learned American circus practices from its leading proprietors—Nathan and Seth Howes, L. B. Lent, John Tryon, Rockwell & Stone, and Rufus Welch. After the death of her husband, she faced the responsibility of becoming both mother and father to her then ten year old son.

Mary Ann Cole

According to Conklin, "She was here, there, and everywhere about the show," and tended to interfere with the duties of others. But when he complained about her feeding the animals without regard for what he had already given them, Cole replied, "Mr. Conklin, that's my mother, and she can do just as she wants to. Don't you pay any attention to it. If she puts hay in where you don't want it, why, as soon as she is gone have your men take it out. But whatever she wants to do let her do it. If she comes in and tells you to kill one of the animals you kill it, and I'll stand back of you."

"I did as he told me," Conklin wrote, "and Mrs. Cole and I later became the best of friends. She said to me once, 'Conklin, don't ever leave Will. As long as Will has a show you stay with him.' And I did."[10]

It is not happenstance that Cole did not marry until he was 38 years old—December 21, 1885. His bride was Miss Margaret Koble of Quincy, Illinois, a non-professional. And it was predictable that Mary Ann was not pleased with the union and did not reside with her son thereafter. But their long devotion to one another was not diminished.[11]

Mary Ann was a pillar of support throughout Cole's sixteen years of circus management. Her managerial talent probably exceeded her ability in the arena, for she had over thirty-five years of circus experience when her son opened his first show. Therefore, we strongly contend that her influence as his constant advisor and as a partner in his success has been too long ignored. Seth Howes once told Barnum that Cole's "mother governs him," and this was undoubtedly true.[12]

Mary Ann Cole died at her home in Paterson, New Jersey, on November 23, 1897, in her seventy-ninth year. Her brother, Thomas Edwin Cooke, also a resident of Paterson, preceded her by two weeks. She was buried in Brooklyn's Greenwood Cemetery beside the grave of her husband, William Cole. Her only son outlived her by eighteen years.

## II

William Washington Cole was heir to a circus tradition that can be dated back to the Eighteenth Century. His great-grandfather, old Thomas Cooke, was touring his show in the mid-1700s—a pioneer of tented exhibitions—pitching his portable theatre at the outskirts of markets and fairs in England and Scotland. As an outdoor showman, perhaps using acrobats, jugglers, and any variety of present day circus acts, he preceded Philip Astley, the so-called "father of the modern circus."

But it was Cole's grandfather, Thomas Taplin Cooke, who was the real progenitor of the Cooke name. Following his marriage to Mary Ann Thorpe on December 19, 1800, he fathered at least twelve children over the course of his career, and perhaps (it is said) as many as nineteen. His progeny produced more Cookes, most of them becoming circus performers; until by the turn of the century there were two hundred descendants of old Thomas Cooke spread over two continents.

Thomas Taplin was born at Warwick, England, in 1782. A man of great strength and endurance, he became a versatile performer, renowned for his Herculean feats, and for his leaping, horsemanship, and rope-walking. Strenuous training prepared him for adversities that were always intrinsic to traveling shows.

After succeeding his father as head of the Cooke circus, he took a troupe to Lisbon in 1816. On the return voyage the ship was nearly wrecked by a storm in the Bay of Biscay. Forty of his valuable horses were lost to the angry sea. Undaunted by this misfortune, Thomas Taplin acquired a fresh stud and then constructed wooden amphitheatres at Newcastle-on-Tyne, Sunderland, Hull and other places. Quite obviously, such distractions did not interfere with his progenic output.

Thomas Edwin was Thomas Taplin's eldest son. He made his debut at eighteen months old and in no time developed into an expert equestrian, wrestler, jumper and acrobat. As a rider, he was expected to rival his brothers but suffered injuries from being thrown out of a runaway carriage and never reached his potential. However, he assumed the proprietorship of the Cooke circus in 1838, and was for a time the "Barnum of England."[1]

William Cooke, the second son, was a rope-walker, gymnast, clown, and strong man. It has been claimed that during a performance in 1842 he stood erect on a tight-wire and revolved one hundred times. His Herculean might was displayed while hanging head downward and ankles strapped to a cable, as he held up a board bearing six children. In such a position, he could hold the girth of a horse beneath him and lift the animal from the ground. Eventually William gave up acrobatics to direct equestrian dramas and train performing animals and, later, to become a circus proprietor.

James Thorpe Cooke, the third son, was the principal rider for the Cooke circus and teacher of the juvenile members. He performed in the manner of Andrew Ducrow, the great British contemporary, enacting scenes on horseback under such titles as "Games of Zephyr," or "The Enchanter of China," as well as depicting numerous characters, including Shakespeare's Sir John Falstaff, Shylock, and the infamous King Richard III.[2]

And there was Henry, less talented but useful in a variety of minor activities that contributed to the success of the Cooke ensemble. He will appear later in our narrative as a continuing member of the W. W. Cole circus.

On September 8, 1836, Thomas Taplin Cooke left from Greenock, Scotland, with his entire company on the chartered ship *Roger Stewart* bound for New York City. During the voyage a granddaughter, named Oceana, was born, who was to mature into a tight-rope walker of international reputation.

The entourage arrived at the New York City harbor on November 20, numbering some forty members of the Cooke family—seven sons, five daughters, and a passel of grandchildren. One of those daughters, and of great importance to these pages, was Mary Ann Cole, barely eighteen years of age at this time.

There were one hundred and thirty people in all, including a circus band, servants and grooms, and a stud of thirty or forty of some of the finest horses ever imported to this date—some full-blooded Arabians and a number of small Burmese ponies. The troupe also included sons-in-law George Woolford and William Cole, clowns John Wells, Joseph Foster, and Robert Williams, rider Henry Needham, and administrative assistant J. H. Amherst.

Amherst, who served as Thomas Taplin's secretary, agent, and general director was an important member of the troupe. He was well known in London as an author, having dramatized several of Scott's novels. At Astley's Amphitheatre he wrote a number of hippodramas, and as an actor he performed *Alexander the Great* at Covent Garden. He has been described as a large, portly man of imposing personal appearance and polished manners, fluent in French, and a respected scholar. All of the advertising bills used for the circus were written by him. "They were really very amusing," wrote Durang, "a kind of equestrian libretto."[3]

Four days after arriving in New York Cooke opened an engagement at Vauxhall Garden, Broadway and Grand Street, where an army of carpenters, painters, and masons had been at work readying the building for the move in. Prices were set to cater to a select audience, with a $1.00 admission for the boxes and 50¢ for the pit. The programs introduced dramatic scenes on horseback and old English nursery tales represented by the children and their guardians, and many other little conceits of that kind. These entertainments were of a novel character, and pleased the respectable element of society, who made the arena quite a fashionable resort.

Cooke's stable of child actors, bred from his own pedigreed line like a kennel of blue-ribbon dogs, met a popular need. This was a period when the histrionics of prepubescents were all the rage. The nineteenth century infant prodigies performed a repertory of difficult characters requiring a mature virility. A public clamor to watch these children enact adult roles created a demand for theatre seats so great that many in attendance were injured in the fray.

Insipid hunger for such gimcrack was set ablaze by Master William Betty, the Young Roscius, but a lad of thirteen years when he made his London debut in 1804. His unmitigated success inspired the emergence of numerous imitators for the next half-century. And at this time Cooke's precocious youngsters, astride ponies, flailing into combat, and transforming the arena into a romantic illusion, carried the Master Betty farce to its fullest.

We learn something about the Vauxhall program from the New York *Commercial Advertiser* of early December. The popular horse spectacle, *The Bedouins of the Desert*, was presented, which included Master George Cooke on two dashing hunters, William and James Cooke as marble statues, Woolford in equestrian feats, and Mary Ann Cole as "The Amazon of the Sun." Mrs. Woolford and Henry Cooke performed on the double tight-rope as a pair of Spanish lovers, while clowns William Cole, John Wells, and Bobby Williams cavorted below. Then James Cooke dashed around on coursers as the "Courier of St. Petersburg." And there were innumerable other Cooke conceits, staged to electrify American audiences. "Of a verity," George Odell once remarked wryly, "There was danger of too many Cookes spoiling the Circus."[4]

The company performed there until mid-February to only fair business. It was then moved to the Bowery Theatre, under the new management of William Dinneford. Why? The *Spirit of the Times* suggested Vauxhall Garden was too far up town.[4] Then at the end of March, Cooke and his company moved again, this time to the National Theatre (formerly the Italian Opera House), under the auspices of James H. Hackett, where *St. George and the Dragon* was staged.[5]

It was a decided hit. The *Courier and Enquirer* acclaimed the equestrian exercises as ably managed, the scenery beautiful beyond precedent, the stage decorations splendidly assembled, dances and marches highly effective; in short, the over-all performance a credit to all concerned. The performance, it said, had elicited loud cheers and hearty applause from the audience.

In mid-April, the circus left for Boston. Horses and actors were placed in residence at the old Lion Theatre where the company went through a rotation of their arenic events until July 25. But all this appears to be a "treading of theatrical waters," while a new circus building was being erected in Philadelphia.

During the latter part of the season of 1837, Cooke, accompanied by J. H. Amherst, applied to Francis C. Wemyss, who held the lease of Philadelphia's Walnut Street Theatre, for permission to use it as a circus. An offer was tendered—three thousand dollars for three months, with a satisfactory security to be deposited in any Philadelphia bank desired by the stockholders, and with the understanding Cooke would leave the property at expiration of that time, and in the same condition as when he received it. Wemyss was favorable to the proposition, but the terms of his lease forbid him to sublet the theatre without the written permission of the board of directors, who in the end flatly refused to accede to the suggestion.

No other suitable arena was found in the city. The Arch and Chesnut Street Theatres, leased to Maywood & Pratt, were unavailable. No building for his temporary purposes was to be had, nor was there a usable site within the business section of the city. So Cooke constructed his own place, a building of stone and brick that seated some 2,000, called Cooke's Extensive Equestrian Establishment and New Arena.[6]

Thanks to the daily announcements in Philadelphia's *Public Ledger*, carefully composed from the plumed pen of J. H. Amherst, we are able to follow Cooke's visit to that city with considerable detail. They illustrate the amazing variety of the company's repertory and confirm its array of talent. The advertised listed events for the opening program is typical, although new acts were later included and others alternated, frequently with re-tailored descriptions to make them appear new: "The GREEK BOY on his Vaulting Pony—the PERSIAN STEED of 5000—MR. JAMES COOKE'S graceful Equestrian Act, entitled the GAMES OF ZEPHYR, and the PLAYFUL CUPIDS—The POLISH BROTHERS—The INFANT

ACTORS will represent a Comic Scene, entitled GULLIVER and the LILLIPUTIANS—Mrs. Cole on her fleet steed as LA BELLE ROSIER—William Cooke's DOUBLE LEAPING—Original Gymnastics, by Mr. Wells—The comic twin Ponies will sup with the clown—James Cooke's new act, EQUESTRIAN OF ALL WORK!—To conclude with a GRAND CORONATION BALL MASQUE."[7]

There were innumerable riding acts, scenic representations on horseback, gymnastics, leaping, pony races, entrée pageantries, pantomimes by the infant actors, living statues, trampoline feats, tight and slack rope dancing, etc. The atmospheric costumes and appointments suggested a variety of distant locales and exotic peoples—Bedouins of the desert, harem maidens, Roman antiquity, English country fetes and pastoral life, mythological kingdoms, the Orient, Tyrolean peasantry, etc.

The daily advertisements, which continued throughout the run, have instilled in us an admiration for the Cooke troupe. It was the epitome of family circus, with everyone contributing to the extent of their particular talents. The star performer was its leading rider, James Cooke, whose presence within each program was highly visible. His brother, William was next in prominence. But the entire company was a well balanced ensemble, with the various artist each getting an opportunity to shine and grow. Indeed we have the impression that this was a school as well as a performing group.

The Philadelphia run came to an end in late December. The company then departed for Baltimore early Friday morning of the 22$^{nd}$. It made its debut for the Chesapeake Bay audience at the Front Street Theatre, called by Durang "the most perfect amphitheatre in America for ring and stage performance blended," on December 28. The program was the same as in Philadelphia, with the titles of acts juggled by the creative Mr. Amherst to avoid an impression of repetition.[8]

The season went well for Cooke for about six weeks and then disaster struck. Between four and five o'clock on the morning of Saturday, February 3, 1838, the Front Street Theatre was discovered entirely engulfed in flames. By this time the fire had reached all parts of the building and its fury was seen bursting from every window and door.

A small fire had occurred during a performance of the *Mazeppa* on the previous night, when a part of the scenery was destroyed; but the flames were quickly extinguished by the stagehands. Or so it seemed. Cooke personally inspected the place before he left for the night. A thick layer of tanbark—a mixture of wood chips and sawdust—was used to cushion the stage for the horses; and although the cause of the greater conflagration, be it by accident, carelessness, or by the hand of an arsonist, is unknown, it was considered possible that Friday's fire, dormant but not completely extinguished, was the basis of the disaster.

In assessing the damage, no lives were lost. Two men who slept in the stable made their escape. There was a vacant lot on the north side of the building, which had prevented the flames from spreading in that direction. However, on the south side, separated by a narrow alley, was an old two-story brick structure, locally known as Gough's Mansion House. It was currently being used as a tavern. This was entirely burned along with some shacks in the rear.

The financial loss was great to both landlord and tenant. The theatre was insured for $3,000, about one-tenth of its worth. As for Cooke, with no insurance, he lost his entire circus, including the fine stud of forty-two horses, fancy ponies, trappings, and a wealth of equestrian wardrobe which he had brought from England; in all, an estimated value of $42,000. He was ruined. "The calamity thus experienced by Mr. Cooke and his family," the *American & Commercial Daily Advertiser* read, "has excited the most lively sympathy throughout the community in which their professional exertions had been the source of unqualified gratification."

Indeed, the tragedy aroused the sympathies of everyone. The good citizens of Baltimore issued a subscription for Cooke's relief. The Baltimore Holliday Street Theatre was opened for his benefit. Bacon's circus, a Baltimore rival, staged a charitable night on February 21. The proprietor also offered his stud of horses, but Cooke refused them. In Philadelphia, Wemyss immediately tendered him the use of the Walnut Street Theatre for a benefit on any night he chose to name. The proprietors of Fogg & Stickney's Amphitheatre in Cincinnati also gave him receipts of a performance. Thomas Hamblin of the Bowery, who had undergone a similar conflagration, presented him with his spotted horse, Mazeppa.

Other persons owning horses came forward with the same liberal donations.

So, at the beginning of March, Cooke was in possession of a stud of horses; not to be compared, however, to those which he had lost. Somewhat recovered, he returned to Philadelphia. The entertainment took up where it had left off, with, of course, the necessary adjustments from the great losses the tragic Baltimore fire had caused. The standard acts remained solid, but there appeared to be only feeble attempts at spectacle. As a result, the season lasted seventeen days before closing.

With his benefit, Cooke's tenure at his circus on Chestnut Street came to an end. Alas! the performances had failed to draw. But now Wemyss at the Walnut street theatre made another proposal to his board for Cooke to do horse pieces at that house. The place being dark, causing the stockholders to lose both theatre and saloon rental, this time permission was granted. So Cooke and his people moved to the American Theatre on Walnut street, a place more suitable for equestrian melodramas.

The first piece was *Mazeppa and the Wild Horse*, which opened on April 2, 1838, with a double company—Cooke's equestrians and a cast of American actors. New scenery, costumes, and accouterments were constructed. It was arranged and directed by Mr. Woolford, who was also cast as Mazeppa, with Olinska performed by Mary Ann Cole. Farces and small conceits previous to the main spectacle were changed frequently, with both Mary Ann and William Cole appearing in them. Following this *The Life of Napoleon Bonaparte* and *The Cataract Of the Ganges* were brought out in excellent style, featuring a beautiful stud of horses in the grand battle scenes. Of Cooke's company, Woolford, Amherst, and Mary Ann Cole had feature roles. On the 3rd of May *Mazeppa* was brought back for three nights, which marked the end of Cooke's American invasion. The final engagement had lasted for only a month.

Durang has written that these pieces also failed. The charm of the company was lost among the ashes in Baltimore. And even Cooke's benefit was a disappointment. So he gave up the ghost on the 5th of May. Poor Cooke! "As honest as the day is long," Durang assured us; and "through all his vicissitudes he left behind him the character of an upright, honest man in all his dealings with the Americans, as well as those of his corps whom he brought here."[9]

It is important to note that Cooke was a victim of his own circus system. He was dependent on the availability of suitable venues in the larger cities or, in the case of Philadelphia, the feasibility of constructing new ones. After the major cities of New York, Boston, Baltimore, and Philadelphia, there was really nowhere to go. His troupe was much too large for touring, too dependent on visual display and too inflexible from family-tied personnel. Whereas the American indoor circuses replaced feature acts with frequency, in Cooke's company there was little room for that to happen. The American managers used these indoor arenas for the winter season; then, went under canvas with a more lean and portable organization for the summer season, performing in communities of most any size. This American tenting style had not yet been introduced to Great Britain.

After an unfortunate year and a half since he sailed from Greenock, Scotland, the American experience concluded, Cooke returned to his native England, soured and resentful, bitterly claiming the Americans had burned him out in Baltimore out of jealousy and had also tried to burn his property twice afterwards.[10] Upon returning to his homeland in his mid-fifties, Thomas Taplin built more wooden amphitheatres and raised more children and grandchildren, thereby establishing the name of Cooke far and wide.[11]

When the Cooke's Royal Circus returned to England, a number of the original company remained in the United States.[12] William and Mary Ann Cole were among them. For whatever reason, they declined passage to their homeland, choosing to remain in this country and take their chances on American careers. Relatively unknown as performers, having been active in secondary positions with the family organization, they faced an uncertain future. But Mary Ann was a Cooke through and through; and from past and future adventures would learn from adversities and grow stronger and more confident with each little success in the offing.

## III

As the Coles waved farewell to the departing members of Cooke's Royal Circus, bound for the British Isles, they must have felt apprehensive about their future. What were their expectations? We can only imagine their dilemma—two youthful circus performers, bereft of the immediate love and support of family, remaining in an unfamiliar country. They were now on their own, no longer part of the Cooke family flock. Although young and callow in the ways of American circuses, they must set about applying their performing skills as a means of survival.

Mary Ann was trained within the family and, as such, must have been a capable rider, a product of the Cooke circus tradition. Still, it is true she was not a leading performer with her father's company, and rarely was involved in a solo act. As we have seen, she was sometimes used in equestrian displays and small dramatic pieces.

Adding to her difficulty, this was a period of American circus development when performances were dominated by men. The women that entered the ring were more apt to be singers and actresses. Occasionally, entrée riders, primarily family members, were used to fill in the spectacle. It would take a few years for that to change, until the Madigan, Gardner, Buckley, and Stickney families prepared their youngsters for the ring. And of great significance, the arrival in this country of English equestrienne Marie Macarte, first performing for the Howes' & Co.'s Circus in 1846, was the distinct prelude to female stardom on American sawdust.

We know very little about William's background. I have found no record of him performing in England prior to his arrival in America. As a member of Cooke's Royal Circus in 1836, he served in a minor capacity. This suggests that he could have been brought into the company through the marriage to Thomas Taplin's daughter, and was in training to become a performer of greater prominence. In his book *Circus*, Rupert Croft-Cooke referred to him as "one of the circus staff."[1] When the Cooke company was at Vauxhall, shortly after arriving in the United States, Cole was mentioned as one of the clowns. Within a year of his coming here, however, he was billed as a contortionist and handler of a trained dog. It can be assumed he worked in the ensemble pieces where characters were necessary for spectacle. We know from the previous chapter that he acted in small farces and short sketches at the American Theatre on Walnut Street. But was he ready to make it on his own when the art of the contortionist was but a secondary event in the equestrian oriented American circus?

It was announced within weeks after Cooke's departure for England that a Cooke's Circus from Philadelphia would occupy a commodious new amphitheatre in Lancaster, Pennsylvania, behind Franklin's Head Tavern, and which was to open on the 21$^{st}$ of May. Among the entertainments was the grand spectacle of *Mazeppa and the Wild Horse*. Mr. Carpenter was the principal dancer; Bobby Williams, the clown; and Amherst, the stage manager.[2] This was most likely a pick-up company of the Cooke people who remained behind. The Coles could have been a part of that group. The stand lasted through the 26$^{th}$. But did they perform at other places under the Cooke title?

Unfortunately, we go through a year of unrecorded activity before we come to the first notice of young Cole's employment. It was at the Military Garden in Brooklyn where a building designated "Saloon" was converted into a theatre after the plan of Niblo's Garden, to be a place for concerts, vaudeville, and the like, conducted within a garden setting. The place was opened to the public on June 19,

1839. It is here that William Cole appeared early in July as the Indian Rubber Man with "his sagacious dog," Billy.[3]

We come across him later in the year, at Peale's Museum on November 11. "Mr. Cole, a man of many forms, whose agile efforts have been the subject of great surprise, will exhibit his astonishing Evolutions, Attitudes, Equilibriums, &c., transforming himself into every possible shape the human frame is, by long and unwearied practice, capable of effecting," the advertisement read. "His great strength of body, and the agility, ease and elegance with which he goes through each feat, must surprise the most skillful observers of Anatomy."[4]

The *Evening Post* reported that the place was attracting large and fashionable audiences. "Mr. Cole's representation of Classic Portraiture are of the most chaste and extraordinary description; his great strength and elasticity of body, and the agility, ease and elegance of his evolutions are matters of astonishment to all who witness them."[5] William appears to be passing the test.

Billy, the sagacious dog, meriting the appellation of "*Le Chien Marvellieux*," went obediently through his well tutored accommodations. This canine feature, along with the human pretzel gyrations of Cole, surely gave the museum and its patrons their money's worth of entertainment. The duo shared the environs of Peale's with a picture exhibit— 200 portraits of the most distinguished American citizens— along with a trio of juvenile dancers, and, not least, the Cosmorama.[6] The engagement ran through December 9, after which William and Billy were supervened by a group of Hungarian vocalist in native costumes.

The next recorded appearance was with Welch, Bartlett & Co. for the winter season of 1839-1840. John Glenroy was a member of that company. In his book of circus memories, he included Cole on the list of performers but made no mention of Mary Ann. If she was with the troupe it was in a minor position.

Rufus Welch, by this time a wise and seasoned circus and menagerie proprietor, took hotel keeper Jonas Bartlett as a partner and purchased the defunct Bacon & Derious Circus from George Cadwallader, who had just foreclosed on management in June of 1839. A Mr. Hopkins was sent to Richmond, Virginia, to take charge of the company; and, without delay, he "dead-headed" the show north and opened in Brooklyn on July 15. From there it was moved into Rhode Island, Massachusetts, New York state, and then New Jersey, closing at Newark in mid-November before opening the winter season in New York City.

This became the Broadway Circus, 509 Broadway, between Spring and Broome Streets. A newly refitted place of amusement, the *Evening Post* described it commodious, capacious, elegant, well adapted for equestrian exhibitions, most comfortably heated, and with every convenience that could be desired. Its opening on November 19, 1839, drew praise.[7]

General Rufus Welch

Although William Cole was included in Glenroy's roster of the Broadway company as a contortionist, he was not there for the full season. We know he was occupied at Peale's Museum through December 9. Winter shows had a practice of changing their programs, sometimes weekly; so performers would come and go throughout the run, while others would remain on for weeks as resident members. Poor William! We take no issue with Glenroy's accuracy of reportage, but in following the daily advertisements in the *Evening Post*, he received no billing whatsoever.

Sometime, possibly by the beginning of May, William and Mary Ann connected with Enoch C. Yale's troupe. This new outfit started the 1840 tour under the title of Yale & Co., but as the season progressed we see the emergence of Seth B. Howes into proprietorship, with the show title changing to Yale, Howes & Co., and finally to Seth B. Howes & Co. The route appears to have been confined to New York state, New England, and Canada.

The Fitchburg (MA) *Sentinel* revealed that Cole appeared twice on the program, once as a contortionist and again with his dog, Billy. As for Mary Ann's presence, this is the first occasion since Cooke's Royal Circus returned home that we have documentation of her being included as a performer. Seemingly the only female member of the troupe, she is listed by the *Sentinel* as a rider in a "two horse *allemande*" with John Shindle. I take this to mean some dance-like movement of horses and/or riders.

The Coles were back in New York City as members of June, Titus, Angevine & Co. for all or part of the 1840-1841 winter season. This organization combined with its menagerie for a stand at the Bowery Amphitheatre, 37 Bowery, opening November 18. It competed for business with another circus at the nearby Bowery Theatre. The major difference was explained in the New York *Herald* of November 30. "The Amphitheatre from its peculiar construction, possesses this great advantage over the common Theatre and other places where the Olympian Games are exhibited: the performances takes [*sic*] place in the midst of the audience—inspiring a reciprocal enthusiasm between the Equestrian and the observer—not in perspective or at so great a distance from the spectator that the feats of the performers cannot be scrutinized. Everything is done here in open sight, and every person within the walls can be comfortably seated, and witness all the entertainments."[8]

The implication to be drawn is that the Amphitheatre's ring configuration was far more audience friendly than the traditional stage/audience arrangement of the Bowery Theatre. We who have lived through the theatrical changes of the past fifty or more years, experiencing such dramatic innovations as theatres-in-the-round, thrust stages, and numerous other small performing venues with an eye toward audience intimacy, can easily relate to the above excerpt.

This rival Bowery Theatre, under the aegis of Welch & Bartlett, had a strong company of artists presenting some heavy equestrian spectacles. The first of these was *The Battle of Waterloo*, advertised as employing a stud of 50 horses and some 200 supernumeraries. This was followed by *Mazeppa* and *Napoleon Boneparte*. Add to this the presence of such notables as the great American equestrian Levi J. North, the talented French rider Mons. LeTort, strong man and versatile performer Herr Otto Motty, and it is evident that the Bowery Amphitheatre faced stiff competition for its share of circusgoers.

This prompted June, Titus, Angevine & Co. to stress a commitment to exert still greater energies in the production of novelty, talent and variety at their establishment, and to guarantee its propriety. "The unquestionable reputation of the audience frequenting the Amphitheatre gives to respectable families the assurance to visit this place of public resort, even unattended, without incurring the smallest personal inconvenience, or the slightest risk of coming in contact with improper characters," the *Evening Post* advertisement read. "The doors of the Amphitheatre are positively closed against all disorderly and notoriously immoral individuals, either male or female, and every feature of the performances given is marked by that due observance to refined taste and modesty which characterize the Legitimate Arena."[9]

In following the announcements in the *Evening Post*, we observed that William Cole was listed for the first week's performances as "the astonishing positionist." He appeared alongside the Ethiopian impressionists Richard Pelham and William Whitlock; rider, vaulter, and slack-rope artist Hiram Franklin; somersaulter Thomas McFarland; clown Dan Gardner; scenic rider T. V. Turner; four-horse rider Nap B. Turner; and the Swiss Brothers (whoever they were). Then, not surprisingly, there was no mentioned of him for the remainder of the run. This does not necessarily mean he left the company at this time. After the first week of the engagement, the advertising focused solely on the starring acts.

There was an announcement on November 30 of the appearance of six lady equestrians "in the most magnificent cavalcade ever presented." Was Mary Ann one of them? We don't know. Until this point we have identified no female performers. But wait. In this same advertisement there was the name of Mrs. Gossin, the beautiful equestrienne from Lexington, Kentucky, and wife of clown John Gossin—her first night in the circle. Then, on December 8, she was teamed with the Swiss Brothers in a set of twelve classical *tableaux vivants* under the title of "Adam and Eve; or, The First Fratricide."

About a week later, on December 14, more names surfaced. Mrs. Dan Gardner rode into the arena as the "Swiss Broom Girl." And, as we were about to think the Coles had left for another planet, lo and behold! this very night the Swiss Brothers and Mary Ann, assisted by the *Corps de Ballet*, appeared in a piece, "The Wreck of Potichinello; or, The Italian Vampyre."

On February 1, 1841, June, Titus, Angevine & Co. unveiled a most impressive spectacle. "The proprietors have the satisfaction of announcing to their patrons and the public generally, that they have completed, after a labor of several weeks, the grand Asiatic pantomimic Pageant and melodramatic spectacle for the introduction of their extensive collection of Wild Animals, in a manner that will eclipse all former efforts by this or any other establishment in the United States."[10] The piece, *Terror of the Forest; or, The Festival of Freedom*, was written and produced by J. M. Amherst, the former Cooke's Royal Circus gentleman-of-many-words.

This extravaganza of man and beast included among its lavish scenic effects the Mahai Tjai or Musical Forest and Hindu Hunter's Hut; every tree alive with real birds and monkeys; colorfully lit fountains visited by long legged flamingos; and grasslands where gazelles were seen grazing. Another scene revealed the Rajah's palace and the chamber of the Golden Curtains, which, unfolding, disclosed "fierce and furious lions, tigers, and leopards, raging to devour the living prisoners allotted for their prey."

Levi J. North

The principal characters were enacted by the Swiss Brothers, LaPetite Caroline, and J. H. Amherst. But they were supported by a horde of actors and supernumeraries and a herd of four-legged extras, as the piece concluded with stage and ring filled with lavishly costumed royal guards, emblem bearers, elephants of state, giraffes bearing costly presents, a magnificent royal chariot surrounded by vivacious dancers, etc.[11]

We are surprised to discover, but pleased in so doing, a benefit for our Mrs. Cole on the evening of Monday, February 15. This should indicate that Mary Ann participated to a greater degree than the advertisements have shown. Part of the program included a pageant entrée entitled "Queen Bodicea and Her Twelve Amazons," with Mrs. Cole and eleven other equestriennes; a spirited act of horsemanship by Master Stevens; a performance by the canine, Billy; a sketch of Flora and Zephyr, on two horses by N. B. Turner and Mrs. Cole; and, finally, a new act on the double-rope by George Sweet and Mrs. Cole.

It has been less than two years since the Cole's were left to exist on their own. Mary Ann, now in her early twenties, and William, probably of similar age, appear to be making progress in their careers. The length of winter employment alone has given them a moderate security. But in a business as tentative as that of the circus their future was surely unpredictable.

## IV

The Cole's found steady employment for the next few years. The experiences under a variety of managements would prove invaluable to Mary Ann in particular when, in the distant future, she would use her acquired knowledge to advise and abet her son in his quest for success.

After their winter season with June, Titus, Angevine & Co. closed early in April, the Coles were engaged for the summer of 1841 with a show under the management of Nathan Howes and Edmund F. and Jeremiah Mabie—the Great Olympic Circus. The Mabies were Putnam County farmers from Patterson, New York, with no previous experience in show business; but their names would be included in the annals of circus activity for several years to follow. Seth B. Howes, for whom the Coles had worked in 1840, served as manager of this fledgling company.

Advertised as the "largest in the world" (an early cousin to "The Greatest Show on Earth") with upwards of eighty men and horses, the circus was a small affair of but ten performers. The Coles, "from Astley's Amphitheatre," were featured, along with James McFarland, the American vaulter. There were two tents, the main one alleged to be 250 feet in circumference, which, if true, made it an eighty-foot round top. The second was used for dressing and rigging horses for the grand entrée.

The circus opened in the Mabies' home town and followed with a routing that included the New England states, New Bruswick, Quebec, Ontario, and New York state, concluding at Somers. It then moved to Boston for the 1841-1842 winter season under Seth B. Howes' management.[1]

Advance advertisements assured the public that the building had undergone extensive repairs and had been fitted up in the best possible style. "Every convenience that can be adapted to a place of amusement will be found there." The private boxes cost $1.00; common boxes, 50¢; the pit, 25¢. Children, when accompanied by an adult, were admitted for half-price. Furthermore, a portion of the house was set aside for the black population.

The Boston engagement opened on November 24. Howes was the equestrian director and leading rider; Charles Bacon, the riding master; and Dan Gardner, the clown. The first evening's program, as advertised, opened with the grand entrée, PEKIN GUARD, OR THE ARMY OF CANTON, representing "all the appropriate Banners, Costumes, &c, of the Celestial Empire." Mr. D. Young, the Indian Rubber Man, came next (where is Cole? you might ask). He was followed by Master James Howes in an act of horsemanship. After some ground gymnastics, Mr. Johnson executed his agility on one, two, three, and four horses. The first half ended with a riding display by Mrs. Gardner.

Following the intermission, Seth Howes and Master James Howes performed the "American Brothers." Turner appeared in the scenic ride of "The Shipwrecked Sailor" and

Mr. Perry did "Osceola, the Flying Indian."[2] Seth Howes returned in a "mythological act" entitled "My Poor Old Grandmother." Turner followed this with his principal riding act. And the entertainment concluded with Pelham's Ethiopian enactments.

The program varied somewhat throughout the run, with an occasional addition of something new. For example, on the 3$^{rd}$ of December a contra dance entrée by Mrs. Cole and Mrs. Gardner was introduced. This may have been Mary Ann's first appearance of the Boston engagement. On December 6 James McFarland, "the 50 Somerset Man," made his debut as champion vaulter.

Cole's name appeared when a December 8 advertisement listed the "Stars for the Week" as McFarland, Turner, William Cole, and Pelham, "with the strongest Stock Company in the United States." On that day he performed with his wonderful dog, Billy. His contribution as a contortionist is not advertised until December 16, leaving us to assume that by then Young, his Indian rubber rival, had unlimbered and left the company.

The Boston engagement ended on January 24, but we believe the Coles remained for Howes & Mabie's summer tour of 1842, which began at Providence, Rhode Island, and followed a similar route as in the previous year.[3] In April a third member was added to the proprietorship, a Mr. Thomas Tufts; but, for whatever reason, come June, Tufts had disappeared.

Clown Dan Gardner was with the company, along with his equestrienne wife, Camilla. This is the first time she is recognized in Thayer's *Annals*, but she will shortly become a rival of Madame Marie Macarte for riding honors. The Gardners were in the process of creating a family that in the next decade would attain true prominence within the circus business.

Howes opened an 1842-1843 winter stand at the now familiar Bowery Amphitheatre, presently called the Amphitheatre of the Republic, on November 7. During the summer the place had been refitted and enlarged to meet a need for greater neatness and comfort. The admission to the boxes and dress circle was set at 50¢; second tier of boxes, 37½¢; and pit, 25¢. Parquet or family boxes accommodating six people could be secured for $3.00. S. B. Howes was the equestrian director and Henry Needham (former member of Cooke's Royal Circus) was riding master. The clowns were Dan Gardner and Sam Lathrop.

For Evacuation Day, celebrating the departure from New York by the British and the triumphant entrance of Washington, on November 25, the front of the amphitheatre was brilliantly illuminated and decorated with national banners appropriate for the occasion.

Sam Lathrop

Withal, the winter season was not going well. A five-year depression that began in 1837 would reach its peak in 1843. The rival Bowery Theatre, which had been offering its usual fare of melodramas and other pieces of popular appeal, resorted to the exhibition of a herd of 25 buffaloes on December 12. These denizens of the western plains appeared in a spectacle of great variety in which they were compelled to ascend high platforms, leap chasms, etc. In consequence of the depressed state of the times, the Bowery management was forced to reduce the price of admission to the following unparalleled low rates: boxes, 25¢; pit, 12½¢; gallery, 10¢.[4]

New York's Park Theatre, too, was in decline by the end of 1842. The plays had not been drawing audiences. The great old playhouse, "Old Drury," was in deep trouble. With the year closing out, manager Edmund Simpson resorted to importing variety performers to augment the regular offerings. As Odell stated it, "But neither reduced prices nor swinging heroines availed; on December 9$^{th}$ I am pained to record that Simpson had called in the aid of Mr. W. Cole, 'the Great Posture Master, or, Chinese Nondescript, a real man of Indian Rubber,' also that of Pelham and Master Pelham in 'Negro Peculiarities, Dances and Extravaganzas.'"[5] Yes, our William, who appeared on the Park stage for a number of days, was among those who exemplified the acts of desperation by management, but to no avail.

Howes & Co. at the Amphitheatre were feeling the pinch of recession along with the other places of amusement. The advertising for December 19 announced the lowering of prices of second tier boxes to 25¢ and of the pit to 12½¢. At the same time we are told that in order to accommodate the immense crowds of visitors to the city during the approaching holidays the management had enlarged and re-arranged a portion of the interior in order to make more space for the cheaper seats.

On December 29 we find the name of William Cole listed in an Amphitheatre of the Republic advertisement. He could have been with the company after leaving the Park engagement, but there was no indication of such in the newspaper items.

Then on January 5, Welch's Olympic Circus, after closing an early season in Philadelphia, moved into the Park, the revered shrine of legitimate drama.[6] Welch consolidated his company with one managed by Rockwell & Stone. John Glenroy, who was with the Welch troupe, wrote, "So with the two companies we had a formidable array of talent, and were entitled to the immense audiences who visited us during our stay of five weeks."[7]

This turn of events caused the Amphitheatre management to make a further reduction of prices. Boxes and the dress circle were offered for 25¢, the second tier for 18½¢, the pit for 12½¢, and the parquet or family boxes for $1.50. Then, in mid-January, the benefit nights began, with Seth B. Howes taking his on the 17th. The final week was announced to begin on Monday, January 23, "in consequence of the Company being engaged to go to Boston." And with this, both circus companies disappeared from the amusement columns, the short winter season put in the deep-freeze by economic stagnation.

There was a change in management for Howes & Mabie's road season of 1843. Co-proprietors Nathan Howes and Jerry Mabie were no longer connected with the organization; Seth B. Howes and Edmund F. Mabie were now the sole operators. The Providence, Rhode Island, *Journal* accommodatingly confirmed that our William was back for what we presume was the third season under the Howes & Mabie title. Although we have nothing to prove it, we have to assume that Mary Ann was also with the company.[8]

The 1843 itinerary was more expansive and varied than in the two previous seasons. After working its way to Buffalo, the show was taken to Detroit by lake steamer. It then followed a route through Michigan, Indiana, and Illinois, and south into Arkansas and Mississippi, finally arriving at New Orleans in mid-December. So successful was this lengthy tour, Thayer tells us, that Howes & Mabie never played the eastern states again.

The Coles must have left the company before it went south. Odell has William at P. T. Barnum's American Museum in early fall of 1843. The announcement of William's engagement there first appeared on September 26. The ad also predicted the appearance of a band of Chippewa Indians and Squaws, all dressed in full costumes and performing on the stage a series of songs, war dances, etc. Alongside were the celebrated war canoes which had recently been used to win a race at Philadelphia. There were also Ethiopian Serenaders; a popular vocalist in Miss Adair; La Petite Celeste, a danseuse; a Mr. Collins, comic singer; a brass band of ten musicians, and 500 curiosities, including the Fejee Mermaid. For only a year after the museum was opened, Barnum had the place operating full tilt. Cole and his performing companion, Billy, hung on for three weeks, ending their run on October 13.

Mary Ann was appearing at the Bowery Amphitheatre for John Tryon while William was at Barnum's. This was Tryon's first of six winters there. The 1843-1844 season was active from September to April, with various performers coming and going during the run.

Following William's engagement at the American Museum, the Coles joined the Rockwell & Stone circus at Niblo's Garden. An ad for the November 22, 1843, opening read: "In addition to a superior Company of Performers in the varied acts of Equestrian Science, the public will be introduced to a new and beautiful Classic Arena and Circus, built and arranged by Mr. Hitchings, Principal Machinist, and decorated by Messrs, Heigle, Duke, White, and assistants from the designs of the best Italian Masters."[9] Henry Rockwell was the equestrian director; Henry Needham, the ringmaster; and Alex Rockwell, the premier clown.

As the run progressed the paper suggested that Niblo's was in an admirable vicinity for the convenience of the fashionable *monde*, and, further, it was gratified by the attendance of the vast number of children, which gave proof that the entertainment was free of anything objectionable.

William's name first appeared in an advertisement for the performance of November 28, where he was identified for his "Unsurpassed Act of Personal Gymnastics." We must wait until December 8 for Mary Ann to be recognized in print, in a "Transformation of Punch and Judy to Zephyr and Flora."

A new feature was added on December 6. The talented Ellsler Brothers, "giving some surprising specimens of gymnasia," were introduced to the audiences of Gotham. The

*Post* writer expressed his great admiration with: "They are beautifully formed, and execute their different feats with great ease and finish. The Trapezium is a novel and wonderful exhibition of strength. The Ellslers performances give a pleasing variety to the entire equestrian exercises of Messrs. Rockwell & Stone."[10]

Levi J. North arrived on December 21. He was freshly returned from his visit to the British Isles where he championed the English vaulter Price in a series of contests. Always a favorite with New Yorkers, he again performed his famous "Sprite of the Silver Shower," and combined a turn with Mary Ann in "Shepherdess and Swain." A benefit was given him on the 28th, billed as his last appearance; but, due to his popularity, he was held over for another six nights.

"The pressure continues unabated, and the sublime performances have attracted more general and fashionable attendance than ever graced a similar exhibition," the *Herald* proclaimed. "There is a principle of sterling worth illustrated in every act."[11] Nevertheless, on January 13 the announcement appeared: "POSITIVELY THE LAST NIGHT OF THE CIRCUS AT NIBLO'S." The management decided to leave the attractive environs of Niblo's Garden for the Chatham Theatre, more centrally located down town. "The lower portion of the city are yet to be enlightened on the merits of this distinguished company."[12] It might be added that the saloons and bars, which had been renovated for the occasion, afforded the public a guarantee of the best style of refreshments.

The show opened there with the grand entrée, "The Royal Guard of Semaphore," in which there were six beautiful ladies. These included Mrs. Gossin, Mrs. Gullen, Mrs. Aymar, and our own Mrs. Cole. The acts of particular mention in the *Herald* of January 31 were: Hiram Franklin, expert rider and vaulter, performing a double somersault on a

49

wildly galloping steed; Eaton Stone in his Indian riding act, wearing an authentic costume given him in Canada two years earlier by an Indian chief; and Cole emulating an Indian-rubber man. The great Levi J. North contributed additional appeal beginning February 9.

At this point in time approximately 20,000 New Yorkers graced places of amusement every evening. This would include the circus, theatres, opera, concerts, balls, parties, etc. Of this number, it was estimated, perhaps too generously so, that upwards to 2,000 attended the Chatham. Among this throng on February 22, the Philadelphia Firemen and their escorts appeared *en masse* to witness Levi J. North ride two of his best acts and Hiram Franklin execute a double somersault and Mr. Cole, "the man without joints," transform himself into shapes not human.

The circus lasted at the Chatham until March 23, after which the smell of horses disappeared and the more tolerable odor of grease paint once more permeated the stage. Mr. William Duverna, in taking over the management of the house, vowed to make the Chatham the people's theatre once again.

We now return to the American Museum as Cole lost no time in re-employing himself at that institution. It was announced on March 24 that the week's attractions included the Kentucky Minstrels, Mr. Cole and his dog, Billy, and other astonishing performances. These would be housed alongside a dreary wax figure display of a group of Indians in the act of murdering a Santa Fe trader. The engagement was successful. Cole and the Ethiopian entertainers received a series of weekly extensions that lasted throughout the month of April.

The Coles' next employment was at the Bowery Circus in February of 1845. We find that the *Spirit of the Times* was supportive, crediting the equestrians with much talent, and showing pleasure that the performances were well attended. The equitation of Mrs. Gossin and Mrs. Cole was noted to be bold, dashing, and decidedly beautiful. Mary Ann was not only getting more recognition but was growing as a performer.

Rockwell & Stone had two units on the road for the summer of 1845. Oscar Stone was in charge of one that remained solely in the northeast—Massachusetts, New Hampshire, and Maine. Alex Rockwell had the other, which started in the northeast but ranged farther afield, eventually moving into Pennsylvania, Maryland, and New Jersey. The Coles joined the latter company at Lowell, Massachusetts, in late April, reuniting in the ring with their English friends Bobby Williams and Henry Needham. The season lasted at least until October 17.

In New York, Palmo's Opera was altered for the arrival of Nathan Howes & Co.'s Circus on January 28, 1846. Here the Coles shared the gaslights with such arenic artists as rider Nap B. Turner, acrobat James Nixon, clown Dan Rice and the sparkling equestrienne comet, Madame Marie Macarte. As Odell stated it, "The entrée changed frequently and piled spectacle on spectacle to overtop similar offerings at the Bowery Amphitheatre." The stand lasted through the end of February, at which time the show took to the road, first Baltimore and Washington, and then into Pennsylvania, New York state, and New Jersey.

Sackett and Covel were the proprietors of the Victory Circus, which was on tour for the 1847 season. These men were unknowns in the circus world before this date and ever after it. Where they came from and where they went is not recorded, and, I might add, of little consequence. The only importance here is that the Coles were members of the company, along with such familiar names as the Madigan family, strong man Mons. LaThorne, rider Charles Bacon, clown John Gossin, and four-horse rider Isaac Sweet. Apparently a Canadian company, the summer itinerary was confined to that country. It no doubt suffered financial problems, because in early August there was a change in proprietorship.

The Coles were back in New York City for the fall season of 1847, working for John Tryon at the Bowery Amphitheatre. The place opened on September 14 with Mary Ann as one of the feature attractions in an act of horsemanship; during which, we speculate, she was significantly pregnant.

52

## V

At some point during 1847 in New York's borough of Manhattan, William Washington Cole was born. His longtime friend, Louis E. Cooke, recalled how "arm and arm I have walked down the street with him and looked up at the windows in the humble house in Houston Street, where he first saw the light of day; therefore, I know whereof I speak."[1] We have seen that the Coles were on tour with Sackett & Covel for the summer of 1847 and in New York City for the fall and winter of that year. But the New York City Department of Records and Information Services, after conducting a search, was unable to find a birth certificate.[2] So the exact date remains a mystery.

Cole was raised and grew to adulthood within the world of the circus. From his early stirrings until he took out his first show, the sawdust circle was his life, and always under the watchful eyes of Mary Ann, his mother and his mentor. For show families, existing totally within the microcosmic world of traveling troupes, teaching and training their progeny or infant apprentices in hotel rooms or on a buggy seat en route to the next stand, isolation from the outer world was common. A circus mother gave birth and moved on to the next town, ready within a matter of days to re-enter the ring. It was not only a financial necessity but a matter of professional pride. Mary Ann was now a seasoned trouper who had grown up in similar circumstances, so inconveniences of motherhood did not interfere with the fulfillment of her performing responsibilities.

John Tryon's season at the Bowery Amphitheatre, which opened on September 14, 1847, gave Mary Ann the most prominence we have seen so far. It is not known just how long she was with the company; there appears to have been a rapid turn-over of talent. Could she have taken a maternity leave at this time? Tryon's management ended by the beginning of December, when Sands, Lent & Co. took temporary possession of the stables; but he was back again beginning January 3, at which time William Cole's name appeared on the roster.

Seth B. Howes had two units of his United States Circus on the road in the summer of 1848. The Coles were connected with the eastern company, which followed the standard route through New York and the New England states. An advertisement boasted of "Embracing by far the largest establishment in the United States, formed of the principal Equestrian, Vaulting, Acrobatic, Pantomimic, Gymnastic, and Comic talent to be found in either Continent."

Well, perhaps not in either continent, but it was a solid group, as good as any in this country. There was Madame Camilla Gardner (at last, a notable American equestrienne), in an act of horsemanship. Her husband, Dan, provided his popular brand of clowning, scenic riding, and comic songs. He was abetted in the ring by another native jester, John Gossin. The vaulting was led by Thomas McFarland, called "the hero of 87 successive somersaults." Include Mr. and Mrs. Cole, the former "the best contortionist in the country," the other "superior in Scenic Equestrianism," and Henry Needham, Mary Ann's brother-in-law, master of the circle. Add to this William Smith, one, two and four-horse rider; Herr Daniel Minnich, a veteran slack-rope performer and strong man; Master Buloid, a juvenile rider; the two Miss Johnsons, *danseuses*; and Joe Mills' band of Ethiopian entertainers.[3]

The advertisement promised a procession into town at about 11:00 a.m. It was to be led by a magnificent Golden Chariot, drawn by twenty cream-colored horses. This previsit announcement was followed by a complete description of the vehicle, representing a most unique piece of press agentry for its day and useful to those who are interested in replicating ancient circus wagons. "The splendor and magnitude of this gorgeous and colossal carriage baffles description. Whoever has read of the Funeral Chariot of Alexander the Great, or the Triumphal Car of Nero, may form some conception of the grandeur of this superlatively beautiful vehicle. The first impression of this splendid effort of Oriental magnificence entering town will be surprised that individual enterprise could attain an object so truly novel, sublime and stupendous—so elegant in its proportions—so grand and classic in its design—and above all, so rich and elaborate in the carving and gilding. The length of the Chariot is twenty-two feet six inches, and its height to the summit of the canopy (which may be lowered at will in passing bridges, &c.) with which it is surrounded is eighteen feet. The Chariot is appropriated to the conveyance of the CELEBRATED NEW YORK BRASS BAND. The invocation and design of this gorgeous vehicle has raised as much admiration as the wonderful exhibition it precedes. The body of the Chariot rests upon two axle trees, inserted into four ponderous wheels, made after the manner of the Grecian chariot wheels in the time of Alexander the Great, the naves and spokes of which are curiously wrought and covered with gold. The body is entirely carved from massive and solid timber, and the external decorations disposed in four relieves, most exquisitely wrought and carved with burnished gold, while the base or ground work is of bronze. The several parts of the exterior are representations of different subjects from the heathen Mythology. At the front in bas relief, stands two figures of Pegasus, raising their wings on either side of the driver's seat. On one side partly to the rear, is the full length figure of Apollo holding the lyre, and that on the opposite side represents Venus as she bears away the golden fruit from her rivals in the garden of the Hesperides. In the centre, on one side, is the figure of Comedy reclining on a shield, and on the reverse that of Tragedy in the same position. A magnificent canopy rises from the afterpart which is gaudily fringed and curtained in silk and gold. The back of the canopy is an apparent support of a full figure of Atlas, and the canopy is surmounted by a coronal or full figure of Pegasus. The interior is lined throughout with the richest crimson velvet, and of sufficient capacity to seat thirty people. The vehicle is altogether superior to the one used by Mr. Van Amburgh or any other that has been seen in the United States, and cost the proprietors upwards of six thousand dollars. The *twenty horses* that are required to draw this mammoth car are driven by Mr. Mark Johnson."[4]

Mary Ann and William were with Howes again the following year, which was primarily an enlargement of the 1848 eastern unit. The 1849 territory included New Jersey, Pennsylvania, New York state, Virginia, and Maryland.[5]

There is no record where the Coles spent the 1850 summer season. We do know, however, they were connected with the National Circus on Ninth and Chestnut Streets, Philadelphia, in September of that year. This organization, which opened to the public on September 2, was called The Great

Olympic Circus (late of the Astor Place, New York). Richard Rivers was listed as the proprietor; Hiram Franklin, the equestrian director. Mary Ann was advertised as one of the principal riders, being in good company with the likes of Silas Baldwin, William Odell, John May, Burnell Runnells, Alexander Rockwell, and George Sergeant.

In 1851 the Coles were with a second unit of J. M. June & Co.'s Great Oriental Circus ("Oriental" because the parade bandwagon was drawn by eight camels), of which Howes was one of the partners. Mary Ann did her exercises of the *manège* and William contorted. Others in the company included Charles and Virginia Sherwood, Thomas McFarland, John Gossin and George Sweet. The show traveled in a New York state and New England territory with a midsummer move into Ontario, Canada. After closing in late October, the outfit was purchased by the popular clown, Joe Pentland.

From here on, the 1850s become somewhat of a puzzle. The engagement with June & Co. is the last season for which we have a record of Mary Ann and William Cole working together, which leaves us with some unanswered questions. Were they unable to find employment as a team? Or was their marriage over? There doesn't appear to have been animosity between them, because, as we have noted, upon Mary Ann's death she was interred alongside William in Brooklyn's Greenwood Cemetery.

The final performing documentation we have of William is with a show in 1852 and 1853. The St. Louis *Missouri Republican* listed him as a contortionist with E. F. & J. Mabie's Magnificent Arena and United States Circus in April, 1852.[6] In May the title changed to Older & Co. The show, which opened in St. Louis, moved about in Illinois, Indiana, Wisconsin, Iowa, and Missouri until November. At that time the title changed again to Mabie & Co.'s United States Circus, combined with Raymond & Co.'s and Driesbach & Co.'s Menageries for a tour of the southern states—Kentucky, Tennessee, Alabama, and Mississippi. The Mabie troupe, and presumably Cole with it, continued on the road into 1853, remaining in the South until warmer weather permitted them to retrace their route of the previous year.

Now the diary of William Cole goes blank. What is more, we have no details of his death. We are told by Louis Cooke that it occurred in 1857.[7] We do not know the cause or where it occurred. His burial in Brooklyn could indicate that he died in or around New York City, but there is no real evidence of that.

We have also lost Mary Ann's activities for a five-year stretch. Could the two of them have left the world of the circus to give their child a more stable life? It is hard to imagine if they were performing somewhere that Thayer in his unrelenting pursuit of circus activity would not have uncovered their trail.

We are re-associated with Mary Ann when she and her son join H. Buckley & Co.'s Circus for the summer of 1857. This could suggest that William Cole died in the early part of that year, making it necessary for her to find employment by a return to performing.

Buckley had made his debut as an owner the previous year. For 1857, however, he added two partners—Stephen S. Babcock and George Passage—a move that allowed a second-year expansion. Starting at Delavan, Wisconsin, the show went into Indiana, Illinois, Ohio, Kentucky, and ended at Natchez, where it was quartered for the winter.

Next, Mary Ann had the good fortune to be employed with the L. B. Lent Mammoth National Circus for the summer of 1858. Lewis B. Lent was a natural showman, having grown up with an eye to the business. His father bought, sold, and leased animals, and for a short period he had a traveling menagerie. In 1834, at age twenty-one, Lewis was an agent for June, Titus & Angevine. In August of that year he purchased an interest in the menagerie of J. R. and W. Howes, a move that began a participation in management that lasted for many years under various titles. He was an all-round circus man and considered to be the best general agent and router of his day. As a proprietor he had an eye for talent and was willing to pay for it. He kept a cadre of some of the same performers year after year. A shrewd, intelligent advertiser, he pioneered the use of "jaw-breaking" circus titles with his "Hippozoonomadom."

The L. B. Lent National Circus was in its second year when Mary Ann joined. The show opened on May 1 at Lancaster, Ohio, where the outfit had been stored for the winter, and made a lengthy tour of Ohio, then into Michigan at mid-July, followed by dates in Ontario, Canada, New York state, and Pennsylvania.

Mary Ann couldn't have connected with a more respected circus company. This is evidenced by an item in the Cincinnati *Daily Commercial*—of a city that was accustomed to seeing many such shows come and go—that lauded the man and his circus operation alike. "His pavilion, which is of mammoth proportions, is spread upon the City Lot, and we invite all who would witness an exciting *roulade* of performance to attend this afternoon and night. Mr. Lent may be justly termed the Napoleon of circus men; he has inaugurated more novelties of high character than any gentleman connected with the profession, and while his name in the country is an endorsement to any concern with which he may be connected, it is equally respected and recognized in Europe. The present company is an embodiment of *samples*. Samples of the best horsemen, gymnasts, acrobats, pantomimists, and of general performers."[8] One has to believe that Mary Ann and her son benefited greatly under this management, acquiring perceptions that could be put to good use in the future.

## VI

The presidential election of 1860 set off a frightful condition of instability. Lincoln had run on the issue of containing slavery, limiting it to the states where it existed. The slave states populations were incensed and there was hostility by many in the territories of Kansas and Nebraska who wanted slave owning rights as well. The trauma that infected the country quite naturally affected the operation of circuses.

Nevertheless, Mary Ann turned a new corner in her life when she and her son joined a Wisconsin-based show under the proprietorship of Orton & Older in May of 1860. Now a widow, she worked under the billing of Mary Ann Cooke. Capitalizing upon the famous name, a month after her arrival the management began interspersing the title of "Cooke's Royal Circus" with its own, and continued the practice for the rest of the season.

Hiram Orton made his debut as a circus proprietor in January, 1854, with a small indoor show in Portage City (now called Portage), Wisconsin. He was formerly a Great Lakes sailor and an operator of a tavern in Indiana before moving to Portage in 1853. It has been suggested that, after having attended a circus performance in Chicago, he was convinced his children could become successful in the ring. He had a total of seven—Miles, Lester, Dennis, R.Z., Hattie, Irene, and Celeste. So he set about forming a show of his own and hiring a few performers who could double as instructors. With three veterans, clown J. A. Gilkison, contortionist J. F. Harvey, strongman Charles Tubbs, and his progeny—fifteen-year old Miles, eleven-year old Dennis, and ten-year old Hattie (the other four were too young to perform at that time), all who learned their arenic feats from others in the company as they went along—he began what was to become a seventy-eight year family business.

After a debut in Portage, Orton conducted an initial summer tour which covered Wisconsin, Illinois, Iowa, Missouri, Arkansas, Mississippi and Louisiana. This first outing did not startle the circus world with its brilliance. In support of this, we learn that after the Ortons succeeded in getting a Burlington, Iowa, license fee reduced, the local paper suggested that "for their audacity to bore the public" they "should be made to pay the full penalty of the bond."[1]

## COOKE'S
## ROYAL CIRCUS.

THIS unequalled European Troupe, comprising all the Great Talent in the Equestrian Profession, will exhibit their Splendid, Novel and Exciting Feats of Horsemanship and Athletic Skill, At KEOKUK, on Monday, June 11th. A Grand Mid-day Performance, commencing at 2 o'clock p. m., and in the evening at 7½ o'clock. Admission 50 cents. Children 25 cents.

Among the superb attractions which distinguish the Royal Circus is the magnificent

### ECOLE DE MANEGE,
By the Brilliant and Dauntless Artiste
**MARY ANN COOKE**,
On her beautiful Manege Horse JUPITER,
**La Petite Laura**
On horseback as the Rose Girl.
**Walter Cooke**
On his wild bare-backed steed.
**Young Lester**,
The Champion Contortionist of Europe & America.
**M. Maddrie**
Will introduce his little sons, with the performing
**Ponies, Cherry and Fair Star.**
A matchless act on two horses by
**Mary Ann Cook and Maurice Mills.**
PROF. CHARLES and his pet LEOPARD
**MAZEPPA.**
The astonishing **Double Summersault** performance, besides many other Great Acts.
The performance will be interspersed by the Gymnastic and Loquacious Drolleries of
**The Court Jester, Geo. Constible.**
The entertainment will commence with
**A Grand Hippo-dramatic Spectacle**,
And conclude with a
**Burlesque Equestrian Pantomime.**
**PROF. REUBENS**
Will form a Procession in his Splendid Chariot, and drive a Mammoth Troupe of beautiful Horses, accompanied by a
**SUPERB BAND OF MUSIC,**
Will enter town at 10 a. m. on the day of exhibition.

**THE SABLE HARMONISTS**
Will give a GRAND CONCERT in the same Pavilion immediately after the conclusion of the Circus performances. [may28d]

The 1855 Orton's Badger Circus was enlarged. Thomas Osborn was added as rider and Joseph Tinkham as leaper. Miles Orton, thanks to a winter of preparation, had become quite an acceptable bareback rider. And there was another half-dozen people of obscure futures. The circus opened the new season on January 1 at Natchez, Mississippi, went as far south as Shreveport, Louisiana, and then worked north into Iowa, Kansas, and Wisconsin.

Beginning in 1856 the organization went out under the title of Orton's Great Southern Circus, which was an indication of a major use of southern territory. Actually, the season opened in Shreveport, then the show went into Arkansas, Missouri, Iowa, Wisconsin, Illinois, and back into Missouri, Arkansas, and Louisiana by the end of December. But the Ortons didn't stop there. After more dates in Louisiana, the show dusted over Texas, Mississippi, Alabama, Georgia, Tennessee, Kentucky, Illinois, and Wisconsin; ending at Portage City on November 9 of 1857 a trek that had taken its sturdy equestrians over the roads for more than a year.

At this time Pardon A. Older bought into the organization and the new name became Orton & Older's Great

Southern Circus for 1858. P. A. Older, who served as business manager, brought more experience to the company. In 1849 he had traded a saw mill in Janesville, Wisconsin, worth about $5,000, for a third of the Mabie circus, an outfit that consisted of some seventy horses, eight wagons, an eighty-five foot round top, and a thirty foot dressing tent. Then he had his own show on the road in 1852. And just prior to joining the Ortons he was allied with Yankee Robinson in a venture.

The 1858 company was solid enough, but not filled with what could be judged top-of-the-line people. There was Mons. Martina, slack-wire walker and contortionist, and his equestrienne wife. The bareback riding was handled by Miles Orton. One of the Orton sisters, called the "Prima Donna of the Cirque," undertook some sort of dancing. The durable Charles Tubbs displayed his Herculean feats along with a show of fearlessness in mingling with performing beasts. Joe Tinkham contributed an ability to tumble and engage in other general entertainments. George Constable was the clown. Add to this a pair of performing lions with the idyllic names of Romeo and Juliet.

The show left Portage City in May and didn't return until the fall of 1860, an amazing twenty-eight month tour. The area covered included Wisconsin, Iowa, Missouri, Illinois, Indiana, Kentucky, Tennessee, Mississippi, Alabama, Georgia, North Carolina, Virginia, back into Tennessee, Alabama, Mississippi, Arkansas, Texas, Louisiana, again Mississippi, Alabama, Kentucky, Illinois, Iowa, Minnesota, Wisconsin, and finally closing, surely tired and bedraggled, on the 15$^{th}$ of September at Rockford, Illinois. Thayer indicates the company was in financial trouble in stating "the record doesn't show how much salaries were in arrears at the closing, but that they were is a fact."[2]

There is little wonder. The premonition of war, which was abroad at this time, was a distraction for the public and a signal for cautious spending. It also inspired a general and fearful stampede of amusement enterprises as they abandoned southern territory for the safety of the North. Particularly, it did not bode well for a show that called itself a "Southern Circus." But if war broke out, the South would be closed to any and all traveling shows whatever the title. So following the end of the 1860 season, for this and probably other reasons, the Orton circus remained in the barn for three years.[3] So ended Mary Ann's first of several years with the Orton organization.

After the closing the Ortons and the Coles took up residences at Independence, Iowa. It was during this time that youthful William Cole had a job as clerk in the dry goods store belonging to a Mr. August Myers, which served as an opportunity to experience the business world outside the show lot.[4]

In 1862 Mary Ann and Miles Orton joined George W. DeHaven's Union Circus for at least part of the season. The show traveled chiefly in Iowa, Illinois, and Indiana.[5] Advertisements audaciously boasted of the best riders, superior tumblers, three clowns, and three equestriennes, "and in fact the greatest combination of talented and salaried performers ever congregated under one pavilion."

Four days after a stand at St. Louis on August 18 the couple were married in that city. Yes, at age 44, Mary Ann wedded the 26 year old Miles. Astonishingly, he was born just ten days before Mary Ann and her family arrived at New York harbor in 1836 for Cooke's Royal Circus' American visit. In spite of the age difference the marriage appears to have gone well for at least a dozen years. Miles became a respected second father to William, welcomed him into the

Orton clan, and gave him the opportunity to learn the ways of circus operation. Mary Ann contributed her knowledge of some thirty years of experience to an Orton company that had never performed in the major population centers of the country.

The Orton circus returned to the road again in 1864, now under the title of Orton Brothers ("Southern" no longer advantageous), because of Hiram's retirement from active management. It started from Independence on April 25 with a troupe made up of Orton family members, Charles Tubbs, James A. Gilkison, and a number of lesser-knowns. Dennis Orton was manager and Miles was the equestrian director, featured rider, and shared a double act with Mary Ann, who also performed her *ecole de manège*. The company was in Nebraska at the beginning of July, making two-day stands with a one dollar admission price. "They have been doing a big business through that country," the report read, crediting it on the absence of circuses in the state for several years.[6]

And no wonder. The issue of slavery had created great animosities among the residents and there were still threats of attacks by hostile Indians.

At season's end the Orton winter quarters was moved to Adel, Iowa. The show had performed there during the summer and Hiram, liking the looks of the place, bought a farm three miles east of town (now called Ortonville).

Travel was often difficult during the immediate postwar years. For the Orton show in particular, the Missouri roads and bridges were in terrible condition. The devastation of the routes of transportation where the fighting had occurred, coupled with an unusual amount of rainfall caused problems of movement. A member of the company wrote: "We encountered the wildest rivers and the roughest roads that were ever navigable! We had to swim most of the rivers, for there was 'nary a bridge, and we frequently did not reach town until two, three, and five o'clock in the afternoon of those days."[6]

Still, the Ortons were welcomed by the war-weary audiences en route, as the St. Joseph *Morning Herald* confirmed. "This institution arrived in the city early yesterday morning very much to the satisfaction of the boys, and located on Fourth and Sylvana streets. It is a very small concern, but capable of containing eight hundred people with ease. They gave two entertainments yesterday and the pavilion was full each time. Those who witnessed the performance were very much delighted."[7]

The St. Paul *Pioneer* agreed. "The performances last evening at the circus were of an excellent description. The house was filled to overflowing and everyone seemed to be delighted. There will be two performances to-day, one for the juveniles, the other for children of a larger growth."[8] The

Ortons' return to the road appears to have been a modest success.

The circus continued in a familiar pattern for the next three years. The 1866 season was opened at Adel on April 21. There was a new 100 foot round top and a new chariot for the band, new baggage wagons and trappings. A ten member female band (some members being boys wearing women's clothing) under the leadership of M. R. Argye was a novelty this year. The season ended on September 14 at Adel, again with a modest roster composed of the Orton family, Andrew Gaffney, William Andrews, James A. Gilkison, and a few others.

The 1867 season opened at Adel on the 20$^{th}$ of April. The main feature was again the cannon ball act of Andy Gaffney. The procession consisted of a band chariot for the

Female Cornet Band, ten "ladies" in all, followed by the "Liberty Car," carriages, buggies, luggage vans, and wagons.[9] On September 30, the show moved to Texas for a winter season. The plan was to remain there for two months, then cross over to New Orleans, where the outfit would be placed on a ship to St. Louis.

Young William Cole became a businessman this year at the age of twenty when he had the sideshow, a privilege which he shared with his step-father. The percentage of the management money and the cash he took from the "rubes" with his gambling device must have given the Coles their greatest professional income.

The 1868 summer tour began at Leavenworth, Kansas. The circus then went into Nebraska, Minnesota, and Iowa, with the expectancy to spend another winter in Texas. Plans were changed somewhere along the line, because the season ended at Adel around November 1.

The circus business in 1869 was disastrous. From the outset until the end the tent outfits suffered cold spells and continual downpours of rain. Out of twenty or more of the leading organizations that began the season only a mere half-dozen went to winter quarters financially stable. The Ortons were particularly vulnerable. Bothers Dennis and R. Z. Orton were no longer with the show. The company included a number of new faces, but Miles and wife, Caroline, Irene, and apprentices Miss Jessie and Master Leon represented the remains of family.[10] The change was not successful.

By the spring of 1870 Miles Orton had joined with John Stowe for the Stowe & Orton Circus. A correspondent from New Harmony, Indiana, wrote of a May 20th stand. "This company have not laid up a day in over a year, and are from the far south. Their outside appearance is miserable, but they have a tip-top show inside." The well-traveled clown,

Hiram Marks, and his daughter, equestrienne wonder child, Minnie, about twelve years old at this time, were mainstays of the company. The Van Zandt Brothers, in trapeze and classic groupings; Leon Munson, contortionist and *chair la perch*; and cannon ball man Andrew Gaffney were repeats from earlier Orton troupes. William Cole had the sideshow privilege and served as ringmaster.[11]

The show re-opened in Louisville, Kentucky, on October 5, for a winter tour of the South by rail. The stock and wagons were left on a farm at Vincennes, Indiana, to winter. At this point the English gymnasts, the Marietta Sisters, were added to the troupe. Their specialties were an aerial act, an outside pre-show double ascension, and the Niagara leap, for which they were said to have been paid $200 a week. To begin this second tour the company had a new canvas, new trappings, and new wardrobe.[12] After going as far south as Florida, the Stowe & Orton circus closed in New Orleans on February 1. The intention was to start on the road for an 1871 season from Vincennes in April, but young W. W. Cole had other ideas.

# W. W. COLE'S
## Great New York & New Orleans Zoological & Equestrian Exposition

## VII

It was inevitable that a young man who came from a long circus tradition and who had learned nearly every aspect of the business would want to have his own company. William Washington Cole put together a starting outfit at Quincy, Illinois, and opened his career in management in 1871. This was the same year that P. T. Barnum, induced by W. C. Coup and Dan Castello, entered his famous name into the annals of the American circus. It was also the year that Seth B. Howes and his nephews brought the core of a circus from England and launched Howes' Great London, a show that continued under that title through 1878. It is ironic that young Cole, barely twenty-four years old at this time, would in a matter of sixteen years be called upon to oversee the circus which still carried the Barnum name, with which Barnum continued to have an important financial interest, and within which had remnants of the demised Howes' Great London.

One might ask how a man that young could find the resources to assemble an outfit capable of competing with the numerous post-war circus establishments. Some have said that his mother's divorce settlement furnished the capital. But the divorce was not official until April of 1878 and the separation did not occur until November of 1873. No, in all probability, Cole was trained by his mother to be careful with his money, which he had received through his labors at an early age and from his returns as a sideshow proprietor and gaming operator. This was probably augmented by his ability to secure credit and by Miles Orton's financial interest in the firm.

We know that at the outset the show title was Cole & Orton's Circus (or Cole & Co's), which would indicate a partnership of some sort. As the season progressed, however, references to the company changed to W. W. Cole's Colossal Circus and Animal Show; again, an indication that whatever investment was made by Orton could have been paid off.

Orton's share of the firm may have been the remains of the 1870 Stowe & Orton circus. We know from the previous chapter the horses and wagons of that outfit were left at Vincennes, Indiana, before a winter tour of the South was launched on rails, which included the purchase of a new tent and other trappings. After the company closed at New Orleans, it is probable that Miles Orton was left with the winter outfit while Stowe retained the stock and wagons stored in Indiana. In a 1911 article, J. Milton Traber stated, without citation, that Cole "came into possession of the John Stow (*sic*) circus."[1] That would give Cole a ready-made show, which needed only horses and wagons.

Carl Landrum, in following a Quincy newspaper of the time, has given us an insight into the acquisition of wagons for the show. Quoting from the *Herald*, he related: "[The E. M. Miller Co.] are now engaged on an outfit for Cole & Company's Circus, which is to be organized here next month to take to the road in April. Several of the heaviest six-horse wagons, warranted to stand any kind of use or road, together with a number of skeleton wagons are now nearly completed. The work to be done by the firm for the circus company will amount to $14,000, the largest order of the kind ever taken by a manufacturer in the West."[2]

A report in March revealed that the circus was organizing in Quincy and that the Miller wagon order was nearly completed. It added that forty horses had arrived and more were expected.[3] The final count was about fifty, probably obtained locally where prices were reasonable. An amount of $20,000 was spent in Quincy alone. But when Cole went on the road he had not completed full payment to the Miller company, so a man was sent along to collect a portion of the receipts.[4]

Miles Orton arrived in Quincy on April 7 and was described as one of the proprietors, although his responsibility within the company had not been defined. As it turned out, he was the equestrian director and featured rider. The plan was to give two performances there on April 23 and then go into Missouri and Kansas, the first stops being Palmyra on the 24th and Hannibal on the 25th.[5]

Cole assembled a meager menagerie by leasing animals from James M. French, who had quarters in Detroit, Michigan, where he stored his zoological members in the winter and leased them out in the summer. It consisted of the elephant Sultan, a den of trained lions, and a herd of camels.

The performing roster was fairly typical of a small western circus. It included Miles and Mary Ann Orton, and the Orton apprentices Master Leon and Miss Jessie Orton; Signor Cappolo, clown and general performer; Lem Munson, contortionist; John Carroll, rider; Paul Schroff, lion tamer (representing French); the Marietta Sisters (Imogene, Millie and Rosalie), aerialists; Albert Richards, Ace Barker, and the Van Zandt Brothers (Abram and Anson), gymnasts; Sam McFlinn and Lee Powell, clowns; and Prof. Manifold's Cornet Band. William Batcheller, an outstanding leaper, joined in September, and was a valuable addition to the company.[6]

References to the season's route are sporadic. They indicate the show remained in Missouri through June, that it was in Iowa in July, and by September in Minnesota. It entered Wisconsin on September 21; but on October 8 upper Wisconsin became engulfed in the first great forest fire of the north-central region, which, coincidentally, began on the same day as the infamous Chicago inferno. Starting at Peshtigo, it raged through six counties and as far south as Green Bay. Careless logging practices coupled with extremely dry and hot weather during the summer and fall accounted for the immensity of the blaze.

This limited Cole's opportunities in the state of Wisconsin. Shortly, the outfit was ferried across Lake Michigan at Sheboygan, thence moved to Grand Rapids and other stands in the Wolverine state before closing at Detroit on October 30 and 31. It is possible that the outfit was stored at James M. French's zoological quarters. At the very least, Cole saved the cost of shipping his animals there.

But the circus found no consolation in Michigan. Devastation similar to that in Wisconsin had occurred there. Coincidentally with Chicago and Wisconsin, small fires ignited in the woods near Holland, a community along the Michigan western shore. High winds carried the flames into the town, wiping out most of the structures and killing horses and live stock. Although only one person died, three hundred families were left homeless. Up the coast of Lake Michigan there was another conflagration that destroyed half the town of Manistee. These fires, driven by strong winds, spread across the state laying waste to forests, fields and farms in eight counties. Eighteen thousand people saw their homes destroyed.

Governor Henry P. Baldwin appointed a number of relief committees to aid the destitute. Citizens throughout the state responded with generous donations. Cole and his company members, in an admirable gesture of sympathy, contributed the receipts for performances in Detroit. "Already disbanded, the proprietors broached the sentiment of the company, and from clown to groom, they agreed cheerfully to the plan, willing to give time and money to the cause. It was advertised that the entire receipts would be given to the Relief Committee and to settle accounts the Treasurer of the Relief Committee has been given the entire charge of the money taken in."[7] So ended season number one.

In summary, the first tour under Cole's direction lasted a successful twenty-nine weeks. It followed a pattern of routing learned during years with the Ortons. His roots were in the West and South, and for the most part Cole moved his company within that territory—the agricultural sector—spent very little time in competition with the eastern shows, and generally kept to the smaller cities and towns.

This was a logical plan. As late as 1870 approximately fifty-three percent of employment in the United States was related directly and indirectly to agriculture, as opposed to twenty percent to manufacturing. The 2.6 million farms in 1870 increased in seven years to 4 million; and, of course, population numbers grew accordingly. This energetic rural productivity lasted throughout the years of Cole's management before receding.

But the show's advertising was far more expansive than what the Ortons' had used. Newspaper column space was enlarged, better pictorial cuts were inserted, and the copy was more provocative. "Await the advent of the Four Co.'s," "Cole's Colossal Circus," "Herd of Camels and Performing Elephants," "Three Great Bareback Riders."[8] Hardly a modest portrayal of a yearling organization.

Cole's early success was later made apparent when it was announced that for the 1872 season the show was greatly expanded, "three shows under two different pavilions." There was new canvas from Martin & Sons of Boston, three tents in all. One was a 120 foot round top, the other two being 100 and 80 feet in diameter. There were some 144 horses and 120 men. Twenty dens of animals, a living seal, and reptiles comprised the menagerie. The museum boasted of four cases of wax figures, Egyptian mummies, relics from the Chicago fire, stuffed birds, and human curiosities. The 1872 procession was enlarged to a bandwagon with sixteen musicians in Prussian uniforms, a tableau car, four performers on horseback, the twenty cages, museum wagons, dromedaries drawing the open lion den, and 100 gray horses imported to Detroit from Canada.

Cole had a strong performing group for a second year circus. Mary Ann's brother, Henry, and his daughter now joined the company.⁹ Henry was an acrobat and tight-rope performer when he visited this country in 1836. According to Conklin, he was getting "along in years" (actually, only four years older than Mary Ann) and played no major part in running things but attended to numerous minor matters and was company for his sister and nephew. Addressed as "Uncle Henry," he was a good-natured gentleman and liked by everyone. By this time he had fathered two great riders in Harry Welby and John Henry Cooke and an equestrienne daughter, Rosina.

THE ORIGINAL, THE ONLY
"GRIMALDI,"
(Geo. H. Adams)
THE BEST TRICK CLOWN IN AMERICA
AND KING OF THE STILTS.

Another British import was clown George "Grimaldi" Adams. He was known and well traveled in England and on the Continent. A kinsman of the famous Cooke family, he would marry Rosina Cooke in 1874. But the real star was champion leaper George Batcheller, whose feats over horses lined neck to neck received laudatory comments from the press all along the route.

The use of a Detroit winter quarters suggests a premeditation by Cole to venture into the eastern part of the country in early spring. The opening in Detroit was advertised under the title of W. W. Cole's Colossal Museum, Hippodrome, and Menagerie.¹⁰ The term "Hippodrome" referred to the arena performance, not a hippodromic style of races around a track within an enclosure which was introduced to this country as Franconi's Hippodrome in 1853 and which would be made even more spectacular with P. T. Barnum's Great Roman Hippodrome in 1874 and 1875.[11] The stand was followed by a route through Canada, and down into New York state, New Jersey, Pennsylvania, Virginia, Arkansas, Tennessee, and eventually into Texas, ending the season at Galveston on January 10 and 11, 1873. This constituted over nine months of continuous travel.

It also displayed a willingness to experiment by taking the show into new territory. Canada and the eastern states were unfamiliar to Cole, although his mother had been there in the 1840s. Going into New York state and Pennsylvania at this time meant facing competition from larger and well established titles. And it wasn't long before Cole headed south into Orton tested territory. He had experienced Texas when the Orton circus went there following the 1867 season.

Few circuses ventured into Texas after the Civil War. It was a rough area with rarely any amenities for travel. A circus performer touring in that state in 1866 exclaimed, "Here they are everything but civilized, whooping and hollering, shooting, and all come to the show with pistols and knives. They shoot through the canvas, call you names that are not very pleasant to hear; and we have to take it all."[12] Later, George Conklin wrote about his experiences in a Texas tour with the Cole circus: "At that time Texas still retained many of the rough characteristics of the frontier. There were many feuds in the state. Everyone carried firearms. Shootings were frequent and accepted as a matter of course."[13]

Cole's advertising resembled that of the much larger Barnum show, both only in their second year on the road.

His newspaper copy contained the same brazen exaggerations. "CIRCUS, MUSEUM, CARAVAN AND AVIARY, 500 Men and Horses, 750 Wild and Tamed Animals, Birds, Reptiles, and Curiosities. A Great World's Fair on Wheels, at an expense of $1600 daily, which it pays out in towns and cities where it exhibits." And his claims grew bolder as the season progressed. Such bravado did not go unnoticed. To his credit, Cole was ever observant of the practices of others, and most importantly those of the Barnum organization.

## VIII

The Great New York and New Orleans Zoological and Equestrian Exposition opened the 1873 season in New Orleans on April 1 for what was to be a legendary tour. This was Cole's first year of rail travel, twenty-some leased cars, which allowed him to expand in both the arena performance and the menagerie exhibition.[1] The move serves as a prime example of how quick Cole was in following the developments of other circuses. The Barnum show, already in the front line of innovation, had successfully gone to rails the previous year. Cole's plan was to eventually get to the West Coast and perhaps even Australia, and he wasted no time in routing the show in that direction. It was reported he paid the Union Pacific Railroad the sum of $10,000 for transportation from Omaha to San Francisco.[2]

It is important in assessing Cole's achievement this season to understand the degree of railroad development at this time. Construction before the Civil War was mostly confined to the eastern half of the country, converging with points along the Atlantic coast and inland reaching as far as the Mississippi Valley. In 1860 the rail mileage total was approximately 30,000, most of which was east of the Mississippi. In all, there were 100,000 freight and passenger cars and 1,000 locomotives.

Following the war the roads in the South were rebuilt and consolidated, and a fervent effort launched to span the distance to the West Coast. The Union Pacific was laid westward from Omaha, and the Central Pacific eastward from Sacramento, until in 1869 they met at Promontory Point in Utah Territory. Between 1865 and 1873 approximately 28,000 miles of new track was built within the country as a whole, much of which was used by Cole in his trek to the Pacific and back this very year.

Paralleling the growth were a number of technological improvements that made travel more efficient, convenient and safe. Among these were steel rails, heavier locomotives and cars, a uniform track gauge (4 feet, 8½ inches), and wider roadbeds. Automatic block signals were introduced in 1866. The Westinghouse air brake was developed in 1869. Around this time George Pullman began production of sleeping cars, and, within a few years, diners, parlors, and drawing-rooms.

Still, in 1873 moving a circus by rail in the West was not an easy alternative. Tracks were built in haste with little attention being paid to adequate grading, substantial roadbeds, and the elimination of dangerous curves. The circus performers had no cars of their own and no sleepers. Often planks were laid over seat backs as make-shift beds. There were no through trains, which meant waiting on a siding for lengths of time. The rails were not uniform from one road to the next; so at each new junction the outfits had to be reloaded onto cars compatible with the change of gauge. To tolerate these inconveniences the rewards had to be promising.

The pre-season *Clipper* had announced that the firm was to carry twenty-two new menagerie wagons; however a later report revealed that there were "sixteen large double-cages."[3] The double cages allowed a greater variety of animals to be exhibited without using more rail car space. The procession was comprised of a chariot drawn by fourteen camels, an elephant, an open den of performing lions, a troop of forty riders, tableau cars, and a number of new cages. One camel died later at Colfax, California, reducing the team pulling the Swan Bandwagon to twelve. There was a small sideshow in which were exhibited a giant boa constrictor, and Mrs. James and her two boys whose total weight equaled half a ton. The outside attraction was performed by Mlle. Christina. She made an ascension on a wire leading to the top of the tent's center-pole. One observer remarked, "The aerial ascension by the young lady who was careless about her toilet was performed in the presence of an admiring multitude—admirers of the garments she didn't wear."[4]

A cage of lions was purchased from John V. O'Brien and George Conklin came with them. "I was sold along with the lions," he wrote later; "that is, it was part of the bargain that I was to go to Cole when the lions did, perform them, superintend his menagerie, and train his elephants."[5] The acquisition increased the cat total to four lions, one tiger, and one leopard; but more important, it brought a top-notch animal man into the organization, one who would remain as a loyal member for over ten years.

The performing company was strengthened from the previous year. This was helped by the addition of Henry Cooke's son, Harry Welby Cooke, a featured juggler on horseback and hurdle rider. He was married to the former Ellen Hughes, daughter of the well-known English circus proprietor. Their daughter Kate also joined Cole as a *manège* rider.[6] W. R. Hayden was the press agent, who would become an important fixture with the show in various capacities for several years.

The tour began with a return to Texas, where the show remained for about a month and a half before moving into Kansas. The Kansas *Saline County Journal* reported that the performances were "the best of a kind that ever came off in Salina."[7] By May 21 Cole was in Denver, where the citizens of that city saw a full menagerie for the first time. The business there was said to be immense, with a five show stand amounting to $12,000. Note that in these western cities the admission prices were $1.00 for adults and 50¢ for children under ten.

Dates in Wyoming and Utah finished out the month, with the final four days devoted to Salt Lake City. A local correspondent wrote, "It was the first large show ever here, and the only menagerie that was ever exhibited here." Each performance was attended by Brigham Young along with his seventeen wives, forty-seven children, and a number of friends. Cole gave him a block of about 200 seats, apportioned off and gaily decorated in celebration of his eminence. A special entrance was also devised, to which Young supplied his own door keeper.[8]

Following dates in Nevada and California, the circus opened to an enthusiastic San Francisco audience on June 19. The reception was such that, after the first week, the run was extended for another seven days. The stand closed on July 6 with a gross of $32,760 for seventeen performances.

Towns in the interior were visited before Cole headed back east. Four sea lions were added in California, said to weigh over 5,000 pounds. "These Monsters of the Deep were captured by an expedition fitted out by the Management of the Exposition at the enormous expense of $30,000 IN

GOLD," the bills read. Fed in view of the audience, they consumed 100 pounds of fish daily. One, a huge, mature specimen in particular attracted a goodly amount of public curiosity. "He is a big fellow and lolls and grunts and barks and hops around to the delectation of the spectators."[9]

Coles newspaper advertisements were boastful and overblown, in imitation of Barnum and making use of his familiar declaration of "World's Fair on Wheels!" They vaingloriously listed four colossal tents and "thirty mammoth dens of living wild animals." They laid claim to fourteen head of camels, fifty snow white cockatoos, the elephant Siam, an exhibit of performing serpents, a den of lions, tigers, and leopards, and a "SUPERIOR CIRCUS" of the most finished artists of the day. The local newspaper writers were particularly interested in the curiosity aroused by the huge sea lion and the impressive ring performances of the Van Zandt Brothers.

The show was back in Omaha for an August 19 stand. It then headed into Iowa, Minnesota and Wisconsin. The St. Paul *Dispatch* was laudatory in reporting: "Cole's Zoological and Equestrian Exposition had two large audiences in St. Paul and the general verdict is highly favorable. The attention to and preparation for the comfort of those attending was especially noticeable, by contrast with other tent shows of the season."[10]

Cole followed Minnesota with alternating dates in Illinois and Iowa until he came to rest once again at Quincy on October 11, where he wintered. The circus had traveled 9,387 miles in 26 weeks—from the Gulf of Mexico to the Pacific Ocean to Lake Superior and finally down the Mississippi—the longest distance that had ever been accomplished in any one season, and surely the most profitable for a single ownership.

It is possible a portion of the profits came from the privileges leased to swindlers. Cole, as a former sideshow gaming operator, obviously condoned the practice as a proprietor. An item in the Salina paper revealed that: "One fellow sweat himself white over the loss of $120 which he lost; another man nearly cried as he saw the gambler's scrawny fingers draw out $60 of his hard earned money; while others, who should have known better, were ashamed of themselves for betting $5 and $10 on a gambler's meanest game—three card monte."[11]

"In the old days the gambler, the pickpocket, the short-change artist, and the faker traveled with the show, and in return for goodly sums of money, paid to its owner, were left undisturbed to prey on the crowd which the circus brought together," Conklin wrote. "The roughest show on the road to-day would not countenance the least of the methods by which great sums of money were regularly taken from the public by swindlers connected with circuses in the late 'sixties and early 'seventies. Some owners tried to justify the practice, in a measure, on the ground that it reduced swindling to the minimum, as crooks were sure to follow a show, and if certain ones were allowed to go as a part of it, and pay heavily for the privilege, their own interest would force them to make sure that all others kept away."[12] These shenanigans, more prevalent in the 1860s, continued into the 1870s, particularly in the new territories of the South and West. When the Barnum show was first organized in 1871, the proprietors hired detectives to accompany the circus to protect the public, and advertised the fact. Shortly, other shows followed and major grift was gradually eliminated.

Sadly, Miles and Mary Ann Cole permanently separated in November of 1873. The reason was clearly defined in the divorce papers with which Mary Ann, as the plaintiff, petitioned the Circuit Court of St. Louis, Missouri, in April of 1878. She claimed that her husband on or about the 25$^{th}$ day of November, 1873, disregarded his connubial duties by forsaking her without cause and taking up with one Lizzie May Hayes and "living open and notorious adultery with her, or committing frequent acts of adultery with her," the facts of which became known to relatives and friends of both parties. Further, she testified that since the date of separation she had not lived or cohabited with her husband and would not or will not have anything to do with him.[13] The Miss Hayes, according to Conklin, was a snake charmer. She had probably been a member of the 1873 company, during which she was engaged in charming more than her reptiles.

Cole went out in 1874 for the "Second Annual Tour." Presumably this referred to year two under the title, "Cole's Great New York and New Orleans" circus. In anticipation of the coming Centennial of 1876, the advertising read, "Wait for the World's Fair" and made use of Zoological and Equestrian "Exposition" following the title. The company had an "English and Cooke" flavor. Along with Mary Ann and William were Uncle Henry Cooke, with his troupe of performing dogs, his daughter Rosina Cooke, *manège* and dancing horse rider; cousin George Adams, clown and stilt walker; and Harry Welby Cooke, with his extraordinary original act of "English Jockey's Pastimes." Add to this two other English imports with European reputations—Elise Keyes, the daring female rider, and David A. Seal, clown and acrobat.[14] Altogether, this was a leap forward in talent from previous years.

Advertisements boasted of a "city of tents which at night [were] so brilliantly lit up with gas that everything [was] discernible as in day." But the greatest lure was still the monster living Alaskan sea lion, purportedly the largest ever captured, exhibited in a mammoth tank holding a large amount of sea water.

The procession included a team of fourteen dromedaries pulling the new golden chariot, *Oriental*. There was a number of riders on elegant horses; an open lion den with Conklin seated inside; forty cage wagons; the African snake handler, Zingra, with reptiles coiling about, in a plate glass serpent den; and the street display concluded with another new feature—a steam calliope "that emits the most ravishing music that can be heard for miles—nothing like it ever seen before, worth 50 miles travel to see."[15]

The show first moved into Iowa, then worked its way to New York state and Pennsylvania, territory rarely visited by Cole. Its popularity was ardently confirmed by Buffalo's *Daily Courier*: "Although the weather was threatening in the afternoon the attendance was large; but it remained to the evening to put the monster circus pavilion to the test. Such an assemblage we have not seen together since Barnum paid us a visit last summer, and hundreds had to content themselves with an occasional glimpse of the performance in the ring. So great was the crowd and pressure upon the ring that the performance did not commence till some time after the appointed time. In order to relieve the canvas as far as possible Mr. Cole authorized his representatives to state that those who wished could have their tickets returned to them, which would be good this afternoon or evening. About five hundred persons availed themselves of the offer, but the great mass seemed disposed to take their chances."[16]

Following the eastern stands the show moved south. It was announced that at Memphis a giraffe, two baby elephants, and three new tents were added for a tour of Texas.[17] The season was closed in the Lone Star State at the end of October, after which the outfit was shipped back to Quincy for the winter, thus ending a tour that had covered nearly 9,500 miles through fifteen states.

Concluding the season's final performance, clown David Seal summed up the lengthy tour with a farewell address:

> Sound the trumpet! Beat the drum!
> And let the world all know
> To-night we end our season
> And give our closing show.
> To-night we are all thinking
> Of the few short hours ahead,
> Of the time to come for parting,
> The farewells to be said.

And I would ask indulgence,
  For I find I can't do less
Than to make, this very evening,
  A short "farewell address";
To take each comrade by the hand,
  And, not without a sigh,
To utter those few little words:
  "Goodbye, old friend, goodbye."
We'll meet again some other day,
  And stand within the "ring";
And when that time comes round again,
  What memories it will bring!
We'll speak of scenes just passing now,
  And tell them o'er and o'er;
Of battles fought with other shows,
  And WON in "seventy-four";
Of the luck we had in starting:
  The snow, the wind, and rain;
The accidents that happened;
  Each well-remembered pain;
Proudly boast of crowded tents,
  North, South, East, and West,
If other shows did well that year,
  *Our* show, of *all*, did best.
And ours was a "youthful captain."
  Young, and smart, and "cute,"
Show after show collapsed and fell;
  *He* never followed suit.
In foresight and in judgement
  He stands "alone" to-day,
A "conundrum" to those showmen
  Whose heads are "tinged with gray."
These are the things we'll speak of

> In the coming future days;
> These are the things we'll think of
> As we part by separate ways;
> And turning our face "homeward,"
> We'll wish each friend "God-speed,"
> Prosperity and happiness,
> With good-health in the lead.
> Then a cheer for the season of " '74,"
> A cheer for its closing scenes;
> A rousing cheer for the "gallant ship"—
> "New York and New Orleans!"
> Hand in hand, with "friendship's grip,"
> We'll reach the parting time:
> "Home, Sweet Home," from our Band will come—
> We'll all sing "Auld Lang Syne."

Sing "Auld Lang Syne" to the first four, successful years of show management under W. W. Cole's name! His circus, with its modest beginning, was now a major establishment in the tented field; and W. W. Cole was fast becoming recognized as a youthful phenomenon, as the Quincy *Daily Herald* proudly proclaimed: "The gigantic exposition known among our citizens as the Quincy show returned to this city yesterday morning, after the most successful seven months campaign ever known among the history of any showman. The genius, tact and excellent management of its young proprietor, W. W. Cole, already stamps him as one of the monarchs among the showmen of the present day, and we doubt if there are any who can dispute the palm with him on the continent to-day."[18]

## IX

The circus, which had been wintering at the fair grounds in Quincy, opened the 1875 tour in that city on May 5—Cole's fifth year in management. The annual pre-season announcement in the *Clipper* revealed that during the lay-off the wagons were repainted by the E. M. Miller Company. The four tents, all new, were made of "longitudinal striped linen cloth, blue and white." The advertising department received twenty-four new lithograph designs. Rail transportation was made up in two sections totaling thirty-seven pieces of rolling stock, including two passenger coaches and one sleeping car. There was a new bandwagon in the procession for Stowe's thirteen member Silver Cornet Band, which, again, was to be drawn by a number of camels.[1] Cole's enlarged sideshow included a four-legged woman, a bearded man, a Scottish giantess, a version of a Wild Man from Borneo, and other less spectacular attractions. The number of employees was listed as 210. There were 90 horses and 9 baggage wagons.[2] I emphasize that all of the above was contained in the pre-season announcement of the New York *Clipper*, and may not be an accurate representation of the actual tour.

George Conklin supervised a menagerie of 29 cages. The zoological specimens included an eland, four sea lions, a talking seal, an African tapir, 17 serpents, a performing elephant, 14 camels, etc. A giraffe was added in September. There was also a manatee, indigenous to Florida but claimed to be the first one shown around the country.

The museum exhibited a giant and giantess, a number of wax figures, and other oddities. A new resident to the wax population was Charley Ross, a child from Philadelphia whose disappearance in 1874 created a *cause célèbre* in the national press. Not wasting an opportunity, P. T. Barnum offered the parents $10,000 for his return and made a deal for the rights to exhibit the boy. Charley Ross was never found. How a replica was created with no model to emulate is a greater curiosity than the wax facsimile.

The arena performance was on a par with the previous year. The riding star, Harry Welby Cooke, was gone, which was a loss; but he was replaced by the clown Hiram Marks and his riding sensation daughter, Little Minnie. The "bounding jockey" ride of Anson Van Zandt was noted by a reporter as "the most expert and daring exhibition of equestrianism ever witnessed," with his leap from the ground to a standing position on his steed, dressed stylishly in his English jockey costume. The gymnastics of The Milton Jaspers and Young Leon's five-horse act were applauded; also the clowning and leaping of "Grimaldi" Adams, the sidesaddle turn of Rosina Adams, and the comical ponies in their seesaw feat.[3] An accomplished equestrian dog that jumped through hoops and over banners while astride a horse and performed other amazing things was particularly pleasing to the children.

Cole introduced serious championship vaulting this year with the pairing of William H. Batcheler and George M. Kelley. At this time vaulters were the elite among gymnasts and acrobats. Their *tour de force* was to run down a raised platform and from a springboard to leap over a number of objects—men, horses, camels, elephants—perhaps turning a somersault or two en route, and, if successful, landing unimpeded on a mat beyond. This was dangerous work, for if the leaper did not alight correctly he stood to severely injure his head, break his neck, or rupture his spinal cord. Therein, of course, gave the act a thrilling appeal to the spectators and created its popularity.

As early as 1810 an Irish clown named Bell was turning a somersault over four horses while with Pepin &

Breschard in Philadelphia. Stuart Thayer tells us that such feats were the greatest addition to gymnastics during the early years of "field shows" when Louis Lipton and J. T. McFarland became the first to be billed as such in the 1840s. A few years later Baltimore's Thomas King, who had joined a circus as a boy, become one of the greatest leapers of his day. While performing in California in 1856 he leaped 31' 7½" over nine horses, an immense accomplishment for the time.

It was during the 1870s and 1880s, however, when vaulters held their most popular appeal. Every circus of any importance required several on its payroll. The vaulting "contests" were arranged to increase in difficulty as the various athletes encountered more and more obstacles, such as animals placed side by side, that created a challenge for the need to leap greater distances, until the final contestant, the featured leaper, was the only one left to commit what seemed to be impossible. The buildup of tension with the audience can be compared to the most dangerous acts of the present day.

With Cole's circus, leapers William H. Batcheler and George M. Kelley "contested" for the leaping "championship of the world." While the show was visiting Glen Falls, New York, on August 6, William Batcheler executed a single somersault over thirty-one horses and followed with a double somersault over twenty-nine during the same performance. The confirming witnesses included Cole, George Conklin, Hiram Marks, and others connected with the show.

Cole introduced more "contests" this year in the form of hippodrome races. The publicity from Barnum's Great Roman Hippodrome and the reports of the huge crowds that attended during the stupendous season of 1874 created national interest in the genre. But unlike Barnum's hippodrome, Cole's races were not within the tent, but rather in a roped-off perimeter encircling the show lot. When space was not available on the lot, a permit to use a public road was secured. There were two-horse chariot races driven by ladies, two standing Roman races, four-horse chariot races, ladies hurdle races, and a race for a purse of $50 by outsiders paying an entry fee.

This half-hour of competition was presented after the matinee, free for all to witness. It served as a unique way to bring a crowd to the lot between shows, giving the annex and candy privileges and outside ticket vendors an opportunity for more sales. But this is the only season the device was used.

An innovation in audience comfort was introduced for the reserved seat section this year. It was a new design of bleachers with foot rests and individual cushioned seats and backs, patented by David. C. Price of St. Paul, Minnesota.

Cole, one of the first proprietors to make use of this improvement, paid an annual royalty to the inventor.[4]

Price's Portable and Detachable Show-Seat consisted of a series of folding seat-boards, foot-rests; and detachable seat-frames, all which could be conveniently packed away for transporting. The rows of seat-backs, giving an appearance of more comfort than patrons had seen before, was an easy inducement for more sales to that section of the tent.

With large crowds the general rule, Cole continued to show his ability for sound management and the accommodation of audience comfort. "There must have been five or six thousand persons in the main pavilion," a Baltimore writer observed, "but the arrangements for seating the multitude were so excellent, and the rule against standing in front of the ring was so strictly enforced, that the whole audience saw every incident of the performance."[5]

The street spectacle, when compared to the P. T. Barnum show or the Howes' Great London, was not impressive; but it was sufficiently splashy to accomplish the purpose. The few people of Rutland, Vermont, who did not appear street-side on August 10 to witness it could only read what they missed in the newspaper the following day: "The procession was a continuous line of glittering splendors and embodied many novelties. The steam calliope attracted the attention of everyone, and the large open den containing Zingra, the African and his monster serpents, was followed by the crowds, as was the open den containing Prof. Conklin and his performing lions and leopards. Among the many novelties in the procession was the band chariot drawn by twelve dromedaries richly and tastefully caparisoned. A gay cavalcade of ladies and gentlemen mounted on fine horses and tastefully costumed was followed by a long line of cages, elephants, chariots, ponies, etc."[6]

There were two free acts prior to the afternoon performance. Prof. Bristol cast off in his balloon, the *City of New York*, shortly before the doors opened.[7] This was followed by Jessie (Orton) Richards' ascension on a single wire to the top of the center pole and back. All done, the newspaper reported, to the hearty plaudits of the bystanders.

The circus performed in Illinois until the middle of April. The May 6 stand, the third of the season, drew an immense business. A correspondent reported, "The street parade, which was magnificent, was viewed by thousands. The wagons and trappings presented a bright and dazzling appearance. The collection of animals is large and they are fine specimens. The circus was one of the best we have seen in Peoria for a long time. The acts were novel and daring, while the *battoute* leaping of Messrs. Kelley and Batcheler elicited the unbounded admiration and praise of the vast audience."[8]

From Illinois the show went into Missouri, Nebraska, Iowa, and Minnesota. On June 19 it enjoyed large audiences in St. Paul in spite of threatening weather. Particularly satisfying to the local patrons were the bounding jockey spurt of Van Zandt and the pedestal somersaulting of the Milton Jaspers. Vaulter Kelley had met with an accident at Boone, Iowa, spraining his ankle, and was compelled to remain there for a couple of weeks. He rejoined the company in St. Paul and was able to make a successful leap over several horses. But he never fully recovered so, in consequence of the disability, eventually left for his home in New York state.

Wisconsin was next. An item in the Beaver Dam *Citizen* revealed that Cole's organization drew the largest audience of any show that had played there in many years. "From seven o'clock in the morning until noon, almost a continual string of teams poured in from every direction." The reason for this large turnout was easily accounted for. The county had been thoroughly advertised. "In nearly every hamlet and crossroads were posted flaming bills."[9]

By July 15 the show began a three day stand at Allegheny City, Pennsylvania, where it was reported: "Notwithstanding the unfavorable weather during the afternoon and evening exhibitions, the average attendance was large. In the ring performances there were several features worthy of special mention. At night Mr. Batcheler attempted to leap over twenty-five horses, neck to neck, but only partially succeeded—alighting, I think, on the twenty-second horse. He afterwards accomplished, with apparent ease, the feat of throwing a double somersault over twenty horses, neck to neck. Minnie Marks did neatly and gracefully an equestrian act, and the riding of Mr. Van Zandt elicited applause. The energetic acrobatic and gymnastic exercises of the Jasper Brothers were very creditable. The menagerie was not very extensive but the animals were in prime condition. In the street parade there were introduced several extra attractions."[10]

From Pennsylvania, the show went into New York state and Vermont. At Rutland the rush to the ticket wagon was immense. Van Zandt and the Milton Jaspers were again avidly applauded, as was Leon's five-horse act. "Grimaldi" Adams was judged to be an extremely funny clown and one of the best leapers in the profession.

New Jersey, Virginia and Maryland followed. There were three days at the famous old Belair lot in Baltimore beginning on September 13. Here Barcheler's vaulting was particularly admired. "It seems incredible that a man should turn a somersault over the heads of twenty-four horses, but one of the bold acrobats in Mr. Cole's circus actually accomplishes the this feat."[11] Nor were the female performers neglected. Jessie Orton Richards was given high praise for her skill and daring on the slack-wire, as was Miss Minnie Marks for her dashing and graceful riding.

The traveling came to a stop at Mount Vernon, Indiana, after which the outfit was shipped to winter quarters at Quincy, marking the end of another profitable tour.

## X

The year of 1876 featured the great Centennial celebration, the Exposition held in Philadelphia from May to November, a huge national museum of arts and sciences. Could circuses compete with it? And if that was not enough, it was an election year, which always interferes with public attention toward amusements.

Cole did not flinch. He expanded the size of the performing arena to two rings and a hippodrome track. This allowed him to translocate his hippodrome races to an oval within the main pavilion. In so doing he became the first combined "hippodrome, circus, and menagerie" company to perform in the United States (Barnum's previous Great Roman Hippodrome was not a circus).[1]

From all reports, audience appeal was highly satisfactory. The track, which encircled the double rings, was 30 feet wide with one lap equaling one-eighth of a mile. The program featured a regular running race of four riders, three of them being ladies, two-horse and four-horse chariot races, a standing-riding race, a liberty race of horses without riders, a mule race, a burlesque race, a walking race, or various combinations of those events. Two of the running horses were purchased at the end of the 1875 season when the Barnum organization held their auction of hippodrome property. "The spectators went wild with delight during the races, and yelled at the top of their voice as the horses sped around the track," so read the Memphis *Daily Appeal*. "They are exciting and thrilling, and by far the most captivating feature of any circus that ever exhibited in this city."[2]

The spread of canvas alone represented an amazing step forward. The performing pavilion was huge, said to be fifteen feet longer than that of the Barnum hippodrome. The four center-pole menagerie tent was 560 feet in circumference; the dressing tent 240 feet. Then there was a 40 by 30 foot cook tent, a 60 by 30 dining tent, and four 40 by 25 horse tents.[3]

The procession included seven magnificent tableaux chariots. The *Neptune* car, 24 feet long and 35 feet in height, displayed Neptune, the legendary God of Water, surrounded by his exotic nymphs. It contained machinery which could raise it to full height or lower it for normal transportation. Built in London, at the time of its purchase it had never been used in the United States. During shipment there was damage to the carving, but E. M. Miller & Co. accomplished a full restoration.

Four other cars represented *Asia, Africa, Europe*, and *America*. *Asia* was drawn by ten camels, *Europe* by eight caparisoned horses harnessed four abreast. The *Conqueror's Car* contained four lions crouched at the feet of George Conklin. There was the Yankee Robinson *Dragon Car* featuring the God of War and attendants. And the *African Car* was the glass-plated serpent den.

Winding up the procession was the wonderful car *America*, containing the Goddess of Liberty, surrounded by figures representing the Army, Navy, Peace, and Liberty.

Built by the Miller company, it was 20 feet long and 25 feet at its highest. Appropriate for the Centennial year, there were life size portraits of George Washington and other Revolutionary War figures, as well as battle scenes, flags and various symbols of early American history.

Also included in the spectacle were four Roman race chariots, each drawn by a four-horse team and four two-horse running chariots, all driven by ladies. The chariots were new, manufactured by Fielding & Co. of New York. The parade harnesses were the work of Quincy's A. B. Willhelm. Filling out the spectacle were the ladies and gentlemen performers on horseback and 30 dens of animals. "The procession will be the most imposing ever seen in this country and will be worth traveling miles to witness," the Quincy *Daily Herald* pledged. "Mr. Cole has spared no expense to make the parade the most gorgeous that will be presented to the public during the Centennial year and it is not too much to promise that the street display will be the finest ever witnessed in America."[4]

The menagerie kept pace with the enlargement of other departments on the show. Management boasted of exhibiting the largest pair of performing lions in the country and the largest living sea lion. Three baby camels, barely a month old at season's start, promised to be a charming feature.

The performers were kept busy, what with two rings and a hippodrome show to fill—"20 different races, 20 acts in each circus ring" the advertising read. The grand entrée was a representation of the continents of Asia, Europe, Africa, and North and South America. The sports of the hippodrome followed, interspersed with performances of the double circus company. This included Frank Gardner, the "English Jockey"; J. C. Campbell, vaulter; George "Grimaldi" Adams and William Ashton, clowns; Jessie Richards, on the wire *volante*; Young Leon (will he ever outlive his youth?), five-horse rider; William O'Dale, bareback rider; George Loyal, aerialist (who threw a somersault while flying from one trapeze to another); the Leroy Brothers, gymnasts; and, of course, George Conklin. The see-saw ponies still teetered and tottered, and Samson, the equestrian dog, returned to zip around the ring.[5]

Again out on rails, the ads boasted of thirty-six cars to transport the outfit. Their arrival at each stand was announced by the firing of a cannon. The sixth season began with dates in the familiar territories of Iowa and Illinois. At the end of June the show made a jump into Canada for a tour that lasted through July. A *Clipper* correspondent reported that "the show was visited by the largest number ever attracted by any show in Montreal, the monster tent being full at every performance."[6]

Cole moved about in New York state and Pennsylvania during August and then headed south into Kentucky and Tennessee. The circus drew nearly 6,000 people at the night performance in Louisville, according to the *Courier-Journal*, "composed of all manner of people, from the gamin, who had obtained his glimpse of glory by odd jobs, to the beauty, fashion and wealth of the city."[7]

An item in the *Daily American* noted that: "Cole's Hippodrome, Circus and Menagerie gives its first exhibition in Nashville this afternoon, in the sulphur spring bottom. The show is probably the largest traveling, three large tents being required for the various parts of the performance. Of its worth, our exchanges speak in the highest terms. It is really a prosperous, honest show, giving a full recompense for the liberal patronage it receives. The performances in the ring are of the most spirited description, consisting of athletic feats, wire walking, bareback riding, feats on the trapeze, chariot races, running races, and many other dashing exhibitions. The menagerie has not a superior in any other traveling show. Some of the animals are extremely rare even in large museums."[8]

For four performances at Memphis on October 2 and 3 it was estimated that a total of 16,000 people were in attendance. The *Daily Appeal* was strong in its praise: "It is the best that has yet visited Memphis in many respects, and the proprietor, Mr. W. W. Cole, deserves the thanks of the public for the efficient manner in which he has organized and perfected the hippodrome and circus, as well as for the great intelligence and appreciation manifested in the arrangement of the menagerie. Mr. Cole is a young man, but is full of the vim, vigor and active zeal that give dignity and strength to the enterprises which seek to entertain and amuse the public. As manager, proprietor and executive, he undoubtedly possesses nerve, tact and intelligence, and all of these characteristics he has most gracefully combined and gracefully utilized in the *toute ensemble* of the largest and most complete traveling show that ever visited our city. Mr. Cole fully merits public patronage, and we are sure his attractions will not be unrecognized by the public."[9]

The circus played Little Rock on October 30$^{th}$ and continued in Arkansas through the first week in November. Then, the season was prolonged by the purchase of the steamboat *Ella Hughes*, which with two barges transported the company along the lower Mississippi, thence the White, Yazoo, and Red rivers, and into the bayous of Louisiana for two months.

At tour's end the *Ella Hughes* was sold to Capt. William Wenzel.[10] The circus then returned to Memphis where the outfit was quartered at the Estes, Fizer & Co. cotton shed on Tennessee Street. The stock, seven camels and 150 head of horses, were pastured in Shelby County on a farm belonging to Major Greer. Because of the late closing, many of the troupe spent the winter lay-off in that city.

During the respite from travel, Cole received a special honor when King Momus bestowed on him the title of Duke of the Realm, as an assistant during Mardi-Gras season. The Carnival originated in 1872, at a time when Memphis had gone through a lengthy period of misfortune—Federal occupation, cholera and yellow fever epidemics, and an invasion of Northern merchants that had forced out local businesses. Thus, the festive February celebrations, which were repeated through 1881, were symbols of local pride and community rebirth. This was illustrated by such lofty conceits as: "Other Cities boast of their public libraries, art galleries, enterprise and intellect of their community, but Memphis and her people can point with true pride to the Memph and its great pageants, combining the most beautiful features of art with the highest excellence of science, history and mythology."[11]

Cole's honorary appointment was not without purpose. When on February 12 and 13 the annual fete occurred, his car of *Neptune*, drawn by fourteen dapple-gray horses, and his *Golden Dragon Bandwagon*, carrying two clowns, were part of the grand parade, and a royal-robed Momus, was seated on the back of the trained elephant, Pete. Other elements of the circus were also part of the spectacle—twenty spirited horses, eight ponies, four donkeys, twelve camels, Roman chariots, and an abundance of costumes and paraphernalia. An appreciative King Momus conferred on Cole the merited title of *Duc de Manège*.

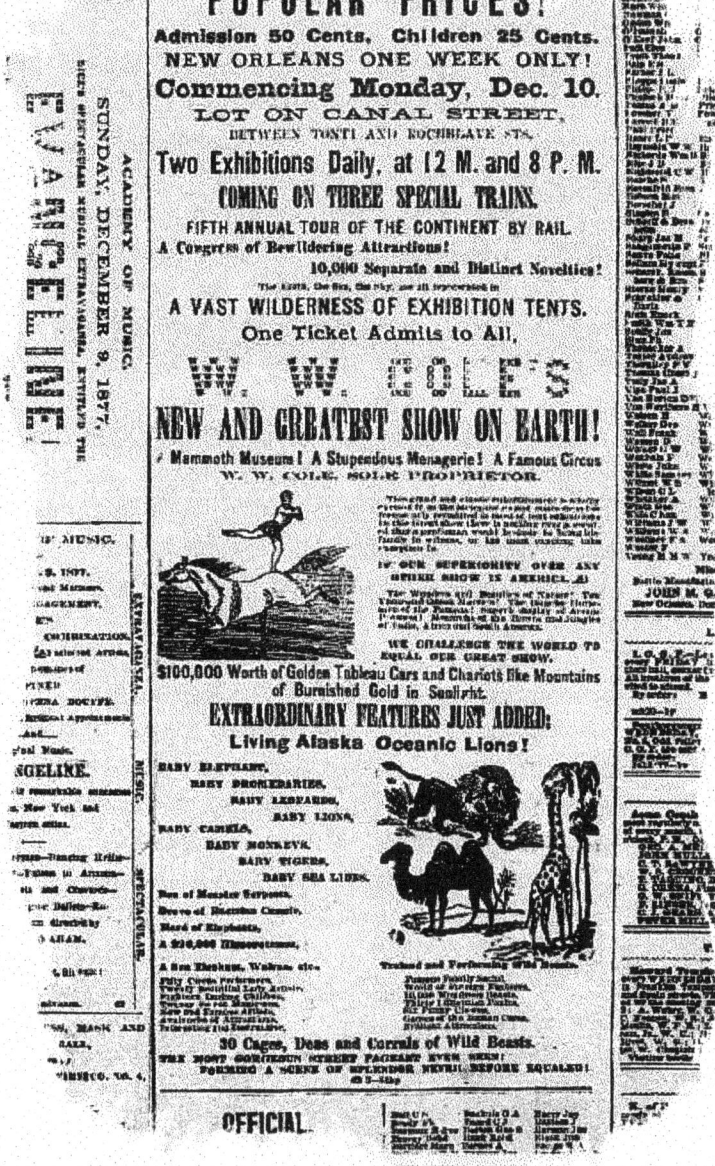

## XI

In 1877 the country was aroused by a national election scandal of the previous year. The Democratic candidate for President, Samuel J. Tilden, polled a 250,000 popular majority over Republican rival Rutherford B. Hayes, and had defeated him in electoral votes, 184 to 163. However, this count did not include the tally of 12 votes from Florida, Louisiana, Oregon, and South Carolina, where the polling was bitterly contested. The dispute was submitted to Congress in which political institution the Republican nominee was selected along party lines. Hayes was elected by only one electoral vote, causing frenetic cries of "fraud!" from ocean to ocean (the readers will recall a more recent and similar controversy). He was thereafter called "His Fraudulency" by his foes. Could circuses overcome this national trauma? The answer is "yes."

Cole's opening on April 2 and 3 was received by a very appreciative Memphis community. He had spent over $20,000 there during the winter, including the sums paid out for meat to feed his menagerie animals and provender for his horses and the employment of local mechanics of various skills in preparation for the new season. "The presence of the circus and menagerie in Memphis has been a great benefit to our people," the *Daily Appeal* announced. "We would be glad to have him winter here again; in fact, for every successive year."[1]

As a show of gratitude, Cole reduced the prices of tickets to 50¢ and 25¢. $1.00 had been the going rate in the South and Far West. "Only fifty cents, and children under ten years of age twenty-five cents, are the lines that indicate the price of admission to W. W. Cole's great show," exclaimed a writer for the *Daily Appeal*; "and we don't see why the idea of cheap admission has not occurred before to some one of the many managers of tent-shows that yearly visit the South." Well, in Tennessee the state license for such exhibitions was anywhere from a hefty $225 to $350 a day, which explains a lot. "The 'cheap rates' is a move in the right direction," he went on, "and there is not the slightest doubt but what Mr. Cole will meet with an enormous success for having been the first to offer them."[2]

**MEMPHIS, MONDAY-TUESD'Y**

**APRIL 2 AND 3.**

CHEAP RATES! TO KEEP PACE WITH THE TIMES!

**Only 50 Cents Admission!**

CHILDREN UNDER TEN YEARS, 25 CENTS.

Congress of Bewildering Attractions! 100,000 Separate and Distinct Novelties! The Fourth, the Seen, the Sky! are all represented in a Vast Wilderness of Exhibition Tents.

**ONE TICKET ADMITS TO ALL!**

Cole understood he could not top what he had presented in 1876 and still turn a handsome profit. A major asset was keeping his outfit to a manageable size; so this year no two rings, no hippodrome races. His show reverted to the original W. W. Cole's Great New York and New Orleans title. The choice was to cut back and rest on the reputation he had established.[3] His advertising stressed such items as the menagerie, the 50¢ admission price, the "1,200 opera seats," and the street pageant.

The 1870s could well be called the decade of the elephants. The phenomenon began early, when in 1871 Seth B. Howes imported ten specimens from Ceylon. The next year Howes' Great London unveiled a five-elephant pyramid act that set a new performance level and was soon copied by the Forepaugh show. Throughout the next several years the herd sizes increased on most of the major circuses until by 1880 Cooper & Bailey exhibited a twelve-elephant military drill, Forepaugh had a herd of ten (although he advertised twelve), and Barnum was scratching to keep in step. This massing of pachyderms was the prelude to the "elephant wars" of the early 1880s.

But unlike his three largest competitors who emphasized their herds of performing bulls, W. W. Cole was content to exhibit only one for most of those years and two at the end of the decade. Nevertheless, his advertising boldly carried the Barnum slogan, "The Greatest Show on Earth."

He had prudently enlarged his menagerie throughout his management until there were some thirty cages of animals and birds—the huge sea lion, a family of young and old monkeys, a kangaroo, an anteater, a walrus, leopards, tigers, panthers, jaguars, etc.—all kept in the finest condition. New this year was a den of laughing hyenas, said to be the first exhibited in this country. But still highlighted in the bills were the denizens that had brought success in the past. The "beast-fish, weighing over 1,000 pounds," the perennial but popular sea lion, was exhibited in a mammoth glass tank filled with water. In that it consumed thirty pounds of fresh fish daily, its healthy diet must have required careful planning while on tour in many parts of the country. The glass den of pythons was another important repeating feature that appeared regularly in the advertising and that held the crowds' attention at each exhibition.

William Batcheler

The highlight of the program was the troupe of vaulters, the largest in the country. The featured act of this segment was a contest between Frank A. Gardner and William H. Batcheler, which was introduced by the now familiar Tom McIntyre.[4] Batcheler, whose real name was Patrick Quirk, had entered the circus business as an apprentice to George H. Batcheler, the famous vaulter and showman, in 1867 and took his mentor's name. The versatile Gardner was, along with his leaping, a bareback rider, hurdle rider, and tumbler. At this time his career was just getting under way.

Frank Gardner

But there were other strong acts, generously praised by the Memphis press at the opening stand. "The superb and graceful riding of young [William] O'Dale was truly the most graceful and picturesque act of horsemanship which we have ever had the good fortune to witness. Without any apparent effort he executed pirouettes and somersaults which were models of beauty and expertness, and, a moment after, rest upon his horse's back in a position which would call up memories of some classic statue carved in marble." Young Leon in his five-horse act "seemed a part of the horse as he guided and put his beautiful steed through a series of evolutions, which prove him not only a finished rider, but an animal educator of rare experience and ability." Others were Anson Van Zandt, Frank Gardner, and Frank Morgan, all of whom rode without saddle. And there was Mlle. Johanna Salomonski who was the premier equestrienne. The Snow Brothers, three in number, accomplished a somersault from shoulder to shoulder and performed their large troupe of dogs and monkeys. "The posturing act of the Snow Brothers was another elegant feature of the enjoyable programme; grace, ease and skill have been studied with earnest application, and combined to add what might be necessary to complete the most finished performance now offered for public admiration." The Lawrence sisters—Sallie, Jennie, and Fanny—were the female gymnasts; Jessie Orton Richards, the *equilibrieste*; beautiful Maggie Claire, single trapezist; and Crossley & Elder, field athletes. The clowns, "Grimaldi" Adams, Harry Long and Tom McIntyre were "in their happiest mood and did not throw out the defunct witticisms of bygone days." For his part, Mr. McIntyre "kept the audience amused and delighted whenever he appeared, by keeping up a running fire of seemingly insoluble conundrums, which, when solved at last, burst out in coruscations of refined wit and laughable oddities." Al Richards, man of many jobs, was ringmaster and "the best that ever appeared in the arena." And let us not forget George Conklin, "a gentleman whose control and influence over the brutes in the menagerie are as strange as they are intense." All this constituted an impressive array of entertainment.[5]

Following the Memphis opening Cole took the show into southern territory. Then by July it was in Ohio, Indiana and Pennsylvania. When at Ashtabula, Ohio, it was visited by a twenty-three year old Walter L. Main. He recalled seeing Batcheler do a double somersault over eighteen horses, neck to neck. "I have seen all the great leapers in the last half-century," he wrote many years later, "and never saw one as good as Batcheler." He added, "It was a swell one-ring railroad circus, with one elephant."[6]

In early September the show was in West Virginia. It played to large audiences at Wheeling on the 6th. The local correspondent reported that the vaulting match between Batcheler and Gardner received great applause.

The company had worked down into Georgia by November. "The name of Cole on a circus bill in this country is the guarantee of a good show," enthused the Atlanta *Constitution*. "The procession yesterday afternoon was immense, and was witnessed by more than four thousand people scattered along the line of march. It was decidedly one of the fullest and handsomest ever made up in our streets.... In the afternoon every seat was taken and the exhibitions in the arena were first class in every way.... At night the crowd was immense. The mammoth canvass was crowded to its utmost capacity. Even standing room in sight of the ring was at a premium."[7] At this time, when Barnum's name meant nothing in the South, Cole's did.

The show moved west from Georgia and closed the regular season with a week in New Orleans at the Canal Street lot beginning December 10. Referring to that date, a *Clipper* correspondent wrote: "On the opening night the attendance was very large, the sale of tickets being stopped at a quarter of eight o'clock, owing to lack of accommodations."[8] Large attendance was also confirmed by the New

Orleans *Times Picayune*: "To leave such business as Cole has been doing here during the past week is like running away from a gold mine, but the show is advertised to show at Donaldsonville on Monday and must leave."[9]

A winter tour was then organized. While in New Orleans Cole bought a stern-wheeler, a cotton and passenger boat, which he fitted up for carrying the horses and people. The women and leading performers had staterooms, while the others slept on cots in shared cabins. A barge towed by the boat served as the menagerie. The show was routed up the Mississippi and sometimes into the bayous amongst the large plantations. When the passage became too shallow, Cole hired flatboats and transferred the show onto them, then reverted to the steamer on his return to deeper water.

This tour closed abruptly at Helena, Arkansas, on January 5, 1878. Conklin explained this unexpected move with: "That year there was an unusual crop of cotton and it was bringing high prices. Everyone was anxious to get his crop into market as soon as possible. The boats could not begin to carry it as fast as it was ready to be shipped, and sometimes a man had to wait for weeks before his cotton would be taken off the dock. Near this town lived a very large planter who had a great deal of cotton which he was anxious to ship, but saw no immediate prospect of doing it by the regular river boats. He had offered to buy the boat and barge and would give Cole such a price in cash for it that he [Cole] accepted the offer."[10]

This ended a successful season of forty weeks, with Cole's being the first circus out and the last one in. The company members that were not needed at winter quarters were paid off and the outfit was put on a freight boat and sent to St. Louis for the remainder of the winter.

As a growing institution from 1875 through 1877, Cole's circus acquired and retained the services of one of the top animal handlers in the business, who was in charge of an expanding menagerie exhibit. The show featured some of the greatest leapers in the country. It was the first to combine a circus program with hippodrome events, which in turn required a larger spread of canvas. New parade vehicles were added to the procession to make it more competitive with the other established companies. And such additions as padded reserve seats and lower admissions for Southern residents gave additional satisfaction. Cole's circus was competing and prospering.

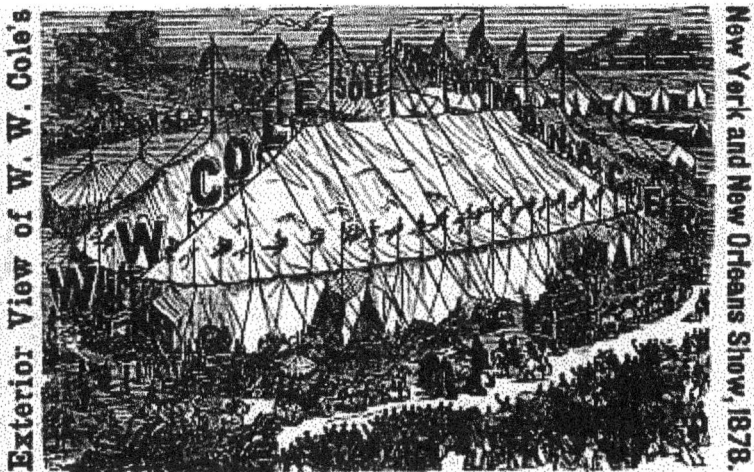

## XII

W. W. Cole made a profitable choice for the season of 1878. He engaged Capt. and Mrs. Martin VanBuren Bates. This unique couple created an occurrence of huge public curiosity that paid off for the show in ticket sales.

Billed as "The Kentucky Giant," Capt. Bates was one of the largest and tallest men in the world, believed to have been 7 feet 2½ inches in height and to have weighed 470 pounds. Particularly admired for his intelligence and kindness, as an attraction, he was not only inordinately huge but was a Southern Civil War hero. A native of Whitesburg, Kentucky, he joined the Confederate $5^{th}$ Kentucky Infantry in 1861 at age sixteen, later transferred to the cavalry, and was eventually elevated to the level of captain. In the fall and winter of 1862-63 his unit was instrumental in breaking up the lawless guerrilla bands that were a menace to the mountain regions. While under Humphrey Marshall's command, he was captured in a raid at Pound Gap and sat out the rest of the war.

After the conflict Capt. Bates moved to Cincinnati where he joined a small circus at a $100 a month salary and expenses. Within a short time he connected with old John Robinson's show and received four times that amount. While booked on a tour of Europe by Judge Ingalls, he married Anna Hannon Swan in London on June 17, 1871.[1]

Anna, "The Nova Scotia Giantess," was born in New Annan, Nova Scotia, in 1846, weighing a whopping eighteen pounds. Impressively tall for a giantess, she exceeded her husband by beyond two inches.[2] Another P. T. Barnum discovery, made through a Quaker friend of the Swan family, she was exhibited at the American Museum in New York alongside the famous Tom Thumb.

The couple were placed for viewing with Cole's circus, not in a sideshow at the cost of another ticket, but in the entrance to the menagerie area on a special platform. Alongside them, reaching only to their knees, were Count Rosebud and Baron Littlefinger, which accentuated the size of all four of the oddities. As the spectators entered they discovered Mrs. Bates in a becoming dress of silk, containing eighty yards of material. She quite captivated them by her graceful manners and polished demeanor. The Captain, in a full dress suit, frank and affable in conversation, also presented a most pleasing appearance.

Louis E. Cooke was in the advertising department at this time, his first of six years with the show. He was born in Jackson, Tioga County, Pennsylvania, but early on moved to a farm in Michigan with his family, where he endured a life of hardship and poverty. "I plowed from dawn until dark with an ox team," he wrote, "and filled my place in the harvest field."

He left home at sixteen and learned the cobbler's trade while attending school. But finding his inclinations were for a higher level of employment he hired on at the Otsego *Herald* as a printer's devil, working nights and going to classes by day. Within a few months he moved to the Battle Creek *Journal*, and then to the Kalamazoo *Daily Telegraph*. During his stay at the latter paper he finished his training and became a proficient job printer, compositor and pressman.

It was in Kalamazoo where he began working as a reporter. In covering entertainment news he was introduced to show life and eventually was getting offers for a job as agent. He finally succumbed to the temptations in 1870 by taking employment in advance of Professor Martino, the California Illusionist.

Louis E. Cooke

A few years later he was connected with the Redpath Lyceum Bureau of Boston, working as agent for some of the major lecturers and concert attractions during the winter season, including Henry Ward Beecher, Theodore Tilton, the Kellogg-Carey Concert Company, the Hyers Sisters, and others.

Eventually he applied for a job as middleman with Cole's organization. The middleman, as Cooke described it, traveled as an intermediary between the advance advertising brigade of agents and billposters and the show. His duty was to keep track of their work, to distribute special advertising bills and supply the various newspapers with copy.

I was engaged immediately," Cooke remarked, "and there began a friendship that is among the most delightful memories of my life."[3]

"Shortly after casting in my fortunes with the Cole Circus," he wrote, "I was promoted to the position of the 'Extreme Advance' agent. I preceded the show and all its agents, exploiting some particular feature that in my judgment was likely to capture the imagination of the general public."[4] One of these was the Bates giants. For this he devised a poster, a huge picture of the Captain and his wife, the largest such paper that had been printed to that time, twelve feet wide and fifteen feet high, necessitating the construction of special billboards along the route.

Cole added more animals to the menagerie this year, obtained at auction of the defunct Montgomery Queen circus. The sale was held at the Exposition Building in Louisville on February 21 by the Buffalo Courier Company that had taken possession of the circus property through foreclosure. W. R. Hayden, Cole's general agent, represented him in bidding for the animals. The purchases, which arrived at the St. Louis fair grounds on the 23rd, included a zebra for $230; a lion and lioness, $200; two kangaroos, $82 each; a wild boar, $5; the elephant Lalla Rookh, $1,500; a sacred cow, $21; two monkeys, $21 each; and the spotted trick horse Humboldt, $280.[5]

The 1878 program, as reported by the Quincy *Daily Herald*, was again a combination of both old and new faces. 1. Grand entry by the entire company. 2. Trained elephants, introduced by Conklin. 3. Leaps, led by world's champion William Batcheler. 4. Principal bareback act by Romeo Sebastian; with Tom McIntyre as clown. 5. Horizontal bar act,

Maggie Claire [courtesy of Steve Gossard, Curator, Milner Library Special Collections, Illinois State University, Normal, IL

Reno Brothers; Pico Adams, clown. 6. Two-horse act by Young Leon and Herbert. 7. Double trapeze by the Claire Sisters. 8. Duo of performing horses, introduced by Sig. Marquez. 9. Herbert Brothers, gymnasts. 10. The Comanche Indian by Sig. Marquez. 11. Flying rings by Maggie Claire.

12. The Principal bareback act by Rosaline Stickney. 13. William O'Dale, bareback somersault act. 14. Leon's seven-horse act. 15. Henry Cooke's ponies and monkeys. 16. Conklin's den of lions.[6]

George H. "Grimaldi" Adams had left the show to devote more time to touring pantomimes. He was replaced by his brother, James R. "Pico" Adams. Their father was the English clown Charles H. Adams, and their mother the former Mary Ann Cooke, daughter of Thomas E. and granddaughter of Thomas Taplin. "Pico," still very young, had served a seven year apprenticeship to the English circus manager Ethardo before coming to this country.

Rosaline Stickney and Romeo Sebastian were strong additions to the riding department. Rosaline, by her friends called "Crissie," was a third generation of important riders. Her mother, also Rosaline, was the daughter of S. P. Stickney, patriarch of the famous equestrian family. Her father, Benoit Tourniaire, was a pupil of François Tourniaire, and the brother of Louise, Theodore and Ferdinand, all illustrious riders. Romeo Sebastian, most remembered for his feat of sitting on a chair on the back of a running horse while reading a newspaper, was the son of Signor Quaglieni, a European performer of note.

This group of quality artists elicited universal praise from the local scribes. In Detroit a correspondent for the *Free Press* wrote: "In the afternoon the mammoth pavilions were filled, and to a thoughtful person the question presented itself: How is it that such a vast assembly will gather in the face of rain, mud and a total eclipse of the sun? At the close of the performance the question had been satisfactorily answered, for the programme gone through with embraced many novelties, innumerable new feats of acrobatic and gymnastic skill; marvelous exhibitions of horsemanship, groups of trained horses, mules, monkeys, elephants, and other animals and exhibitions of wonders almost incomprehensible."[7]

A unique advertising device this year was a throwaway fold-out six inches wide and four inches high. When opened, the item extended to some ten times its width, its pages extolling the great double circus troupe through a panoramic illustration of its street parade. The front cover revealed a vast field of canvas (see page 127); the back cover the "Interior of W. W. Cole's Grand Traveling Zoological Gardens."

The following illustration, copied from the inner back cover of the fold-out, gives us a vision of the configuration within the performing tent with the use of both ring and stage. We can also make out a band of musicians and a minstrel troupe significant of the concert. Further, we can see that the hippodrome track, installed two years earlier by Cole, has now become a permanent area.

The Topeka *Daily Blade* stated that the menagerie was arranged for the convenience of spectators by being in a separate part of the pavilion from the circus and "so placed that all can see without being crowded."[8] This suggests that Cole had dispensed with an individual menagerie tent, using the main one for the exhibition of both wild and human animals; but, this is misleading. A description of how the Cole circus tore down its tents and loaded the outfit for the next stand, quite vividly described in the Wamego, Kansas, *Tribune*, leaves no doubt that there were separate canvases—the main tent, the museum, the menagerie, the dressing and assembly tent, and the annex—and two trains of railroad cars to transport them all.[9]

Cole opened the season with a week stand in St. Louis on April 29 and played to large turnouts.[10] Following, the first leg of the tour took in Iowa and Minnesota. The *Pioneer Press* describe the circus day excitement that occurred in St. Paul. "So eager were the people to witness the performances of which the free exhibition has given such promise, that almost before the vast canvas was spread, and the thousands of seats in place, a grand rush commenced." The paper praised the bareback feats of Sebastian, who threw a somersault through a balloon, never failing to land on the flank of his galloping steed; also Batcheler's double somersault over eighteen horses, the chaste wit of clown McIntye, the intrepidity of Conklin, and the skills of a number of other artists.[11]

The tour continued into Kansas and Nebraska. While at Topeka the *Commonwealth* expressed its pleasure with the street procession. "It was gorgeous to say the least, and everyone remarked, 'what splendid horses and what good condition too,' in which they were correct, for never has such a large number of well kept horses been seen in Topeka." The paper also found the full house performances deserving of commendation.[12]

While exhibiting in Clay Center, Kansas, Capt. Bates escaped the ninety-eight degree heat by taking a swim in a nearby river. The incident created quite a stir in this small community. The local *Dispatch* commented, "Several citizens went down to see the fun and report that was by far the best part of the show. The Captain is a number one swimmer, and was not the least bit bashful about pulling off his clothes before the crowd of spectators."[13]

From Kansas, the show moved east to Illinois. The Quincy date was like a home-coming, as the company was happily received by the press. "Quincy has a warm place in its heart for W. W. Cole and will give him a welcome today.... There are a number of Quincy favorites with the show, the sight of whom will be good for the eyes." Four veterans were given special attention. Fred Levens, treasurer from the very outset, was fondly designated with "genial as of old." Joe Gulick, the calliope player, was remembered as "the backward shot and vocalist, who can sing all day and make up his song as he goes along." Tom McIntyre, who had been in business there a few years back, "and furnished more fun for the town than any other man in the same length of time," was fondly anticipated. And Prof. John Evans, the lecturer, was expected to lift his melodious voice in introducing the 'tallest people in the world.' "John was educated for a Roman Senator and when he gets to talking 'makes Rome howl.'"[14]

Then on to Michigan and a successful week in Detroit where "the evening performance was greater than in the afternoon, while the entertainment was in every way as pleasing, with the addition of the delightful glitter of elaborate wardrobes under the hundreds of gas jets which lighted the huge tents."[15] Cole was congratulated in having kept faith with the public by presenting everything just as advertised, an observation that was voiced repeated from season to season.

Dates in Canada followed (while there, it was announced that Cole gave a donation of $500 to the Memphis Relief Committee to benefit the yellow fever sufferers); but by October the circus had moved south. A Richmond, Virginia, correspondent revealed that attendance there was disappointing, probably because the circus lot was too far from the city's center of activity. North Carolina and Tennessee were next, prior to closing the season in Knoxville on October 18. The show then returned to winter quarters at St. Louis, thus concluding a typical Cole season, efficiently managed, financially successful and relatively trouble free.

St. Louis *Post-Dispatch*, April 21, 1879

## XIII

Cole entered the 1879 season with a bold display of confidence within his advertisements: "The proprietor of this vast and unparalleled consolidation of interesting and attractive features has, for the season of 1879, through a life-long experience and a lavish outlay of money, the pleasure of placing before the public the GRANDEST EFFORT OF HIS LIFE, by procuring all the attainable novelties of the BRUTE CREATION from all quarters of the world, and in connection wherein will be found the most conspicuous Riders, Gymnasts, Grotesque and Acrobatic Male and Female artists to be found in any part of the world."

His *Avant Courier* boasted of "500 Zoological Wonders in the Menagerie"—well, maybe, if you counted the side-poles. But it did contain a reasonable collection of rare animals. Among those listed were Asiatic elephants, a giraffe, lions and tigers, a black leopard, camels and dromedaries, a Tibetan yak, an eland, tapirs, a zebra, apes and monkeys, etc. The advertisements claimed thirty-five cage wagons, which we believe were still the short double-compartmented kind that were loaded crossways on railroad cars. Comments from the press assured us the animals were all in good condition. And, again, within the same canvas stood the very affable Bates couple, greeting the public as it passed through the entrance.

The *Clipper* announced in 1878 that railroad cars ordered by Cole were under construction in St. Louis. It appears he took possession of them this year if the advertisements, "coming on my own railroad cars," are to be believed. We have found no other source for authentication. The number of cars circuses claim to have is always unreliable and varies from one account to another. Sometimes this incongruity can be more justified with cars that have been leased from the railroad companies, allowing more flexibility in their usage. But still, as in most circus matters within this period of operation, items of information are shuffled and dealt out by creative press agents.

At season's end the New Orleans *Daily Picayune* characterized Cole's circus train with: "The traveling equipment of the concern, with its thirty cars and two Pullman coaches, cars for the working men and the stock, all handsomely painted and lettered, 'Cole's New Orleans and New York Circus and Menagerie,' is a show in itself."[1] Thirty cars for Cole's growing institution is possible if they were of the thirty-five to forty foot length that was still in common use at this time.

Cooper & Bailey's Great London introduced electric lighting to the circus world this season. The generator and accompanying lamps were manufactured by the Charles F. Brush Company of Cleveland, Ohio, to which the circus proprietors paid $15,000 for the exclusive right of use under canvas. The system consisted of an engine with an armature that averaged 750 revolutions per minute and which powered twelve carbon-pencil burners, creating light of an extreme whiteness as contrasted to the yellow, smoky, flickering jets of contemporary circuses. In response, Cole acquired an electric lighting system during the course of the season, although we don't know when. Advertisements through July make no mention of it.

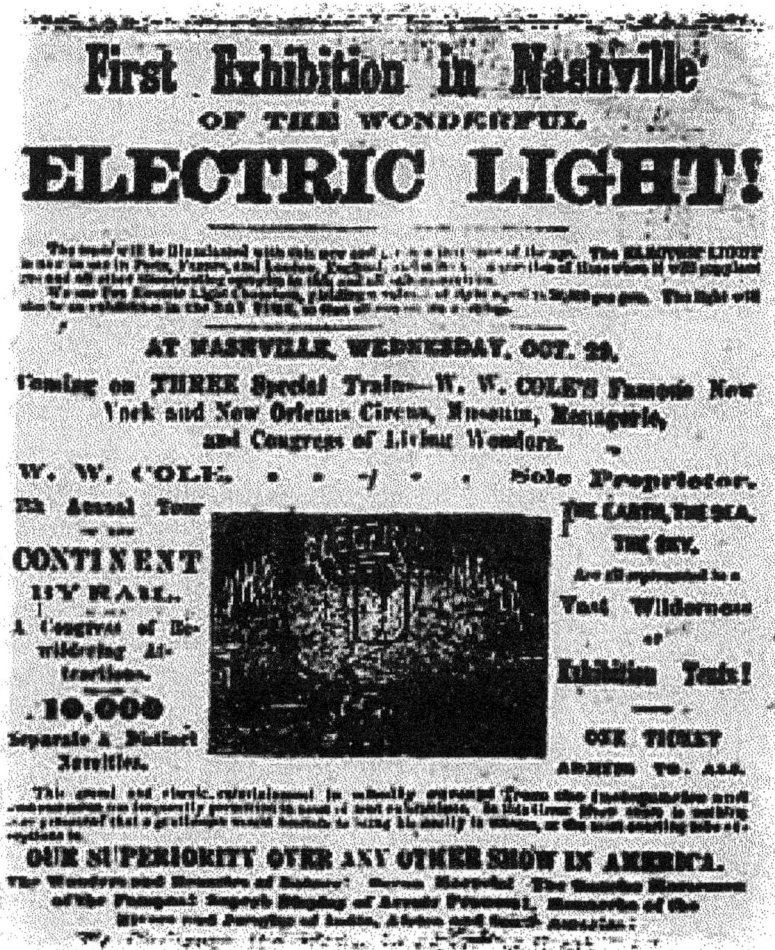

Prior to the acquisition of an electrical system the show's *Avant Courier* stressed the benefit of illumination with gas. "Our Mammoth Tents are lighted with gas, which is manufactured especially for our use, so that the actors, great Hippodrome Chariot races, animal curiosities, and all other features of this magnificent exhibition, can be seen as effectively in the evening as during the afternoon. The odor of kerosene, which is so offensive in many exhibitions, is entirely avoided."[2]

The use of electricity becomes prominent in the show advertising and newspaper accounts in late October and November. The Nashville *Daily American* found it to be the most notable feature of the entertainment. "In the darkest night the tents are as light as in the full glare of day."[3] The Savannah *Morning News* observed that "the tents were brilliantly illuminated with the electric light, which was quite an attraction." The illumination was said to come from one of the Brush Dynamo Electric systems manufactured in Cleveland, just as was Cooper & Bailey's. It was run by a thirty horse power steam engine, giving it a capability of handling sixteen lights, each equal to thirty-two five foot gas burners. The menagerie tent was brightened by three of these and the main tent by six.[4]

On April 21 the Cole circus opened in St. Louis, where it had been wintering. The *Post-Dispatch* reported that the various departments were in excellent condition, money having been lavished with a free hand on preparations for the season. The opening performance reportedly went without a flaw, save for a ring horse which, for want of practice, gave Carlotta Wambold an ugly toss. "The lady, by the way, has made an innovation in the old style of dressing to ride. Instead of looking like an umbrella, she has very sensibly donned tights, which are much more graceful and becoming."[5] Then, during Conklin's encounter with the cats, which closed the program, he was viciously attacked by a frustrated tiger; but before real damage was done the animal was permanently bestilled.

Along with the above, the 1879 arena was enlivened with the high flying Claire Sisters[6], a bicycle spectacular, and an amount of roller skating. William O'Dale was the bareback rider; and Tom McIntyre, Pico Adams and Dan Kennedy were again the clowns.[7] Acrobat George Dunbar did a double-somersault from a giant swing. The performing elephant Siam was trained to stand on its head, play a hand organ, kneel down to receive passengers, shoot a pistol, ring a dinner bell, walk a tight-rope, and dance on its hind legs.

Strong man Mons. De Ruth caught cannon balls from a gun that was loaded in the presence of the audience. An occasional miss, which allowed the ball to crash through a huge barrier, only proved that the projectile was heavy and forceful. Apparently the feat was not particularly well received. The Louisville *Courier-Journal* called it "about the poorest thing in the show."

There was also "The Man of Fire," direct from Europe, Sig. Peluzio Cardozo. Clothed only in a slight garment of his own invention and supplied with eye protection, he entered a booth of flames, hot enough to "roast a fowl," where he remained fully ten minutes, walking, standing, sitting in full view of the audience. This sounds to me like a feature reserved for the concert.

In 1877 the Barnum show introduced a liberty act of six Trakene stallions from Prussia, which turned out to be a great hit with our horse dependent society. Not missing a bet, Cole acquired his own group of stallions for 1879, three blacks and three grays, that under their insightful trainer, William Organ, performed a drill-like routine, waltzed in couples, stood on their hind legs, rolled barrels, performed on a see-saw, etc. The highlight came when one took an extensive leap over the others.

It was announced in the *Clipper* that Cole had "eyes on the golden shores of the Pacific," and that the show would be in Colorado by May. But on May 21 it was still in Kansas. The Atchison *Daily Champion* confirmed this date in the following item. "Cole's circus came yesterday, and with it came the swarming multitudes. Countless farm wagons filled with people—and nobody has found out yet how many men, women and children can get into a two horse wagon—poured in on all the roads. Cataracts of pedestrians came pouring down all the hills of Atchison into the hills of Commercial street. All the people who could squeeze into the upper front windows from one end of the street to the other did so. At last came the cavalcade, passing, as Frank Everest says, 'like an oriental dream.' It took in only about half of Commercial street, whereat the people who were left out of the line of vision waxed furious. The elephant was greeted with the usual enthusiasm and was followed up the street by the usual number of tender youth, each with his 'letter in the post office.' The big tent was crowded both afternoon and evening. The general performance was an average one, though the trapeze performance by the sisters was excellent. The cannon ball catcher couldn't catch at night, on account of the bad light, he said, but accidents happen in the best regulated circuses. The side show should get a new hurdy-gurdy. The instrument on hand at present is too slow, and has a depressing effect on the multitude. Other improvements might be suggested, but the Cole show will pass muster and certainly amused an immense number of people yesterday."[8]

An item in the *Clipper* reported that Colorado was visited to "very large business," the tent being filled at nearly every stand. But good attendance aside, the trip was responsible for a serious mishap. At Pueblo the two elephants, Pete and Siam, were transferred from their special broad-gauge car onto a flat car to make the trip on the narrow gauge Denver and Rio Grande road. The train left the rail yard at 6:00 p.m. on the 11th of May under pleasant weather conditions, but while crossing the Divide a sleet and snow storm came up. By the time the circus arrived in Denver the twelve year old Pete had caught a very bad cold. The animal lingered until the 15th before dying quietly.[9]

I have no explanation for the change of plans, but after playing dates in Colorado Cole's eyes turned eastward and the show headed for the mid-West—Wisconsin, Illinois, Indiana and Ohio. For a Ft. Wayne stand on July 15 a correspondent wrote: "The street-pageant was very fine, the ring performance only fair, there being much sickness among the performers and animals."[10] This may have been due to the extreme mid-summer heat, which was soaring into ninety degree temperatures. At Muncie, one of the sea lions, unaccustomed to Indiana dog days, showed symptoms of heat prostration, but a vigorous swabbing with ice water and intense fanning brought about a return to normalcy.

At Indianapolis the parade left the grounds earlier than usual, at nine o'clock, and the ticket wagon remained open all day to relieve the crowds from the unfriendly rays of the sun. The local assessment was positive, the company having recovered from heat shock. "The ring performances were among the best seen in that city for several years, while the animal department, though not large, was varied and pleasing."[11]

Indeed, there was consistent praise along the route from the local press, exemplified by Wausau's *The Torch of Liberty*. "It is fair to state that the ring performance, the trapeze, the trained animals and exhibitions of muscular development surpassed everything which has heretofore exhibited in Wausau"[12] And the LaCrosse *Republican and Leader* agreed. "The animals in the menagerie were in good collection, the performing stallions were marvelous, and the entire performance in the ring was interesting and meritorious"[13] The Sheboygan *Times*, in concert with its colleagues, stated, "It made the best street parade of any circus that has been here for some time, and inside the canvas its exhibition and ring performances were of the highest order of this class of shows."[14] The Appleton *Crescent* conceded that "there was one feature of the show, of a very commendatory character, and that [was] the very gentlemanly and ladylike bearing of all the principal participants, rendering it a pleasure to meet with them socially."[15] And the Indianapolis *Journal* of mid-July commented on the bright appearance of the costumes and carriages and extolled the quality of the arena program: "The acrobatic and gymnastic performers under the canvas displayed greater skill and agility than any that have been given recently in connection with other circuses; while the horsemanship deserves to rank high among displays of the equestrian art."[16]

An unfortunate incident occurred in late September. A lion escaped from its cage somewhere near the city of Defiance, Ohio. It ended up in a farmer's barn, where it unceremoniously killed and ate a cow. The beast was recaptured and hurried on its way to the next stand. The owner of the cow, we must assume, received appropriate payment for damages incurred.

The company left the Midwest at the latter part of September and headed south—Kentucky, Tennessee, Georgia, etc., with admissions now at 75¢ and 50¢. In Louisville the crowds were immense. In the evening many were turned away while a similar number stood throughout the performance. "The circus is fully up to, if not really above, the average, as circuses go," we see in the *Courier-Journal*. The writer was glad that the clowns got off very few jokes, that the stale witticisms that are common with circus jesters was "conspicuously absent." He continued to be candid in his observations, finding the bareback riding "not remarkable"

and the menagerie only "fair." And as for the six performing stallions (there were only five at this performance), one of which was supposed to leap over five others, "There is no such leap made by any of Mr. Cole's horses, and the management, it seems, ought to be aware that it is the poorest of poor policies to advertise it." On the other hand, he expressed admiration for the Livingston Brothers, the horizontal bar exercises, the leaping of Frank Gardner, and the aerial display of the Claire Sisters, particularly Maggie Claire "in her graceful and daring feats in the ring and in descending the rope."[17] The paper also showed amazement at and admiration for Capt. Bates, a fellow Kentuckian, calling him an Apollo Belvedere in form, perfect in proportions and a physical Goliath.

The circus met with equal popularity in Nashville. "The best order was preserved and no accident marred the enjoyment of the immense audience present," so stated the *Daily American*. Because of the reduction in admissions (50¢ and 25¢), the concert and sideshow did a large business. It was estimated that between 5,000 and 6,000 were packed together within the tent and another 300 were unable to gain admission.[18]

On to Savannah, Georgia, where on November 11th the citizens were to experience electric lights for the very first time. But old Dame Fortune was irritable this day. The show train, which was to reach the city by eight in the morning, was stalled on the Savannah and Charleston Railroad when the locomotive gave out. It's arrival three hours late, which necessitated scratching the grand street parade, disappointed the huge and expectant crowd. Still, by one o'clock the lot located on the Whitaker Street line was crowded, mostly with ladies and children; but to their dismay the matinee had to be delayed until three o'clock. "As was predicted, the immense tents were literally packed," so informed the Savannah *Morning News*, "in fact at one time locomotion was almost impossible in the menagerie tent, so dense was the crowd. After viewing the animals and the giant and giantess, the crowd slowly moved on to the circus tent, and in due time were all seated, every bench and chair in the extensive pavilion being crowded.... The crowd at the performance last night was simply beyond expression, and it is estimated there were fully seven thousand five hundred people present. Never has such a jam been seen beneath canvas in this city, and hundreds were turned away."[19]

The circus opened for a week in New Orleans beginning on the 24th of November. "Last night W. W. Cole's Circus and Menagerie opened on the Rocheblave and Canal street lot to a perfect mass of human beings gathered beneath the mammoth canvas," read the *Daily Picayune*. "Over four thousand persons must have gained entrance before the managers stopped the sale of tickets and closed the doors against further admission."[20] Seemingly, the mass of people anxious to attend was consistent throughout the run. "The trouble has been to accommodate the crowds with seats, and hundreds have been turned away at each exhibition."[21]

There were several dates in Mississippi before closing and returning the outfit to St. Louis for winter storage.

Cole's ability as a circus proprietor is proving undeniable. He has shunned opportunities for personal recognition and, unlike Barnum and Forepaugh, refused to have his likeness plastered on his advertising paper; yet throughout the preceding years of management he has acquired and maintained a position of respect from the people and places visited. The following excerpt from the Leavenworth *Daily Times* is an example of this: "There is no traveling entertainment exhibiting beneath the canvas that is better and more favorably known than that of W. W. Cole, which exhibited here yesterday afternoon and evening in a pavilion which it is not exaggeration to say was completely packed each time. Mr. Cole, though young yet—but thirty-three—is undoubtedly second to no manager in the country in the point of success."[22]

Aided by his mother, he was observant of every detail that made a positive impression on the public and that was conducive to running a "well-oiled" operation. "The excellent discipline and management of the troupe is everywhere to be seen," the New Orleans *Daily Picayune* confirmed. "The exhibitions given are as orderly and refined as seen at a regular theatre. The members of the company and employees, about the exhibition and while stopping at a first class hotel here, have left the impression that circus men can be temperate, well behaved gentleman. This speaks well for the profession, and shows an improvement over the rough flat foot circuses of the olden time. The energetic manager who is conducting this great enterprise so well, and making his business keep pace with the requirements of the times is deserving of the success he is receiving."[23] So much for nine years of prudent and resourceful management.

## XIV

Cole would now set out on one of the longest continuous tours ever attempted, a trek that stretched as far away as Australia and the South Seas and back again. It might be noted that there was danger of the idea being rejected at the outset. J. B. Gaylord, the general agent, wired his boss that everything was so expensive and the prospects so dim that the project should be called off; but Cole, in his foresight, ordered his agent to complete arrangements as planned.[1]

His confidence may have been bolstered by the many circus attractions he had assembled.[2] Along with the Bates giants there was a performing Spanish bull, a leaping horse and six trick stallions, the see-saw ponies, the three aerial DeComas, the riding and leaping of Frank Gardner, and much more.

On exhibition was a mammoth ox named Kansas. It was raised on the farm of J. S. Metzler near Burlington, Kansas. Advertised as the largest beef animal ever bred, it appeared with a standing offer of $5,000 for its equal in weight, beauty and size. To confirm this, Cole's advertisement referred to the *National Live Stock Journal's* report on the 1879 International Live Stock Show in Chicago where, so it said, there were but two animals that exceeded 2,800 pounds in weight; whereas the Cole bovine tested the scales at 3,100, and from nose to buttock measured twelve and a half feet.³ This was not a sideshow attraction, but was exhibited for no extra cost. The circus personnel must have felt comfort in the thought that if business turned sour they could at least feast on sirloin steaks for a time.

In the menagerie were the now famous sea lions, including a baby some six months old, a two-horned rhino, fifty white cockatoos, a wild boar, a tapir, monkeys of every age, four elephants (a record number for Cole), sixteen camels, etc. The popular Bates giants were stationed there on a platform ready and willing to answer questions from the passers-by.

The program, the order of which we have adapted from an October *Daily Alta California*, contained nineteen acts.⁴ 1. The Grand Cavalcade and Carnival Parade introduced elephants, camels, horses, ponies, ladies and gentlemen, and concluded with a star quadrille on horseback. 2. A

Spanish bull from Madrid (with his picador handler, the very gifted Señor William Organ) performed like a trick horse, rearing on command, waltzing, jumping high gates, firing a pistol, mounting a pedestal, and walking on its hind legs. The act concluded with a sham bull fight, in which, after ferociously charging his trainer, the animal gored the man to death and carried him out of the arena on his horns. The bull was said to have exhibited "almost human intelligence and skill in some of its feats, and ha[d] evidently been trained with marvelous skill and knowledge of the capacity of animals for instruction."[5] 3. Capt. Bates and wife, in their third season with Cole, were introduced. 4. Notably, there were the amazing DeComas, recently arrived from Paris. "The aerial bicycle act by the three Frenchmen was the most dangerous, thrilling and marvelous act we have ever seen," wrote a correspondent in Leavenworth, Kansas.[6] The eldest of the brothers rode a bicycle on a cable stretched between two center-poles, and suspended from it was a double trapeze on which the two younger men performed daring feats as the vehicle was peddled back and forth. "The act is not only one of rare beauty," a St. Louis *Post-Dispatch* reporter declared, "but it is sufficiently thrilling to make the blood tingle in the veins of the most phlegmatic spectator."[7] 5. *Battoute* leaping included twenty-four performers. Champion leaper, Frank Gardner, had a standing offer of a clear $1,000 to anyone who could match his feat of performing a double somersault over twenty-two horses. 6. The pair of trained horses Humboldt and Hindoo, introduced their remarkable skills, and Humboldt's leaping ability as he went through fire. 7. Ella Stokes performed as the leading female rider. This young lady was the daughter of Spencer Q. Stokes, and sister to two other female talents, Kate and Emma (and would in a short time marry circus proprietor John B. Doris).

Tom McIntyre was clown to the act. 8. An unexplained buffoonery, "If I Sat in the President's Chair," followed. 9. A horizontal bar act was composed of George Dunbar, Reno, Livingston and Murtz. 10. The six trained stallions went through a program of waltzing in unison, of marching, drilling, standing erect, and walking around the ring on their hind feet. 11. Maggie Claire displayed her beauty and her skill on the flying rings. 12. Frederick Barclay, veteran performer, gave an exhibition of riding. Pico Adams performed as clown. 13. The Livingston Brothers returned in an acrobatic routine. 14. Frank A. Gardner saddled up as a bounding jockey. 15. William O'Dale rode a five-horse act. 16. Frederick Barclay returned as a scenic rider with "The Comanche Indian." 17. The ponies Beauty and Butterfly raced around the ring with their monkey riders. 18. There was a camel race. 19. Conklin concluded the program by entering his den of lions and coaxing them into obedience, making them tumble and jump, and finally putting his head in the mouth of one of them.

Cooper & Bailey's 1879 use of electricity proved to be highly successful, which led to other shows promoting an imitation of it in 1880. W. C. Coup's New Monster Shows boasted of a "$15,000 Electric Light." The Sells Brothers proclaimed their use of "the Great Perfected Electric Light." Old John Robinson inserted "New Electric Light Show" in his lengthy circus title. So it could be expected that Cole would not be outdone.

His 1879 experiment with electricity, a modest demonstration of the new miracle, must have signaled a need to upgrade to a more effective system. So in the off season Cole went to Philadelphia in an attempt to get permission from James A. Bailey to purchase a lighting system resembling the one that Cooper & Bailey had so successfully employed,

Fred Barclay as "The Wild Comanche Chief"

to be used in territory where their show would not be exhibiting. But Bailey shrewdly declined to share his exclusive use.[8]

So Cole returned to his 1879 system or acquired a generator similar to Bailey's. The advertisements revealed that the electricity manufactured by the "Brush Dynamo" process using a Fitchburg engine produced light for twelve lamps (a later claim was sixteen). "No extra charge was ever made for the light," Louis E. Cooke recalled, "although it proved such an attraction that the price of admission was often increased for the night show, and especially was this true during the Southern tour, where the writer boldly advertised the 'Electric Illumination More Dazzling Than Daylight Down in Dixie.'"[9]

>THE ONE GREAT SHOW OF THE WORLD,
>EMBLAZONED AND ILLUMINATED WITH THE
>GRAND ELECTRIC LIGHT.
>It supplants the sun and turns night to day. In comparison with which all other lights glimmer with an uncertain and feeble vigor.
>**EQUALS 30,000 GAS JETS,**
>and is in operation Day and Night, producing a
>LITERAL BLAZE OF STUPENDOUS SPLENDOR.

So read a St. Louis newspaper advertisement for the opening week of the season.[10]

James W. Davidson, a resident of Austin, Minnesota, who visited the Cole circus that year as a small boy, offered these recollections: "On show day, near the marquee there stood a large wagon vibrating with the power from a high speed steam engine turning what appeared to be a simple cylinder (the generator) and operating at that hour merely as a ballyhoo. Once under the big top, we observed the wiring and the glass globe, but the actual exhibition of the light ablaze awaited the concert that followed the main show. As dad and I saw it at the matinee performance, we used the daylight as an excuse for going again at night when the effect would be more brilliant."[11] If this observation is correct, Cole utilized the electricity in the afternoon concert merely as an enticement to observe the lighted arena at the night performances. The Galesburg, Illinois, *Republican-Register* described such a scene with: "To crown it all, the immense tent was brilliantly illuminated with the famous electric light, producing 'rays of stupendous splendor.' It is no exaggeration to say that it turns night into day; all other lights have sickly hue compared to it. The apparatus used for manufacturing this light is driven by a thirty horse power engine."[12]

Louis Cooke created a "Pictorial Primer for Boys and Girls and Older Children," within which were descriptions in rhyme of the many attractions, with each verse representing a letter of the alphabet (an example is included below).

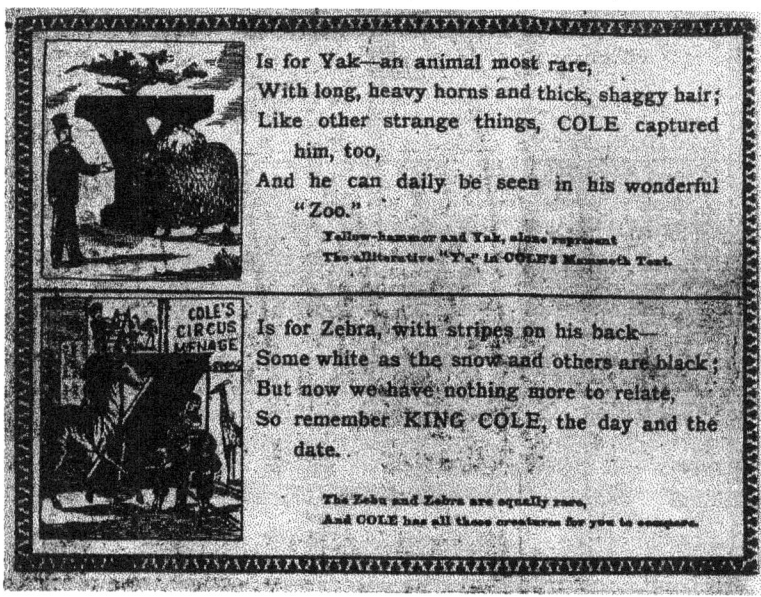

The 1880 tour, under a new canvas, began with a week's stand in St. Louis on the lot at Twelfth and Locust Streets. The opening was on the evening of April 12$^{th}$. It was revealed in the *Post-Dispatch* of the following day that the debut was a bit rough: "Owing to its being the first night there were several delays in the programme and it dragged somewhat."[13] But the shaky start did not discourage attendance.

On the night of the 14$^{th}$ a demonstration was to be given from the top of the highest building in the vicinity. An electric lamp, placed in front of a powerful reflector and powered by the circus generator was expected to illuminate the show grounds and all the streets adjacent. The event was supervised by a Mr. Lawrence, representing the Cleveland Electric Light Company. A similar experiment had been attempted in Cleveland some time earlier to great success. It was purported that the brilliancy of the light enabled people to read from copy more than a mile away. Unfortunately, on this occasion, the electric plant refused to accommodate the expectant spectators because of some wire failure.

Following the successful week in St. Louis, the first stops were in the mid-western states, where the show drew a repetition of favorable responses. The Indianapolis *Journal* testified that: "W. W. Cole has the best circus that has visited Indianapolis this season, which is saying a good deal. It is complete in everything that goes to make up a good show, and the large crowds in attendance yesterday testified to its merits by frequent and long continued applause."[14] The Effingham *Democrat* pronounced it the best that ever visited their city: "The performances were all new and novel and well given, the paraphernalia new, neat and clean, and the employes, instead of being bullies and thugs, were persons of gentlemanly deportment."[15] And the Galesburg *Republican*

*Register* concurred: "May 19 was the day a small boy, and a great many of the older ones, looked forward to with a throbbing delight. That was the day announced for W. W. Cole's Great Circus and Menagerie to exhibit in Galesburg. The day has come and gone, their hopes have all been realized, and Mr. Cole fulfilled his contract with profit and honor to himself."[16]

Eventually the circus began a lengthy route that would end on the West Coast, a trek that encountered continued success along the way. By mid-July the tour was centered in Kansas, where the Leavenworth *Daily News* affirmed what other papers along the line had disclosed: "As a whole, the show is certainly complete; not one objectionable feature could be pointed out. There was no annoyance from ticket sellers and lemonade and peanut vendors; but contrary to what is frequent, these and all other attaches are gentlemanly in their actions. W. W. Cole will have a big season in Kansas."[17]

"The Only Electric-Lighted, Sun Eclipsing Big Show That Ever Crossed the Great 'Divide'," the bills read as the company continued its westward move. Denver was played to crowded houses. The *Daily News* showed pleasure in its response to a July 26th performance: "The arenic display is unusually good. True the old acts that delighted us in boyhood are done again, but they are done better. The novelty of the programme is the bicycle ride over a rope stretched from one pole of the tent to the other—performed by three Frenchmen named DeComas. While one rides a bicycle along an ordinary rope the other two perform upon a trapeze suspended from the wheels of the machine, which is a very daring and startling feat. The riding is remarkably good, Barclay in his bare backed act doing some startling tricks in a graceful manner, and Frank Gardner, as the jockey rider, does some wonderful things, one of which is jumping upon the horse's back and alighting upon his feet, while the animal is in full gallop. The trained stallions are very interesting, but perhaps one of the best things ever seen among trained animals are the two ponies, Humboldt and Hindoo, who get upon a see-saw and ride up and down, apparently enjoying it as much as any two boys ever did riding on a plank over a gate."[18]

The stand at Salt Lake City opened on August 10 with the *Desert Evening News* announcement: "The circus and menagerie arrived in town about nine o'clock this morning, and took up its stand upon the 8th Ward Square. By noon the whole of the tents, etc., were erected ready for the afternoon performance. Prior to this, however, there was a grand procession through the streets which was witnessed by thousands of people.... The circus itself, just adjoining the menagerie, is very commodiously arranged. The seats are so placed that all can see, and anyone wishing to be in reserved seats can be accommodated in that way by a payment of twenty five cents extra."[19]

During the seven years since Cole journeyed to the West Coast many new towns had been established, some in the remotest mountain areas of the country, which created great hardships in getting to them. The thriving mining community of Leadville, Colorado, for example, was at the end of the line of a single narrow-gauged railway that had not been fully completed. The circus counted on the possibility that track would be finished into the town by the date billed. This miscalculation forced Cole and his people to haul the equipment by horse and hand two and a half miles up the mountain to their destination. But it proved worth the effort. It was the first circus ever to visit Leadville and money was there to be spent. Admission was raised to one dollar and fifty cents for reserved seats. Lemonade sold for twenty-five cents a glass.[20]

When the show finally arrived in California the Los Angeles *Herald* welcomed it with approval. There was admiration for Gardner's vaulting over three elephants and nine camels and his double somersault over a long line of them. William Organ's six stallions were "the miracle of an age which [was] making steady advances in subjecting the brute creation to intellect." In addition: "These stallions alone [were] enough to make Cole's circus the leading attraction of the day. They [did] almost everything but talk, and they [were] perfect beauties." Gardner's bounding jockey was the "prince of the sawdust arena," showing feats of horsemanship "not-a-whip short of the marvelous." The teetering ponies, see-sawing on a plank stretched over a barrel, were comical to the extreme. And O'Dale's five-horse riding was a thing to be cherished. But the real novelty was the illumination of the tent by electric lights.[21]

The Southern California tour was rewarded by remunerative box office figures. The gross at Anaheim was a full $4,000; for San Bernardino, $5,000; and for Los Angeles, $12,000.[22] The circus then moved on to Bakersfield, Fresno, and the final stop at San Francisco before embarking for Australia.

Cole arrived in San Francisco seven years after his first visit, when the tents were originally set up at the sunken lot on the corner of Jackson and New Montgomery Streets, and settled in this time at Seventh and Mission. In imitation of the 1879 Cooper & Bailey circus, when a grand electric street parade was given on the eve before opening in the larger cities, Cole introduced San Franciscans to his own illuminated procession on the night of October 8.

"In 1880 he has come back to pay us a second visit whilst on his road to Australia," an item in the *Chronicle* revealed, "and though one of the youngest managers in the profession—he is but a trifle over thirty—has brought such a show, and is already conducting things in such a way as prove him to be one of the most go-ahead and enterprising entrepreneurs of ring amusement." The writer continued by drawing a succinct portrait of the young proprietor: "Mr. Cole looks younger than he really is, is quite mannered, of very few words—the very opposite, in fact, of his press agent, Albert Richards, who is all bustle, activity and go."[23]

The circus opened to turn-way business on October 9, a success that continued for nine days, during which fifteen performances were given. "The acts follow one other in the most rapid succession, there not being a single wait," one could read in the *Daily Alta California*. "The merits of the arenic performance are very high, and we do not think it too great praise to say that it is the best one that has been given in this city."[24]

When the San Francisco stand came to an end the circus company with all its equipment was loaded on the *City of Sydney* and sent forth to the land down under. This lengthy sea voyage would cost the management $17,000 in each direction.[25]

# Royal Performing Stallions

## XV

The company sailed on the *City of Sydney* on October 23 with passages paid for sixty people or more.[1] Louis E. Cooke had left for Australia in advance of the show on September 25 with seven assistants and over thirty tons of lithographs and other printing, a full year's supply. He also took a set of electrotype plates to use for all of the letterpress work. "It was my ambition to make the printed matter as distinctly American as was the show," he wrote.[2]

The performing company was made up of people that had been a part of the tour to California, augmented with a number of new faces. In the first group were William O'Dale, George Dunbar, Fred Barclay, James Campbell, Burt Richardson, Daniel Kennedy; the Livingston Brothers, and clowns Tom McIntyre, and Pico Adams. Among those added were Linda Jeal, "Queen of the Blazing Zone, in her Daring flights on a Bareback Horse, Looping through Hoops of Fire"; Wooda Cook, "Fearless Horseman and Somersaulter"; equestriennes Elena Jeal Ryland and Adelaide D'Atalie; Millie Turnour, "the Beautiful and Dashing Empress of the Air"; William O'Dale Stevens, "introducing the Dancing globes, Electric Table, the enchanted Cross, etc.";

and a band of war-dancing Yuma Indians led by Dick Deadeye. Murtz, Dunbar, and Adelaide D'Atalie took over the aerial bicycle act from the DeComas. Other features included illumination by electric lights, the trained stallions, and "1,000 thrilling novelties."

Linda Jeal

The departure from San Francisco was rocky. After leaving the harbor the boat encountered huge swells which made the un-seaworthy performers desperately ill. The only exception was bareback rider Wooda Cook who, as George Conklin put it, "had been so drunk in San Francisco that it was necessary to carry him on board."[3] But the passage was even worse for the animals. Because of the cramped boat space the horses could not lie down. The constant standing made their legs swell, so slings were devised to allow relieving the weight on them whenever they tired.

Honolulu was the first stop but only for an overnight. The island royalty visited the boat with a band of fifty musician and native men and women entertained the now bored passengers by diving for coins in the shark-infested water. Then the boat took a direct route to New Zealand, which lasted some twenty-one days. The New Zealand visit was a means of breaking up the long trip, giving the human and animal cargo an opportunity for a rest and to acclimate them for the arrival at Australia.

The enthusiastic reception was altogether surprising to the management. The first port of call was Auckland, where the circus remained for two weeks, first to make repairs and get the animals in shape and the second week for performing. The opening day was November 29 and success was immediate. In referring to the Auckland stand a correspondent revealed that the American company played "to overflowing houses, and turn[ed] away hundreds at every exhibition."[4] This was followed by five days in Wellington beginning December 1, then to Christchurch and Dunedin for ten days each, the transportation of the show being accomplished through chartered steamers.

It was the Wellington stop where misfortune struck. Before opening, a wind storm came up with sudden rage. The canvas was lifted up and torn to ribbons. Everything was flattened. The backup canvas, never unloaded, had been sent on to Christchurch.

"We certainly made a mistake, Louis, when we let that canvas go through." Cole calmly remarked to Cooke.

"There won't be a boat this way for a week and it'll take some time to patch this one up. Louis, do you think we could rent the opera house, so that we could show there tonight? We might as well begin arrangements for the next day or two at least."[5]

William O'Dale Stevens

By 11:00 a.m. that day the opera house was made available. Cooke then rushed an advertisement in the newspaper and arranged some printing with a job press to alert the citizens of Wellington that the evening's bill at the opera house was, with the exception of riding, a full and complete performance. What's more, he had the band back on the street within an hour. "When the doors opened that night," Cooke stated, "there was a crowd sufficient to fill the opera house twice over."[6]

Meanwhile, the city was scoured for sail makers and other workmen, who were offered extra pay to assist in rapidly restoring the battered canvases. Work progressed all night and by matinee time the next day the main tent was ready for use and the performance came off on time.

The show opened at Dunedin on December 23 to large business which continued throughout the visit that closed January 1, 1881. Then there was one day in the city of Balclutha and two days in Invercargill before the circus left New Zealand, stopping at Hobart, Tasmania, for a stand before crossing to the Australian mainland.

The mainland was reached at Adelaide, where there was a ten day stand. Again, they played to full or near full tents. "At several of the performances hundreds were turned away, unable to gain admission."[7] Then the itinerary included Melbourne for ten days, followed by a five-week railroad tour that hit all the principal cities as far as Queensland. Rail travel was used for the interior dates, boat travel for the coastal ones. The final stand was in Australia's largest city, Sydney.

In all, the entire visit, quoted Cooke, was uneventful but most prosperous. "We were everywhere received in the most kindly manner, and as it was our business to amuse we tried to be pleasant."[8] A *Clipper* writer agreed: "The success throughout the colonies has been something unprecedented, and the show has been greeted by enthusiastic audiences at all places of exhibition. The troupe of performing stallions are a special attraction, and seem to be particularly pleasing to the Australians. Frequently the spectators rise and greet these equine actors with rousing cheers."[9]

Australian circus historian, Mark St Leon, gives us a somewhat different summary of the show's visit. Agreeing that it was a highly profitable tour, he asserts that Cole's "sharp business practices provoked the ire of many of his unsuspecting colonial patrons." He cites an example from the *Town and Country Journal* when, at Tamworth there were three booths available for the five shilling tickets and only one for those selling at three shillings. The overcrowding at the cheaper place encouraged many patrons to give up and shell out the extra shillings for the more available but more expensive tickets.[10]

St Leon acknowledged that, as with the earlier visit of Cooper & Bailey, the street processions, an apparent novelty at the time, greatly impressed the Australian public. In quoting from the Sydney *Morning Herald*, he wrote that the parade in that city was headed by a buggy carrying none other than W. W. Cole. This was followed by the band chariot drawn by two white horses, nicely caparisoned (not the dozen camels used on the mainland); ladies and gentlemen riders; two small ponies, one of which was carrying a clown; six elegant horses, "richly trimmed and ridden by knights in medieval armor"; five performing stallions led by attendants; a number of closed cages, with the exception of Conklin's den of lions; and, finally, the elephants.[11] This represents a similar pattern used by Cole and others in the United States, but, as with Cooper & Bailey before him, it exemplifies the extent that circuses reduced and contracted stock and equipment for overseas travel.

Understandably, there was resentment of the American invaders by the native Australian circuses. The large drawing power of the Cole aggregation certainly affected their attendance. At one point riding star Gus St Leon, of the St Leon circus, issued a challenge "to any equestrian in Cole's company for a stake of one thousand pounds."[12] There was no response from the visitors' camp.

While the circus was still in Australia, Louis Cooke was sent to India to see about extending the tour there, but decided that further travel in the region was not feasible. Cole was not about to repeat the mistake that Cooper & Bailey had made when they ended a successful tour of Australia by extending it to South America. All the profits were wasted away there through difficulties of transportation and other problems and James A. Bailey brought the show back to the United States penniless.

Cooke also went to Samoa and the Fiji Islands in a search for museum curiosities. He was successful in acquiring a number of artifacts and exotic birds. Live entertainers were also contracted to enact their ethnic and tribal customs.

There was a troupe of East Indian performers—"Nautch Dancers or Whirling Dervishes"—which included jugglers and snake charmers. They executed "Mysterious Incantation Scenes, Feats of Necromancy, Patagonian Dances and Pastimes, presenting a performance identical with the romantic histories if these Strange and Weird People, who have been secured and transported to this country by [Cole's] special direction, at a cost of 30,000 rupees." In addition, there was a band of "South Sea Savages, or Maori War Dancers, tattooed from head to foot," and a group of Oriental acrobats—Bedouin Arabs—"The Marvels of a Nation Noted for its Muscular Men."[13] The search completed, Cooke preceded the show back to the United States to prepare for an eastward tour.

Cole and company sailed for home from Sydney on April 21, 1881, returning on the same boat on which they left San Francisco months earlier. Again they stopped at Honolulu for supplies, but again the stay was very short, terminated by the discovery of smallpox on the island.

"It was early in the day when we sailed into the Golden Gate," Conklin recalled, "and everyone was more than anxious to get ashore, and all expected to [within] a few hours; but the anchor chain had hardly commenced to rattle through the hawse hole when a boat with a quarantine officer ran alongside and the doctor shouted to the captain, 'Did you stop at Honolulu?'"[10]

Yes, of course they did, but there was not a single case of sickness on the boat. "No matter, thirty days quarantine aboard ship," was the edict. But there was a short supply of food for the animals and everyone was anxious to stand on solid ground once again. It all fell on deaf ears; food would be sent out so the animals wouldn't starve. Asked if they could get word to their representatives on shore, the authorities said "No, and no notes can be sent." What a dilemma.

Fortunately the circus had three advance agents already working San Francisco—Louis E. Cooke, Charles T. Sivalls, and J. B. "Daffy" Gaylord. When these men learned of the quarantine they did what agents are paid to do, they made the "fix."

"At twelve o'clock that night we went ashore," was Conklin's last words of the matter.[11] How easy to imagine the relief and ecstasy of all concerned as they re-entered their homeland. And how satisfied Cole must have been with the journey. The five months of stands in New Zealand and Australia profited him a clear and astounding $150,000.[12]

## XVI

W. W. Cole's *Avant Courier* for 1881 made much of the visit Down Under, calling it "one of the greatest triumphs yet recorded in the annals of travel." It was touted to be the most profitable series of successes ever known in show history. "In every city where exhibitions were given it was found necessary to close the ticket office, and thousands were daily turned from our doors, unable to gain admission to the main tents.... Upon our arrival in the leading cities, the Government officials issued proclamations granting half-holidays, in order that the citizens might witness the grand street-parade, which in all cases called forth thousands upon thousands of spectators, who completely swarmed the streets and housetops for miles and miles."[1]

Once in San Francisco, Cole began refurbishing the entire outfit in preparation for the move east. The company personnel remained essentially the same.[2] Added were souvenirs of the Australian tour—Arabian gymnasts, Hindoo snake charmers, a troupe of Maori war dancers, some East Indian jugglers, kangaroos, emus, and a collection of native animals and birds from the South Sea Islands.

The tents were again set up on the lot at the corner of Mission and Seventh Streets and, after a morning procession, the two-week San Francisco stand opened on the evening of May 23. During the time out of the country Murtz, Dunbar and Adelaide D'Atalie developed the aerial bicycle act the DeComas had performed on the show earlier, which allowed a spectacular event in the program without Cole having to hire special personnel for it. The above three artists merely "doubled in brass." The thrilling exercise consisted of Murtz riding his bicycle on a single wire with Dunbar and D'Atalie working a trapeze dangling beneath. The critical moment came when Murtz balanced himself on his head on the bicycle's seat.

Along with that were the various equestrians—the double horsemanship by the Jeal sisters, Wooda Cook's bareback feats, as well as O'Dale's and Barclay's; the *battoute* leaping, gymnastics and acrobatics, racing camels, trained elephants, horses and ponies, the ever present Conklin and his ferocious cats, and the novelties brought back from the South Seas. Oh, yes, an albino buffalo had been acquired along the way.

Charitable institutions were recognized at this stand. The unfortunate children of the Hebrew Orphan Asylum were guests for a matinee performance on the 25th, the young charges of the Ladies' Protection and Relief Society on the 26th, and those of the Protestant Orphan Asylum on the 27th. "Every part of the program was interesting," the *Daily Alta California* writer confirmed, "and, as a whole, the entertainment furnished here is the best of its class ever witnessed in California, and fully merited all the applause and praise it received."[3] Cold weather was claimed to have interfered with the early attendance, which may have influenced the lowering of the admission price to 50¢ for the final week.

## A Snow-White Buffalo!

The run concluded on the night of June 5. The show then played a week in northern California—Redwood City, San Jose, Oakland, Antioch, Sacramento, and Stockton. The Sacramento *Bee* declared it to have attracted the largest audience under a spread of canvas ever assembled there. "In every respect the show is first class," the item read. "The spacious enclosure was thoroughly illuminated by 16 Brush dynamo electric lights, the motive power for which was furnished by a 20 horsepower engine.... Every act was given without delay, the brief intervals between the arranging for the appearance of each artist in his or her specialty being well filled with jokes and funny acts."[4]

Turning south, there was a stopover at Los Angeles on June 13. "The mammoth tent, with its corresponding vast seating capacity, was taxed to its utmost at the evening performance," related the *Daily Herald*. The newspaper, reflecting the sentiment of an entertainment starved city, expressed amazement at the brilliance of the electric lights and the magnificence of the grand entrèe, "the display of elephants and camels being remarkably fine."

**MDLLE. LINDA JEAL,**
By all Nations crowned Queen of the Blazing Zone, whose Equestrian Feats and
**Perilous Flights Through Hoops of Fire**

"Dropping the regular order of the program, which, by the way, was not adhered to," the writer continued, "the features of the evening's entertainment which pleased us most were, first, the somersault equestrian act of Wooda Cooke (sic). Assisted by [a] neat clown performance of McIntyre, this was a quite enjoyable episode. Cooke is a daring and successful equestrian and was greeted by applause at all stages of his performance." Secondly, he found the bareback riding of Miss Addie D'Atalie a pronounced success. "This young lady, who is only nineteen years old, and who is as pretty as a peach blossom, has made wonderful advances in professional accomplishments and aplomb since she was here a year ago." He was also impressed by the Murtz, Dunbar and D'Atalie aerial bicycle feat, Linda Jeal's juggling on the floating wire—"the Jeal sisters generally were a host, contributing markedly to the sensations of the evening," the equillibrist performance of William O'Dale Stevens, and the wonderful stallions (now reduced to five because of one death).[5]

Continuing on, the circus moved over the just completed Southern Pacific Railroad on "The Finest Train of Cars in the World," as Cole stated in his *Avant Courier*. "I own every car in my train, built expressly for my use," was his claim. The number of rolling stock stated in advertisements often varied from city to city, and the count by the press as the train rested on local sidings was also questionable; but it can be estimated that the total number of cars was around twenty-five with lengths of fifty and sixty feet. They were new this year, built by a firm in St. Louis. In all probability the shorter cars used in 1879 and 1880 were disposed of before the show left for Australia.

The 64 foot No.1 advertising car (shown on the next page) was the fancy domain of Louis E. Cooke and his crew, said to have been built at a cost of $7,000. The seating and sleeping compartment, occupying one end and containing four double seats and eight folding double-berths, was twenty-five feet long. There were also spacious lockers where the advertising material was stored—bills, lithographs, etc.—each variety in a separate bin. The next compartment, in the center of the car, the office and reception area, was an upholstered and decorated space nine feet square. It was embellished with pictures of circus people and with various relics of the South Sea's tour. It also housed a couple of live cockatoos that passed the time with attempts at the human voice. The final compartment was the work room with exactly everything that was needed for preparing the advertising. There were also the necessary toilet facilities where water was supplied by a compact brass siphon pump. The exterior of the elegant car was painted with decorative representations of animals and scenes of performing artists. We have not been able to find a description of car No. 2, but suggest the accommodations were similar.

The circus performed at San Bernardino, Yuma, Tucson, and other points along that line, being the first show through the territory by rail. One hundred horses were contracted for a wagon trip through Arizona. For the privilege of seeing a rare circus the public was charged $1.50 to $2.00 general admission and $1.00 for reserved seats. "The country was sparsely settled and water tanks were far between," Louis Cooke reminisced, "but bless me how the 'dobe dollars' did roll in!"[6]

At Tombstone, in Arizona Territory, a vicious windstorm caught the tent and all that was in it, lifted it into the air, and deposited everything in a mass upon the ground. A center-pole and a number of seats were broken and an employee injured. Fortunately, the accident occurred an hour or so before show time with no audience in the tent; otherwise, there could have been a large number of deaths and severe injuries. The final performance there was presented in the open air and well attended by nearly 5,000 spectators.[7]

Colorado was next. The Pueblo *Colorado Chieftain* heartily approved of what was presented on this occasion: "This city and surrounding country had the pleasure of witnessing two of the best performances ever seen under canvas, and right royally did our people turn out on this occasion, as the large canvases were crowded to their utmost capacity, fully 5,000 people being present at the afternoon performance, and nearly twice that number were present at night, and we will venture to say that every one went away fully satisfied.... Fourteen lady equestriennes were in the grand entree, twenty leapers went over the backs of as many elephants and camels, with double and single somersaults; a beautiful lady did an elegant act of juggling on the slack wire; the somersault act of the pad rider was admired by all; two beautiful young ladies appeared at the same time in the arena on dashing steeds, going through balloons and over banners and hurdles, which brought down round after round of applause. Another young lady rode, drove, and managed seven horses with the utmost skill and daring. The see-saw ponies, the racing camels and George Conklin's performing den of lions, wound up the performance. As a whole the performance was far above the average, and what makes it so pleasant for an audience, there are no waits between acts, as they go in and out in rapid succession. The vast tents were lighted up by the Brush Dynamo electric light. A forty-horse power engine is in use to generate the electricity, which diffuses a most brilliant and dazzling light, making everything as bright as a noon day sun."[8]

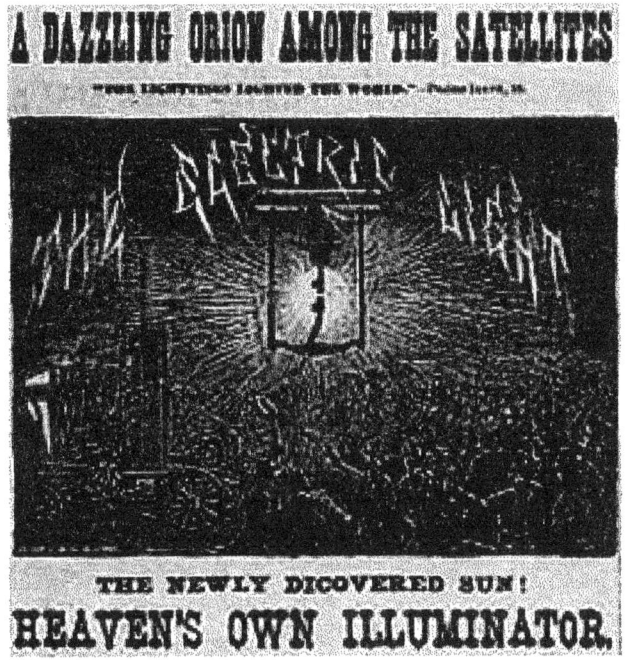

The company eventually went north into Canada, crossing the continent, and then back into the eastern United States. By August 29 it was at Windsor, Ontario, just across the river from Detroit. Large crowds were drawn from both cities. A *Clipper* correspondent determined that the performance was "of the good, old-fashioned kind, in which the minstrel-show agents, song-book and peanut vendors and lemonade peddlers figured prominently, but unpleasantly."[9]

The show spent two weeks at the Dominion Exhibition in Halifax, Nova Scotia, commencing September 19. By October 8 it was back in the United States, where, at Portland, Maine, it played to a small audience in the afternoon, but a large one in the evening. The season came to a halt at Providence, Rhode Island, before going into winter quarters at Utica, New York. "Thus ended the longest continuous tour in this and foreign countries on record," Cooke declared. "We had not missed an advertised stand or date. We closed with a round profit of more than one-third of $1,000,000"; and, we might add, consumed an aggregate of some 28,000 miles.[10]

## XVII

The Cooper & Bailey circus merged with P. T. Barnum's following the 1880 season to form Barnum's Greatest Show on Earth & the Great London Circus. This new and mammoth organization made its debut in the spring of 1881 in a huge tent with three rings of simultaneous activity and set a new standard for the circus world. The show carried 250,000 yards of canvas, with the circus tent seating 15,000 people, including the 5,000 reserved seat chairs. There were twenty trained elephants and an unprecedented number of animals in the menagerie. The museum was headlined by none other than Tom Thumb and Chang the Chinese giant. All this was assembled and guided by the great James A. Bailey.

Cole, just back from the Australian trip that year, was in no position to be competitive with the larger show. But in 1882 he picked up the challenge by using two rings and a center stage. The single ring and stage configuration that was a particular feature of his 1878 circus had been abandoned for three years as part of the economizing traveling gear for the overseas venture. But with the Barnum show going to three rings, an expansion became a necessity for all the major circuses.

P. T. Barnum's huge elephant, Jumbo, which had been purchased from the London Zoological Society, arrived in New York harbor aboard the *Assyrian Monarch* on April 9, 1882, where it was met by thousands of curious people from the city. It was already the most famous animal ever exhibited because Barnum, the master of hyperbole, had worked his way with the press to create a public anticipation and genuine enthusiasm for its American arrival, a Jumbomania that only a Barnum could accomplish. The animal had cost him $10,000 plus another $1,000 for shipment to New York. But there was no doubt within the masterminds of circusdom that, even for the high cost, Jumbo was a phenomenal addition to the combined shows of Barnum, Bailey and

Hutchinson, who now had, and who would promote extensively, the largest mammal in the world.

At the Charles Reiche & Bros.' Stables in Hoboken, New Jersey, the largest elephant in the United States (Jumbo not yet having arrived) was to be sold at auction on the 25th of March. The Asian male had been giving kiddie rides at Coney Island but was becoming too temperamental to safely continue in that capacity. The upcoming arrival of Jumbo having created an interest in its purchase, several prominent circus proprietors were on hand for the bidding.

After learning of the Reiches' intention to dispose of a large elephant, Cole and Louis Cooke went to Hoboken to examine him. He was not as tall as Jumbo but was somewhat heavier. How do you define the "largest creature in the world," by height or by weight? They quickly decided that he would be a great advertising feature and thus entered the auction with serious bidding.

John B. Doris was first to make an offer of $2,000. Cole easily raised it to $3,500. Doris responded with another $500. Cole again raised the bid to $4,500. John V. O'Brien briefly entered the contest with $4,550. Doris went to $4,700. Then Cole and Doris countered each other until the final offer by Cole ended the matter with $6,600. The New York and New Orleans Circus had purchased a Jumbo-type pachyderm to be used competitively against the Jumbo craze for $4,400 less than what Barnum had paid for his elephant. This new acquisition was designated "Samson."[1]

The rewards of publicity began early. When it was time to ship Samson to winter quarters at Utica, Cole and Cooke realized he was too large to fit into an ordinary stock car; so a crate was built to be carried on a gondola or flat car. But to Cole's surprise and his press agent's delight the specially constructed conveyance was too tall to go through the

Hoboken tunnel. The solution was to walk the animal around and add the top layer of the crate on the other side. "What excellent matter this made for our press work," Cooke wrote later.

Size, which had always been an advantage in elephant ownership, was now a must. Before the season opened Adam Forepaugh, proprietor of the circus most competitive to Barnum's, bought the huge Bolivar from the VanAmburgh people, which set the stage for the three largest elephants to be publicized by the three circuses most capable of using their advertising skills. "Here commenced what was known as 'The Elephant War' between the big shows," so wrote Cooke.[2]

"The elephant war waxed warm and heavy," he continued. "If pitted side by side or put upon the scales, there would not have been much difference between the monsters, but Jumbo's prestige, added to the Barnum name, made him invincible. All of us kept up the battle, however, flooding the country with posters, hand bills, press work, and every device to attract attention to the big fellows."[3]

Cooke was not lax in trying. For example, he devised a stunt for potential newlyweds, young couples, to be married on Samson's back, and gave away silver tea sets as inducements. Local Sunday school classes were made offers to ride in the animal's large howdah during the street parade. Among his many press releases for distribution was the rather silly poem below.

"Samson is an elephant,
His back is strong, his trunk is long,
And big as big can be.
He falls in love with all the girls
And sets them in a flutter.
The ladies sigh and say, 'O my!
He's just too utterly utter.'"

Jack Shumake was Samson's driver but Conklin was the handler for as long as Cole owned him, that being until

1886, after which he went with Conklin to the Barnum show. So he was very familiar with the elephant war. "As soon as Cole bought Samson he at once began to bill him as the largest one in existence," Conklin wrote in his book. "I think probably Cole's statement came nearer the truth, for while Barnum's elephant may have measured a little more in height and had larger ears, Cole's had by far the greater bulk and weight. In addition he was much more intelligent, being an Indian elephant, than the Barnum elephant, which was African."[4]

The press in various cities were encouraged to witness Samson being unloaded from his special railroad car. Both Cole and Conklin were there to entertain questions and enhance the rivalry between the two large beasts. The stratagem worked to their advantage, as an excerpt from Cleveland's *Plain Dealer* reveals.[5]

"How does Jumbo compare with this elephant?" George Conklin was asked.

"Well, I dunno," he replied, "but since you ask me I will say that Jumbo may be a little taller but is not so ponderous or presentable an animal as this. Jumbo is old and lean and ragged."

"How old is this elephant?"

"He is fifty years old. Lalla Rookh, our next largest elephant, is seventy-five years old. The other three elephants, Jim, Tom and Lizzie, are much younger."

Conklin continued giving the Cleveland reporters information. "It takes thirteen gallons of neat's foot oil or twelve pounds of coconut butter to grease his skin. He is twelve feet and seven inches high, sixteen feet around the belly and weighs over seven tons. Samson was purchased from Mr. Charles Reiche, of Hoboken, New Jersey, by Mr. Cole about a month ago, and was shipped to Utica in a gondola car. Mr. Reiche is the biggest animal dealer in this country and this elephant was captured by his men in India. Jumbo comes from Egypt. Egyptian elephants have a bow-shaped hump on their backs and it is this that gives Jumbo his tall appearance."

The 1882 season opened at Utica, New York, on April 22. There were two pavilions, with the first housing both the menagerie and museum. As the Janesville *Rock County Recorder* reported: "The scrupulous neatness of the place, and the fresh, bright appearance of the long line of elaborately decorated cages, cars and dens, will at once strike the attention. The zoological collection is really superb. It will delight the student in natural history, while the monkeys and elephants will furnish a feast of amusement for the little folks. The elephant Samson is a veritable monster. So fine a herd of camels as is shown has rarely been seen in this city."[6]

The performing tent was professed to seat over 12,000. The Grand Rapids, Wisconsin, *Reporter* called it "unquestionably the largest ever spread in the city."[7]

For the outside attraction there was a balloon ascension and Japanese daylight fireworks. The balloon was in command of Signor Gomez, who made a daily voyage from the show grounds around noon, ascending to a height of about 1,000 feet, while a man performed on a dangling trapeze. The fireworks were curious and inexplicable, filling the air with various quaint objects—dragons, serpents, insects, birds, etc.—things real and things unreal—appearing in vast numbers, the execution of which was claimed to be a Japanese secret. And, not least, the giant elephant, Samson, gave rides to the children before the performances in a specially made howdah that could carry eight or ten of them at a time.

Repeating from 1881, the aerial bicycle feat still had Murtz on the wire, Frank Livingston had replaced George

Dunbar, with Adelaide D'Atalie (now using the name of Addie Austin) completing the trio.[8] Frank Gardner was still leaping over any number of obstacles and finishing by double somersaulting over five elephants (three of which were standing on tubs) and four camels. His wife, Mildred, was a *manège* rider. The equestrianism, all done without a pad, was divided between Rosina Dubsky Murray, Addie Austin and Frank Gardner, the two ladies performing their skills in a mock competition.[9] Blondin, the Australian rope-walking horse amazed, as did the tattooed Maori warriors, the Bedouin Arab gymnasts, and the six European stallions.

New were the bicycle-riding Lane Brothers, who performed upon a stage placed in the center ring and "displayed some extraordinary powers of agility and skill, setting the laws of gravity at defiance, and using the spider-like wheels with as much ease as boys use a hoop."[10] There was Capt. A. H. Bogardus, the crack rifle shot who had won the American Shot Championship in 1871, then went to England in 1875 and defended his title there until returning in 1878. He worked with his sons Eugene, Edward, Peter, and Henry (Edward and Peter were at home this season). There were the Russian roller skaters, including the only female skate performer. The Topeka *Capital* enjoyed a skating sketch by the lady and two gentlemen, a pair of them appearing on the platform as novices. "The large tent full of people resounded with roars of laughter."[11]

The itinerary was in reverse of the usual this year, going from east to west. Following the Utica opening, April was devoted primarily to New York state. The weather was a factor during this early part of the season. At Buffalo, cold and rain prevented the street parade of May 4, but the attendance was large at both afternoon and evening performances. "The throng was indeed vast, and as well pleased and orderly as could be asked, the excellent manner in which everything about the show is systematized in no small degree contributing to the comfort of its multitude of patrons."[12] On the second day there was a large crowd in the afternoon and an immense one in the evening, so filled there was room for no more. In Albany, audiences also defied the cold for a large turnout at both performances.

By June the show was in Indiana and Ohio. We learn from the Indianapolis *Daily Sentinel* that the tents were set up at Tennessee Street, just south of the Vandalia Freight Depot. The parade on the morning of June 12 was considered the finest that had ever been transported around the streets of Indianapolis; the elephants, including Samson, were judged to be fine looking beasts; and there was admiration for the freshly painted wagons, all of which showed off to good advantage. Both afternoon and evening performances played to turn-away audiences. The presence of pick-pockets did not seem to diminish the pleasure of the entertainment; and the newspaper allowed that "Mr. Cole and his show will always be welcomed back to Indianapolis."[13]

The *Plain Dealer* was succinct in its response to the Cleveland date: "Cole's circus, the first of the season, drew great crowds yesterday afternoon and last evening. The menagerie and the ring performances were much admired. The tents will be struck after tonight's show."[14] The Batcheller & Doris Inter-Ocean show followed Cole's into Cleveland for the next two days. Recalling the aggressive bidding for Samson, a rivalry was forming between Cole and Doris.

Cole was in Kansas by July, then moved north into Minnesota and Wisconsin. The Janesville, Wisconsin, *Daily Recorder* found the parade to be above average and "an excellent fore-runner of the feast that was to follow." There were approximately 6,000 people present at each show. The paper made special mention of the roller skating and bicycle riding, finding them "not only marvelous but decidedly interesting, and oft times thrilling." There was nothing to offend but much to satisfy and astonish. "Mr. Cole evidently possesses the Aaron's rod of all the great caterers for public amusement and instruction."[15] While in Janesville the Cole baseball nine, apparently proud of their successes on the diamond, challenged a team of school boys to a game. In the end the circus athletes left town embarrassed by the losing score of 14 to 8.

At Grand Rapids, where some 7,000 people turned out from a twenty mile radius, the performances were judged to be the best in many years. In Watertown the crowds fell short of what the Batcheller & Doris circus had attracted; and Cole was scolded for not showing everything advertised, the balloon ascension and pre-show fireworks having been omitted.

September and October was devoted to the southern states. Cole's past popularity in Memphis assured him of a large turnout in that city. "The people expected to see a superior menagerie and a grand ring performance," the *Daily Appeal* announced. "They were not disappointed.... In both the menagerie and circus departments, the show is all that could be expected."[16]

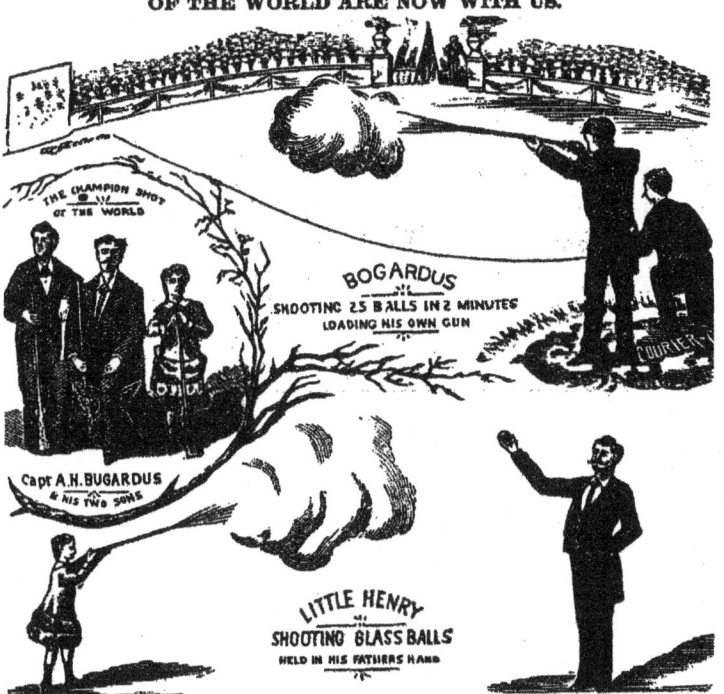

The street parade drew particular praise from the *Daily Arkansas*: "The circus parade yesterday was the finest Little Rock has seen this year, and most of the paraphernalia seems new and bright. The elephant 'Samson' is certainly a monster, and fully as large as newspaper columns give him credit of being. The camels in the lead of the procession, drawing the grand car, were objects of great curiosity."[17]

A tragedy occurred at Lonoke, Arkansas, when doorkeeper Michael Longmire was shot and killed. He had had some altercation with a man while at his post; but everyone thought the air had cleared, when a gun was fired and Longmire exclaimed, "I think I am shot." He was escorted to the dressing tent by two colleagues. A third ran after the culprit but the man escaped through the aid of friends. Treasurer John D. Evans accompanied the dead man to his resting place in DeSoto, Iowa.

"He was a most exemplary man, kind to a fault and as harmless as a child," Cole wrote to the *Clipper*; "also a most trusted employee of mine for twelve years' standing."[18]

The season was finished off in Arkansas and at the end of November the outfit was again shipped to St. Louis for storage at the fair grounds.[19]

## XVIII

Cole created his largest and most powerful company to date for the season of 1883. There were the two rings and a raised stage and thirty-five acts on the program. The show traveled on from twenty-five to thirty-six railroad cars, all painted milk white with red lettering shaded in black. The big top measured 250 by 400 feet.[1] The menagerie was greatly enlarged. The acts in the arena were represented with unusual variety and headed by the greatest bareback rider of the age.

The advertising pattern Cole had developed through the years was to go sparingly on newspaper space and spend heavily on billing. Generally, an ad would be placed in local papers about a week before arrival and perhaps nothing on the day of performance. Of course the pattern changed when there was opposition from other circuses. But Cole put out lots of paper and kept his bill posters busy. He was probably the first to use a number of 100 sheet stands of lithograph paper when and where such could be displayed to advantage.

Ernest Cooke, agent for Cole, arrived in New York aboard the *Celtic*, a steamer of the White Star Line, on April 7, 1883, bringing with him a number of performers, including a troupe of a dozen Bedouin Arabs, who had made the long trip from Constantinople. Cooke, who was to be Cole's principal clown, heard of their amazing accomplishments and followed them from place to place until he was able to convince them to come to America.[2]

The Arabs were taken immediately to the Westminster Hotel where rooms had been chartered for them. After remaining in New York a few days, they moved on to Chicago and their quarters at the Sherman House. Creating the appropriate curiosity and press responses there, they continued on to St. Louis for rehearsals that would soon be under way. Their performance consisted of sham battles, knife-throwing at each other, forming lofty pyramids, leaping over lines of fixed bayonets, somersaulting over high objects, and other such athletic feats while holding swords, cutlasses and daggers in their hands. The largest performer held eight men aloft with a total weight of 1,300 pounds. In addition, the eleven males and one female performed in scenes depicting forms of desert life. In the street parade they were displayed on the backs of camels and Arabian horses.

The Arabs would share Cole's billboard space with champion American bareback rider, James Robinson, giving the circus a strong and appealing program. A slightly built man of about five feet four inches in height and weighing 130 pounds, he was forty-six years old at this time. "One wouldn't take him to be the professional circus man that he is, as he is modest and unassuming, and seems a kind and agreeable gentleman," wrote an interviewer for the Sadalia Bazoo.[3]

James Robinson

Robinson had worked for most of the major circuses (the exceptions being Forepaugh's and Barnum's, strangely enough) and had taken a show out under his own name. Considered the greatest bareback rider of the century, George Middleton once wrote of him: "When he walked in the ring to begin his act, with a whip in hand, and jumped on the back of his bare-backed horse, one was impressed at that minute that he was 'it.' He had that style and grace and finish to his act that no one else ever had that I have ever seen or heard of."[4]

Robinson was riding the same horse he bought in 1871. "He is reliable," was his explanation. "I never saw a horse whose gait was smoother, and he understands what is expected of him thoroughly. I do not give my horse credit for intelligence, but rather believe he acts from habit. He has done those things so often that he knows just what is expected of him and he does it."[5]

Along with these great features, there were the performing stallions and elephants; the bicyclists; simultaneous riding, hurdle riding, and other feats of horsemanship by ladies; the aerial art of Nestor & Venoa; vaulting; the ceiling walking of Aimee Austin; Russian roller skaters; Blondin, the Australian wire-walking horse that carried a man on its back; exploits of aerial bicycle riding, and more.

New for the museum was a wax statuary collection representing all the presidents of the United States from Washington to Arthur. There was a likeness of Guiteau, the notorious assassin; financial monarchs such as Gould, Vanderbilt and Blaine; and many of the crowned heads of Europe.

"The most perfect order existed everywhere and at all times, evidencing the strictest surveillance by competent superintendents, and excellent system of discipline," read the St. Paul *Pioneer-Press*. "As an amusement caterer, W. W. Cole's name is a power in the land and with such exhibition as he now possesses can aught but add to his enormous wealth and excellent reputation."[6]

In a rare interview with a writer from the Sedalia, Missouri *Bazoo*, Cole stated that the show carried 250 people, 150 of which were workmen, the others being actors, musicians, and associates. There were 160 horses, including forty that appeared in the ring. As for salaries of the performers, James Robinson received the top money of $350 a week and expenses; Frank Gardner, $250; Aimee Austin, $150; the two trapezists (presumably Nestor & Venoa), $100 each; the Arab troupe, $600; and the remaining ranged from $15 to $75. The expenses on the road averaged from $1,900 to $2,000 a day and at winter quarters $250."[7]

The circus played three dates in Missouri before officially opening the season in St. Louis on April 23 and, with the exception of the first day when there was threat of rain, played to turn-away business all week.

The itinerary was not typical of Cole's other seasons. There was no direct route apparent, but a scrambling in and out of states and back again. Following St. Louis there were dates in Missouri, Arkansas and Kansas. Heavy rains spoiled the day in Ottawa, Kansas, but nonetheless the *Republican* responded positively: "The exhibitions of Cole's circus were of course given under the most unfavorable of circumstances, yet we have heard nothing but commendation of it. It was really excellent, and considering the natural condition of the track and apparatus after and during the soaking rain, extraordinarily so. Many of the feats were novel, and all well executed; particularly the trapeze performance, the ceiling walk, the bicycle performances, and the marvelous feats of strength and agility of the Arab troupe." But the writer couldn't resist stating that "the concerts, of course, were an unmitigated swindle." Amid or because of the horrible weather conditions, poor James Robinson led with his nose while performing with a hoop, a mishap that required minor surgery and perhaps the application of heavy theatrical makeup at the next stand.[8]

After Kansas the show was in Missouri, Iowa, Illinois, and Iowa again by June. In Des Moines there was the typical anticipation of the morning procession. Interested spectators arrived from in and out of the city, "and while the country people selected the most eligible positions on the sidewalk and street corners, the city people peered copiously from the second story windows of the business blocks, each proprietor or tenant seemed to have invited a bevy of ladies and children friends to his window observatories." A writer for the *Iowa State Register* evinced admiration for the quality and condition of the animals and the attractiveness of the wagons and costumes. Outstanding were the two steam calliopes—one of which was driven in a mechanical chariot—the four elephants in tamden harness hauling a golden show wagon, two excellent bands, and the open cages of lions and snakes.[9]

Wisconsin was visited in mid-June to more large turn-outs. At Milwaukee, "The tents pitched at the corner of

Tenth and Clybourn were visited by vast numbers at both the afternoon and night shows," the *Sentinel* confirmed. "At the evening performance the doors were closed and hundreds turned away, unable to gain admittance because of the crowded condition of the tents."[10]

The Appleton *Post* made reference to a common complaint of many municipalities after a circus has left. "Cole and his elephant are gone and with them many hundreds of dollars of Appleton money." The criticism of the arenic performance was positive, however, and the proprietor was commended that he did not have "such a gang of roughs and thieves following him up as Forepaugh did." It was also reported that the Humane Society's attempt to stop the performances because of the danger involved was "all talk," since a net stretched under the athletes removed all risk of injury.[11]

The Racine stand posed somewhat of a dilemma locally. As we all remember, school children were wont to skip classes when the circus came to town, if not go to the matinee at least to witness the parade. On this date Cole's arrival coincided with the first session of school, enrollment day. The *Daily Journal*, responding to innumerable complaints from the youngsters, went on record as agreeing with them, advising all who wished to skip the Monday session to do so and then be enrolled when they arrived on Tuesday.[12]

The following day the paper carried a response from a reader, writing under the identity of Publicus, who expressed real anguish at the *Journal's* rash advice. "Is the circus so good in influence, so powerful an educator, so important in giving a child useful impressions of life that he should avoid school for the sake of it?" Publicus questioned. He reminded the paper that the daily expense of Racine's schools amounted to about $200, a sum that would be spent uselessly if a large number of absences occurred. "Publicus is unquestionably right," was the *Journal's* reply.[13]

Cole was in Minneapolis giving four performances on the 4$^{th}$ of July, but, even with four, all of the crowds could not be accommodated. From Minnesota the show trains went into what is now North Dakota, and Canada's Manatoba Province. The Jamestown, North Dakota, *Morning Alert* reflected a general satisfaction: "The street parade was splendid and the exhibition all that was advertised and more. The management and actors are clever and sociable people, and the work gang above the average of that class of men in respectability."[14]

After returning to Minnesota, the itinerary took the circus into Wisconsin, Iowa, Missouri, Nebraska, Iowa and Wisconsin again, then Illinois, Missouri, and back into Kansas by fall.

Returning to Ottawa on October 2, the circus was received quite differently than in their earlier spring visit: "Cole's circus did not give that degree of satisfaction yesterday as it did on its appearance here last spring. The street parade, while it was composed of a goodly number of animal cages on wheels, was nothing at all brilliant or 'gorgeous'— there was nothing of the 'glittering pageant' about it that was advertised. At the grounds two small rings contained all that was offered for the amusement of the goodly crowd that assembled, and the acts were in the main common-place. The performers appeared to be careless, and in a hurry to get through with their several acts. There was a noticeable lack of several prominent features that were shown here before, and that were really good. Even the Arab troupe has dwindled into insignificant numbers, several novices of pronounced Caucasian type appearing for the nonce as brown-faced children of the desert. The circus as a whole was not good."[15] After four months on the road the smell of fresh paint had worn away and the general appearance become bedraggled.

Humboldt was played the following day, where 400 feet of billboards had been erected on the north and east side of the park. The *Union* proclaimed them "about the best and most attractive show bills we ever saw." Here the company was visited by the great Dan Rice, who was temporarily residing a short distance away in Garnett, awaiting settlement of back wages from the recently demised Nathans & Co. circus.[16]

At Witchita on the 9th a storm hit the show, creating serious damage. Two days later Cole's beleaguered company performed at Marion in a drizzle without the canvas top. But, according to the *Record*, "The folks were there in great numbers."[17]

Problems followed on the 13th at Parsons. Although the *Daily Sun* estimated that not less than 8,000 people witnessed the matinee, filling every seat and leaving no standing room, and attendance nearly as great repeated in the evening, during both performances "advantage was taken of the immense crowd and every known scheme of robbing the people was resorted to." Again, the complaint we heard during the Australian visit: only one 50¢ admission office but a dozen men working out of satchels, selling tickets for from 60¢ to a dollar. There was also an indication that customers had been short changed. The *Daily Sun* summed it up with: "The show is a good one, but the people connected with it are hard characters, to say the least."[18]

Cole was in Texas by mid-October, where he remained until the first of December. If the reception at San Antonio was typical, the Texans were pleased with what they saw, in spite of the $1.00 admission price. The *Daily Express* report revealed pleasure with the length and variety of the parade. Special commendation went to the performing elephants, with particular astonishment at the size of Samson.

"The leaping corps, headed by the champion Frank Gardner, was also a wonder in the ring, while the bicycle and high wire acts called for and received full recognition. Aimee, a thirteen-year-old sprout, made a decided hit in walking the ceiling head downward.... In opposite rings was Jas. Robinson, of bare-back fame, contending against young Leon, a by no means slow adversary, for the honor of the world's plaudits. The Arabs in their tumbling, balancing and pyramid work gave a fine exhibition of what endurance and perseverance will accomplish."[19]

Following Texas, the show when into Louisiana. After closing in New Orleans on December 15, there were eight stands in Mississippi, wrapping up at Holly Springs on Christmas day. In all, the 1883 tour had taken the New York and New Orleans Circus into eleven states, two territories and one province, a distance of 17,083 miles, during a season of thirty-five weeks and five days.

## XIX

The New York *Clipper's* pre-season account of the 1884 Cole circus gives us a general idea of its immensity, which was reflected in the new title of "W. W. Cole's New Colossal Shows, Consolidated 3-Ring Circus, Menagerie, Gallery of Wax Statuary, Russian Roller Skaters, Elevated Stage, Encyclopedia and Races." The accompanying statistics reveal that the show had 260 horses, plus ten performing stallions, four trick horses and six ponies, a school of comical donkeys, racing pigs and riding goats, monkeys and dogs. There were fourteen tents, 185 employees, twenty-three baggage wagons, forty-eight white cages with landscape and animal paintings. The street procession was said to be divided into three sections, each led by a brass band. There were eight tableaux cars, six open dens, a number of loose-lead animals, and twelve Arabs mounted on Arabian stallions.[1] I again remind the reader that the above represents information sent to the *Clipper* by a show official and that it may contain exaggerated claims and/or pre-season speculation that did not materialize.

The forecast was to visit California, Oregon and the western territories, and perhaps make another visit to the South Seas. It was asserted that the show had an exclusive contract with all western railroads that prohibited interference from opposition. The rolling stock, made up of all sixty foot cars, numbered twenty-eight, with two used for advertising. And, as in the past, Cole owned all privileges.[2]

There was a large company, many of whom had been with the show for years—Anson Van Zandt, Young Leon, George and Hattie Dunbar, the Livingston Brothers, John Murtz, Dan Kennedy, Burt Richardson, and, not least, Tom McIntyre, who was there for his twelfth year as equestrian director. Wooda Cook was back, replacing James Robinson as the top equestrian, most likely at a slightly smaller salary. Cook, who had been with the show on the Australian tour, was a first-class rider but he certainly did not have the national appeal of Robinson.

"The circus is so large that it takes three rings and an elevated stage to give all the performers a chance to display their various acts and personal accomplishments," so reported the Topeka *Daily Commonwealth*. "The only fault to be found with this truly enormous show is that it is too long. Forty-five acts are given at every performance. It combines a circus, menagerie, theatre, roller skating rink, gallery of wax statuary and a dozen other complete exhibitions—all in one."[3] The above quotation should be interpreted as counting either the stage or the hippodrome track as the third ring. This arrangement—two rings and a center stage—was used in 1883 and during the years that follow. However, it is possible, although we have nothing to prove it, that the stage could be struck during a performance and its space used as a center ring.

Wooda Cook

Similar to the previous year there were aerial bicyclists, roller skaters, the troupe of Bedouin Arabs, a lady ceiling walker, Roman gladiators, rival riders, wrestlers, gymnasts, and leapers, and a learned pig race with a monkey jockey. All this was displayed on what was advertised as "three rings and a stage," which may explain the *Daily Commonwealth* reporter's confusion. Featured this year were the seven Sutherland Sisters with tresses seven feet long, highly advertised but apparently reserved for the annex and/or concert.[4]

The menagerie was stabled in two tents. In the first, a large canvas capable of holding 2,000 spectators at a time, was the ring of cage animals; and in the second the herd of elephants, including Samson and a new import from Burma, the group of camels, the Shetland ponies, the cage of lions, the white hippopotamus, the two-horned rhino and the white buffalo.

Louis E. Cooke still gave the press an opportunity to tour his handsome rolling facility, the Cole No. 1 advertising car, conveniently parked on a siding. "Every season for the past five or six years it has been the pleasure of *Commonwealth* reporters to visit, look through and write up advertising cars, but nothing of the kind ever stood on a side track in Topeka that was more elegant, convenient and attractive than car No. 1 of W. W. Cole's great show which arrived here Sunday at noon and remained until 12:30 last night, before it was hooked onto the hind end of a Union Pacific passenger train and went west."[5]

The reader may recall that the car was decorated with relics from the South Seas tour, acquired in Australia, New Zealand, and the Sandwich and Fiji islands. Among the lot was a pair of cockatoos, one rose colored and the other golden, that could carry on an amazing conversation. An emu skin, lined like a sleigh robe and with decorative feathers varying in length from a few inches to two feet or more, made an attractive conversation piece. A boomerang, representing Australia, was an item certain to interest the 1880s visitors. The walls were filled with photographs of members of the circus community and Cooke's family and friends. All of which formed a mini-museum-like atmosphere for affecting special treatment to members of the press and other local people of importance.

This was the year of the infamous White Elephant War, a supreme struggle for dominance between Barnum, Bailey & Hutchinson and their most aggressive adversary, Adam Forepaugh. Barnum announced in June of 1883 that his agent in Siam, J. B. Gaylord, (the reader may recall that Gaylord was a former agent for Cole) had informed him that he was about to make a deal for a White Elephant. Albino elephants were held sacred within the East Indian culture and, as such, were almost impossible to obtain. The reported purchase turned out to be ill-advised, as the elephant died aboard ship. Nevertheless, by November Gaylord had succeeded in buying another so-called white specimen from King Theebaw of Burma for £40,000.

When Adam Forepaugh learned of this he set a plan in motion to create a White Elephant of his own. From the able pen of press agent Charles H. Day a story was concocted and then released in January of 1884 that, through an agent in Gibraltar, a White Elephant had been secured and was being shipped to the Forepaugh quarters in Philadelphia. This immediately began a war of words in the country's newspapers that lasted throughout the season.

Forepaugh's "Star of Asia" arrived in New York on March 20 and in Philadelphia two days later, the *Clipper* announced. An observer found it to be ashen gray in color, quite light enough to distinguish it as elephant white; but, for reasons known only to the Forepaugh people at this time, the beast was kept blanketed. The realization of a "whitewash" would come later.

We have no intention of getting into the Barnum/Forepaugh elephant hullabaloo. It is pertinent only because of what followed. In February the New York *Clipper* carried an item revealing that W. W. Cole had received a cable from his agent, Ernest Cooke, whom he had sent to Burma, that read: "Have purchased a sacred elephant much whiter than the one recently shipped from here. Fifty thousand rupees is the price paid. Will depart by first steamer."[6] Cole was once again attempting to counter Barnum's moves with one of his own.

Cole's "White Elephant" was qualified descriptively as the "white faced sacred elephant" in his newspaper ads, in contrast to claims of complete whiteness by his competitors. "Now when we speak of a white elephant," Louis Cooke informed the reporter for Atchison's *Daily Champion*, "don't imagine that I mean an elephant as white as a Troy laundered shirt front, for such a beast never did and probably never will exist. But the spotted or piebald creature, before whom the Buddhists bow with deified veneration is termed sacred and by them called 'white,' and one of these we have; but in order not to mislead the public in the matter we shall frankly state that the purely white elephant is a myth."[7]

Rehearsals began for the 1884 season in St. Louis on April 18 and the opening was set for Monday the 21st on the grounds at Twentieth and Chestnut Streets. For the previous Saturday there was to be an after dark illuminated street parade—weather permitting. "Night Transferred Into Day!" the advertising boasted. But weather did not permit and indeed the opening, too, was postponed until the following day, when the usual morning parade was arranged in spite of unpleasant conditions. Yet the matinee and evening shows were well attended.

"The performance was, without question, one of the very best given here," the *Post-Dispatch* reported, "and demonstrated most perfectly that it is not necessary for enterprising managers to keep in the same stereotyped track in

W. W. Cole's sacred "white elephant"

presenting attractions." The writer observed that the double ring and elevated stage were occupied constantly and gave at the same time varied and non-conflicting offerings. "At a word, Cole's circus is, beyond a doubt, one of the very best ever exhibiting in St. Louis."[8]

The *Globe Democrat* found the performers to be excellent: "Each was a star in a particular line, but the marvelous ceiling-walking by Mlle. Aimee, who is appropriately styled the human fly, excited the utmost astonishment. The troupe of Arabs gave the crowd some marvelous leaping and tumbling exhibitions, which were no less remarkable than their feats of strength and picturesque groupings in the form of pyramids. The show contains a host of fine athletes and a galaxy of graceful riders, ladies and gentlemen. The horsemanship of Leon (no longer 'Young'), who stands among the first equestrians in the country, was one of the praiseworthy features of an entertainment startling in novelty, endless in variety and of absorbing interest." The writer felt the menagerie had been strengthened from the previous year and that the seating arrangements under the mammoth canvas were admirable, allowing perfect viewing of all "three rings."[9]

A week later the circus was in Kansas. The Kansas City *Chronicle* reported early success. It was estimated that at night there were fully 15,000 under the canvas and that the doors were closed at 7:30 with thousands turned away. The number 15,000, however, was most likely more than what the tent could accommodate.

The season had barely begun when Cole faced a battle with John B. Doris' Great Inter-Ocean circus.[10] This rivalry had been brewing for some time, possibly dating back to the aggressive bidding between the two proprietors for Samson. It would become a nasty and expensive contest in the weeks to come.

Cole was running eleven days ahead of Doris in Kansas at the beginning of May, but not far enough to avoid getting slapped in the rear. Doris was a capable showman who consistently put together a strong company of performers; and, in 1884, somewhat stronger than Cole's. Featured were the Salbini Troupe of French bicycle riders, the Moore Family of roller skaters, three acrobatic Siegrist Brothers, iron-jaw lady Millie De Granville, the classical posturing Macarte Brothers, clown Johnny Patterson, Prof. Hamilton and his dogs, the Fisher Brothers, and three well known riders in Willie Showles, Ella Stokes, and Sallie Marks.

It must be added, however, that Doris was always teetering on the edge of going under. A billing war with a wealthier opponent was risky business for him.

To illustrate how expensive a conflict of this nature can be, we refer to one carried out in 1881 between the Barnum and Forepaugh shows in St. Louis, which was documented in the *Post-Dispatch* at the time. Previously, the largest quantity of paper put up in that city was in 1879 by the Great London show, which amounted to approximately 18,000 sheets. But in the war for St. Louis between these two great arenic organizations Forepaugh used 22,000 sheets and Barnum exceeded that with 23,000. The *Post-Dispatch* reported that "both Barnum and Forepaugh [had] flung painted banners to the breezes, and millions of quarter-sheets, dodgers and various other devices, that kept the Times Printing Company's presses going night and day for weeks." Both shows spent extravagantly for painted banners and additional newspaper space. The total expenditures of each circus was estimated to be some $16,000.[11] There is no record of what it cost Cole and Doris in their quest for dominance.

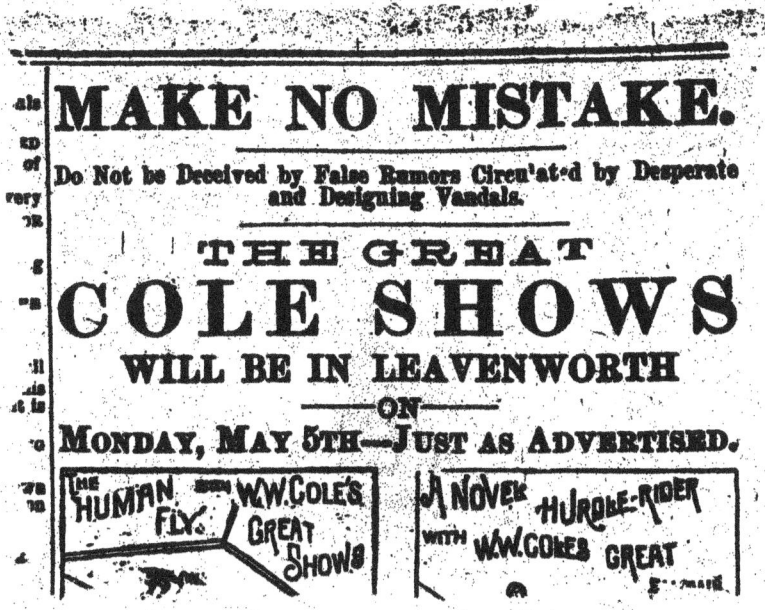

## XX

The 1884 billing war between the circuses of Cole and Doris for the ownership of Kansas was confined to various days in April and May. Cole's circus was set to appear in Topeka on April 29. Doris' was booked for some days later. Being second could mean second best at the ticket wagon, therefore "YOU MUST WAIT," his ads read, "THE BIG SHOW WILL NOT BE IN TOPEKA UNTIL FRIDAY, MAY 9."[1] The first of the bitter confrontations occurred here.

Cole's advertising car, under the direction of W. C. Boyd, arrived on March 24 and thoroughly papered the town. The crew was back on April 6 to re-paper and hit the places that had been missed on the first visit, then left a little past midnight of the following day. Newspaper ads began on April 10. Doris' lithographs were first posted on the 18th; but, in opposition, the Cole No. 2 car, under Ed H. Madigan,

Wires, Cole's "confidential agent" was present at this time doing whatever "confidential duties" there were to be done. On the 24$^{th}$ four horsemen from Cole's circus rode through Topeka, blaring trumpets, handing out show literature and proclaiming the virtues of the coming event. Doris' bugle brigade followed a week later. His car No. 5 arrived on the 25$^{th}$ and re-billed the city (Doris did not have five advertising cars).

John B. Doris

As usual, it was Louis Cooke's job to feed a glowing image of his circus to the hungry press. "It is a very easy matter to talk about big shows but quite a difficult thing to organize one," he contemplated to the writer for the Topeka *Daily Capital*. "There are several important qualifications necessary for the successful organization and maintenance of a really great amusement enterprise. The first thing needed is money and lots of it. The next is an extensive and established reputation, such as I know W. W. Cole to possess. New and novel features are also quite necessary, and this season we have been particularly careful to discard all old features and people and to not only replace them with new acts and new faces, but to add every decided novelty that money could purchase or advanced ideas suggest."[2]

An item appeared in Topeka's *State Journal* on the 25th that listed Doris' roster of performers and announced the show date. Cole countered with an article in the same paper on the 28th. "Everybody is waiting for the promised great circus festival which will be inaugurated here tomorrow, when W. W. Cole's colossal shows open their doors to the public," was the proclamation. "This is the greatest entertainment to which the people of this section of the country have ever been treated." The overblown item boasted of sixty acts in the arena and 100 cages in the menagerie. "Cole is undoubtedly the best show on the road, press and public uniting in so declaring it."[3]

Of what Cole announced as featured acts, Doris announced he had more. Cole advertised his $100,000 sacred elephant, Doris followed with one, named Theodora, that cost $110,000. Cole's claim of twelve genuine Arab acrobats was countered by Doris' fourteen Turks. If Cole had a troupe of Russian roller skaters, Doris had one from Siberia. Each was attempting to outdo the other.

The Cole circus got off to an unfortunate start on show day when the train did not arrive at Topeka's Union Pacific depot until 8:00 a.m., due to being held on a siding seven miles east to allow another train to pass on its way to Kansas City. By 10:00 a.m. a huge crowd had gathered for the street procession, only to be kept waiting until some time around 12:30. The *Mail* called the parade far from imposing. Apparently the late arrival not only delayed the start but caused the management to shorten its length. The *Capital* stated that the spectacle was but three blocks long. As for the performance, it was "very slim, and but few, if any, new or original features were introduced." Further, the *Capital* complained, "The tendency to cut short every act and rush things through was plainly noticeable, especially in closing up the menagerie before time was given half the people to view the wonders." The *Commonwealth* included an even harsher remark. "Cole's circus, considering the time it has been on the road this season, is said to have congregated as grand an array of 'crooks' as the most exacting might wish."[4] Not a pleasant recommendation.

Doris fared much better. The street procession, which began on time, was observed by the *Commonwealth* as being "so much finer, grander and more extensive than Cole's that an attempt to compare the two would be mockery." The *Mail*, too, was more favorable toward the Inter-Ocean. "Doris' circus gave two exhibitions in Topeka last Friday, and all who went said they thought the performances much better than Cole's. There is a bitter rivalry between the two shows, which appears to have been started by Cole."[5]

Both circuses played Lawrence, Cole on May 3 and Doris a week later with only minor skirmishing. Cole published an excerpt favorable of his company from the St. Louis *Globe Democrat* in the Lawrence *Journal* on April 29. Doris then followed two days later by inserting an unfavorable one from the Topeka *Daily Capital* of April 30, and concluding with: "Now people of Lawrence and surrounding country we would advise you to wait for Doris' greatest show on earth. Don't be deceived. The date is positive. Remember the big show don't come until Saturday, May 10. Save your money until then."[6]

Nevertheless, Cole received a friendly reception at Lawrence. "Mr. Cole certainly has a great show," the *Journal* concluded, "and he has the good fortune to have a first-class management in all respects. He will be welcomed back should he return to our city again."[7]

The sharp attacks picked up again at Leavenworth. Just a day before his arrival, Cole devoted a large space in his advertisement to a scathing rebuke of Doris and his Inter-Ocean circus. "I refer you to the published bill of sale of the little Doris Circus for an exact inventory of everything that he exhibits. He does not own it, as it is in the hands of his lenient creditors. Finally and frankly I will say: Mr. Doris, your Little Circus is Doomed to an Early Death from the fact that you advertise everything and exhibit little or nothing! There is no Two-Headed Lady in the Doris Circus, yet such an attraction is boldly advertised! There are no Turks in the Doris Circus, but you will see white men painted and palmed off as such! There are no Russian Athletes in the Doris Circus, although they are a principal feature on the bills! There is no White, Sacred, or Albino Elephant in the Doris Circus as no animal of any kind had been purchased by Mr. Doris in 2 years! There is no Herd of Elephants in the Doris Circus. He has just two very ordinary ones. There is no Bovalapus in the Doris Circus. A common buffalo cow is all he has. There are no Lion Slayers in the Doris Circus. Two moon-faced monkeys are the stock in trade. There are no New Features in the Doris Circus. Every act is old and can be seen in any show. There is nothing great about the Doris Circus except its indebtedness. Its people are ill-paid, ill-provided; its horses are ill-kept, ill-fed, ill-looking; its managers ill-advised financial wrecks. A CHALLENGE TO A DELAPIDATED CONCERN would be worse than 'fool's folly.' At one time I offered to loan Mr. Doris $10,000 (to cover one of my deposits inviting him to an open comparison), and take a mortgage on his show for the amount, but that time has passed. The show is now out of his hands and beyond his control, 'as attests the annexed bill of sale,' etc. However, I will donate $10,000 to any charitable society in Leavenworth, that the Mayor and three other responsible citizens may select, if all that I have stated above is not 'AS TRUE AS SCRIPTURE.' Very respectfully, W. W. COLE, Proprietor of the Great Cole Shows."[8]

Doris responded in the *Evening Standard* of May 2. "To the Common Sense of the American People—My situation has been called to a program emanating from W. W. Cole, an envious rival showman, which is the most astounding, disgraceful, cowardly and mean act of the period, and such a deed as should bring the blush of shame to the face of the proprietor; certainly his conscience will smite him. The intent of the shameful assault undoubtedly being made for the sole purpose of damaging my character and the business interest of my great shows. I have no desire to enter into any newspaper controversy with Mr. Cole, but will seek redress in a legal manner and not on windy effusions in public prints. I feel charitable toward Mr. Cole for his weak mindedness, but if he persists in resorting to these silly subterfuges for the purpose of advertising his show and damaging my character and reputation, I shall most unwillingly be compelled in my own defense to unravel the history and working of Mr. Cole and his executioners and assistants from their commencement in show life, regardless of the mortification and shame that it may reveal. I furthermore warn Mr. Cole, his agents and employes, that if they continue hereafter to print in newspapers, handbills or other publications or circulate or distribute any printed statement injurious or damaging to my character, or the business interest of my show, I shall immediately institute legal proceedings for damages against such parties. Your obedient servant, John B. Doris, Sole Owner."[9]

This denunciatory give-and-take was of little benefit to either party. The Leavenworth *Evening Standard* was satisfied with the May 5 Cole date, although the evening performance was but half full due to rain. Doris, arriving two days behind, was more fortunate. The *Times* rated his the best show that had performed there in years; and, although the morning of the 7th was rainy, causing the circus to set up at Cherokee and Twelfth streets, two blocks from the lot originally contracted, the tent was well filled for the matinee and, weather clearing toward evening, the night attendance was even better. Both shows had suffered heavy losses from the very disagreeable weather for the past two weeks. Indeed, at Rich Hill, Doris was forced to give a hall show because of flooded grounds.

The war continued in Atchinson with the posting of similar diatribes and the outlay of twice the usual amount of money being spent for advertising. The press releases are the only items of evidence still in existence, but the reader can be assured there were thousands of spiteful pieces of literature concocted by the rival agents and energetic attempts to cover each others' stands of paper by the bill posting crews.

And to make things more complicated a third party entered the fray—Sells Bros.' Monster Fifty Cage Menagerie and Great Four Ring Circus—which was to perform at Atchinson on May 25. The *Globe* of May 3 stated: "In this issue will be found special announcements from the three circuses which are to be in Atchison this month, and they are worth reading, for more spirited examples of literature have not appeared in these columns before in years.... The result of the amazing war now in progress will be that all of the circuses will be well patronized, for the advance agents have created a desire on the part of the people to judge for themselves."[10] And the judgment was again in Doris' favor, both in performance quality and in attendance.

A moment of truce occurred on the morning of May 8 when the Cole and Doris trains simultaneously halted in East Atchison for a ten minute delay. Cole was bound for

St. Joseph, Missouri, and Doris, just coming from there, was on his way to Leavenworth. The two managers had a congenial talk on the station platform and, in parting, wished each other success. But the war continued unabated.

The St. Joseph stands were the closest to actually "day-and-dating", coming as they did twenty-four hours apart, Doris on May 6 and Cole on the 7th. The first volleys were lofted by Cole with his ads appearing in the St. Joseph *Daily Herald* on April 16 and 25. Doris answered with an ad on the 27th and two more on Sunday, May 4. The Sells Bros. got a shot in, also on May 4, with a reader that indirectly accused its competitors of false advertising. In this same publication was a card by Doris in which he quoted excerpts purportedly representing adverse reviews of Cole's Kansas City appearance. These dates would also suggest the arrival of the advertising cars and their billing crews. The number of "rat sheets" distributed and the amount of billboards papered over can only be imagined.

An item in the *Daily Herald* on Doris' show day carried a boast quite obviously inspired by a press agent. "Of the superiority of this show too much cannot be said (but, of course, too much had already been said). It comes here with the strongest recommendations from the press wherever it has exhibited, and our citizens can rely on its being just what it advertises to be. Its attractions are numerous, and every promise made by Mr. Doris concerning the performances will be carried out to the letter."[10]

On this same day were items for both Cole and the Sells Bros. Cole's referred to the "scurrilous and defamatory article" that was published in the Sunday columns, calling it a most malicious libel from first to last and "a paid advertisement written and arranged by the little opposition show, seeking to curry favor by circulating all sorts of infamous reports concerning the great Cole shows, which are too well known to permit of any question as to their integrity or superior worth." Cole again accused Doris of "floundering in the quagmire of bankruptcy" and of advertising "his own little cross-road exhibit" falsely. The show, Cole's retort stated, had no two-headed lady, no Turks, no Russian athletes, no Siberian skaters, no three ring circus, no sacred elephant, etc. The Sells item, mentioning no other show by name, but avowing its own superiority in truthful advertising, claimed its place as "the largest and best of all tented exhibitions in America... and one that it will pay to wait and see. Don't forget the date, Wednesday, May 27."[11]

Because of a blockade of freight cars, Doris' company did not arrive in St. Joseph until noontime on show day, causing disappointment to the crowds that had been waiting since nine o'clock. Once the parade occurred it was judged by the *Daily Herald* to be "a very ordinary affair." The matinee did not commence until three-thirty and, as a result, was hurried through. "Nothing of a very startling nature was expected, and few were disappointed. An occasional feature of the arena was passably good and affected applause, but on the whole little enthusiasm was manifested. The actual comment was that the spots on the sacred elephant existed more in the imagination of the glib-tongued ring master than in reality."[12]

The *Herald's* appraisal of the Cole show on the following day was quite different. In spite of rain, there was a large turnout for the procession. "It was by all odds the grandest pageant that has appeared on the streets of St. Joseph this season." The doors were opened on time and the tent was "crowded to apparently overflowing in the afternoon, and the exhibition gave such universal satisfaction that the attendance in the evening was even larger."[13]

Within two days Cole had left the fray in Kansas for dates in Nebraska. The Doris circus did not follow, but when Cole moved into the state a Doris agent had decorated the walls of Nebraska City with: "Stop thief! Farmers stay at home! A terrible pestilence is about to visit Nebraska City, May 12, 1884, in the shape of W. W. Cole's circus. Farmers, for God's sake remain at home. This show is composed of the worst and most desperate organized bands of thieves, cut-throats, plunderers and housebreakers. Protect your homes and barns, keep your guns loaded at home, for when they start out they present the appearance of bloodthirsty desperadoes. Don't leave your house on May 12."[14]

By June, Cole had moved into the Northwest—Montana, Washington, Oregon and British Columbia. The show traveled over Northern Pacific rails which had been partially completed in 1883 and which connected with the Oregon Railroad and Navigation line. "We took in the northwest, including the Puget Sound country, and in many cases we showed in towns that had never seen an elephant," Cole agent W. C. Boyd recalled. "Our business throughout the northern and western trip was immense—the best, I think, that the W. W. Cole show ever had."[15]

The Butte *Inter Mountain* reported that the circus which visited there on June 17 had "knocked the Robinson show of last year all hollow." "In every feature it is superb," it continued. "Every performer is a wonder, the human fly being particularly so. The circuses of Barnum and Forepaugh may have a more widely extended reputation, but in point of variety and interest of their attractions, Cole is fully their equal."[16] But there was skepticism that if Cole did not know of the swindling going on by his employees "he was a fool." Of the 7,000 to 8,000 people that attended the circus, there were no reports of pickpockets, but twenty-six people were reported hoodwinked. In response to these assertions, Cole refunded $312 wrongly taken by the candy peddlers and extra ticket sellers.

"This is the first stigma that has ever attached itself to my circus," Cole disingenuously stated. "I have remedied the matter as much as possible. No one, to my knowledge, has been financially injured—save myself."[17]

For the June 26 date in Walla Walla, Washington, all kinds of vehicles loaded with men, women and children came from the surrounding counties and by ten o'clock every available space was filled along the parade route. Unfortunately, the circus train was again late in arriving, causing the procession to be delayed until noon. "The parade was magnificent and elected rounds of applause," the *Union* read. "The band wagon drawn by camels and another by elephants 'took like wild fire.'"

Discomfort from waiting for the parade to commence aside, the tent was filled to the brim for the matinee, including the temporary seating erected to satisfy the overflow of 1,000 spectators. "In all particulars Cole's circus takes the lead over all circus troupes that have visited the Northwest," the *Union* writer concluded.[18] And a satisfied W. W. Cole stated that Walla Walla was the best show town he had experienced since leaving Salt Lake City.

Word of questionable practices continued to precede the show. The Ashland, Oregon, *Tidings* reported on July 4 that a number of thieves were following in its wake. "When the rush comes after the doors open," the item read, "a number of self-appointed assistants string out with tickets and do not return change, when any is to be returned to the purchaser."[19]

The same day, however, the Portland *Standard's* report was positive: "The circus is complete in its appointments and program, and it is not probable that another on so grand a scale will visit Portland in years."[20]

Expectant Vancouver citizens expressed pleasure when the circus appeared in their city at 11:00 a.m., Thursday, July 24. Hundreds of people were on hand for the unloading from two steamers and a barge that had transported the troupe up the coast from Astoria, Oregon. However, the appearances, with audiences estimated at 1,000 in the afternoon and 2,500 in the evening, received a mixed review by the Vancouver *Independent*. "As to the circus performances, there were some very good and interesting features, and some that might have been better." The writer approved of the bareback riding, the tumbling, the tight-rope walking, and the trained horses. "Although there were some who seemed to be dissatisfied with the show, we think, taking it all together, it is the largest and best show that ever visited these parts. We will say, however, that the performance given in Portland was somewhat better than here. Be it as it may, we can all say we saw the 'big show,' and if some think the circus wasn't worth a dollar, they must admit the menagerie was."[21]

Portland was re-visited on July 30. The writer for the *Oregonian* was impressed with the novelty within the program. "A man might spend $50,000 a week in salaries, and he could not engage talent which will give a performance that does not bear some resemblance to some other circus performance; however, he can secure some novelties and the very best of old style attractions. Cole has done this, and he does not give a single dull act."[22]

Trouble came when the elephant Samson broke his chains at Hailey, Idaho, on August 4. As was the custom, Samson had carried a howdah full of children in the street procession. After being brought back to the menagerie he proceeded to overturn the lion cage in which Conklin had been riding, knock four horses to the ground, killing two, and then charge after his handler. Fearing the menagerie would be totaled, Conklin mounted a horse and lured the malcontent into the adjoining fields where several shots were fired into his tough hide. He was eventually subdued, chained and returned to the circus lot, but with thirty bullet holes to show for his cantankerous spree.

"I have often laughed when I have thought of the spectacle we must have made," Conklin wrote later in his book. "I was dressed in a suit of tights covered with shining spangles, had a great leopard skin around my waist and hips, and was mounted on a bronco with a Mexican saddle and bridle elaborately ornamented. The elephant had on all the parade trappings and great saddle, and as he ran the colored velvet blanket blew out from both his sides like huge wings."[23]

Cole ordered the animal severely punished. "I remonstrated with him, telling him it was not necessary, that the elephant had given in and was behaving himself, and that it would do no good," Conklin recalled, "but Cole thought he must be punished until he squealed." We won't get into the unpleasant details that followed, only to say that the big guy refused to squeal, but when he was let up about a half-hour later he could barely stand and could not bend his trunk. For more than a week he was fed by hand and given water with a force pump.[24]

The tour, which covered territory west of the Missouri River, from the Mexican border to British Columbia, ended at Salem, Missouri on October 25. With no plans to lengthen the season by going south, which had been a familiar pattern in the past, Cole must have been anxious to put the outfit to rest.

The two rings and a stage, expensive featured acts, and large crowds along much of the route, appear to have created a loss of perspective for management. The Atchinson *Globe* expressed one of the concerns with: "Were we to find fault with W. W. Cole's tented exhibition, it would be that it lacks inside management. Mr. Cole has as many expensive features as any manager on the road, and plenty of fine horses and capable performers, but the programme is not rendered with snap and vim which a circus audience enjoys."[25] It appears that expansion went against Cole's style and created a departure from his established philosophy of not losing sight of details. This year the show suffered from its own success.

VACQUEROS of MEXICO.

## XXI

The 1885 tour for W. W. Cole's New Colossal Shows was confined to states east of the Mississippi. Preparations began for the season in April at the fair grounds winter storage facility in St. Louis. The opening was scheduled for the week of the 20$^{th}$ on the lot at Nineteenth and Pine Streets. Threatening showers interfered with the first day's procession to some extent, deterring the usually high public turnout. But in the afternoon, in spite of poor weather conditions, thousands of children were admitted free to the matinee. In reality, this could be considered a full dress rehearsal. "The first performance is always attended by friction, as the ring management is never in good working order," the *Post-Dispatch* observer wrote, "but yesterday's performance gave fine promise and last night it passed off smoothly to the delight of a large audience."[1]

The museum was in a separate tent this year. It was a typical sideshow, which could be entered for the sum of 10¢.

## W. W. COLE'S NEW COLOSSAL SHOWS

### PROGRAMME OF PERFORMANCE.
#### SUBJECT TO CHANGE.

GRAND OPERATIC OVERTURE.......................... PROF. A. D. GOOD, Leader

| 1. | 2. | 3. |
|---|---|---|
| RING NEAREST MENAGERIE. | STAGE. | RING OPPOSITE END. |

1. OPENING DOUBLE PROCESSION, introducing Costly Clad Knights and Dames, Armored Warriors, Natives of all Nations in Costume, Richly Caparisoned Elephants, Dromedaries, Zebras, Ponies, Beautiful Horses, Loose led Hippopotamus, Samson, largest of all animals, Elk, Deer, and Elegant Wardrobe, Trappings, Banners and Flags.

2. Five Minutes with Mexicans, not a Circus Act, but an introduction of them in Costume; also showing their manner of Lassoing, and Riding Bucking Bronchos.

| PERFORMING HORSES, T. B. McINTYRE. | PUNCH, THE CLOWN ELEPHANT, | Performing Elephants, GEO. CONKLIN. |
|---|---|---|

**ÆRIAL BICYCLE RIDING**
SIGNOR MURTZ AND LES FRERES GILLETTE.

| 20-CLOWNS-20 | ALL IN THE RING at ONCE | TWENTY OF THEM |
|---|---|---|
| DOUBLE HORSE RIDING Mons. and Madam HARVIE. | | Comic Song by the Clown ERNEST. |

PROGRAMME CONTINUED ON NEXT PAGE.

Excerpts from Cole's *Daily Programme*, East Saginaw, MI, June 9, 1885

For that small token one could see a living two-headed cow—eats with two mouths, has four eyes, four horns, one body; also Miss Annie Howard, the Tattooed Lady, and Frank Howard, her tattooed counterpart; Col. Steere and wife, the smallest married couple living, a combined weight of but sixty-five pounds; Miss Annie Bell, the California Giantess; Miss Aggie Zoluti, the Albino Lady; Fatima, the living Half-lady; Lieut. Allen, ventriloquist; Prof. Cazanovia, magician; and various other wonders.

## PROGRAMME—Continued.

| THE FLYING TRAPEZE<br>The Austin Sisters. | The HUMAN FLY<br>M'LLE AIME. | The SWINGING TRAPEZE<br>The Maretta Sisters. |

### BATTOUTE LEAPING BY THE COMPANY,
LED BY MR. JOHN WORLAND AND MR. CHAS. RENCH.

| Bareback Somersault Riding<br>JAMES LEON. | CLOWN ERNEST AND HIS<br>DANCING GIRAFFE | JUMPING JOCKEY<br>A. D. VAN ZANDT. |

### BICYCLE RIDING
THE LIVINGSTONE TROUPE.

After the Circus is over, in this same Tent, and using the Large Stage, a Mammoth Company will appear in a varied and pleasing Entertainment. TICKETS 10 CENTS.

| Balancing on Aerial Bar<br>Miss ROSE MARETTA. | JAPANESE PERCH<br>L. S. VICTOR. | Flying Rings<br>Miss MAY MARETTA. |

### M'LLE ELIZE AGUZZI
The Greatest of all Riders, will next appear.

EDDIE EVANS AS CLOWN.

### MESSRS. DUNBAR and VERNON
IN AERIAL FLIGHTS.

PROGRAMME CONTINUED ON NEXT SIDE.

The concert, held in the main tent after the show, introduced "25 Artists in latest Songs, Dances, Burlesques, and Sketches," not to mention an illusion of The Floating Lady and the surprises of mesmerist Prof. Handy. All for a dime!

The arena program consisted of the usual leaping, tumbling and acrobatic work, along with the specialty and featured acts. Anson Van Zandt repeated his jockey riding and other equestrian feats. He was joined in these by long loyal James Leon (at last he has a first name). The very versatile Aimee Austin again performed her ceiling walking and doubled with her sister, Rose Dubsky, on the trapeze. The *Post-Dispatch* writer assured his readers that her human fly

## PROGRAMME—Continued.

### The Abdallah Ben Said Troupe of Arabs
**TWELVE IN NUMBER.**

| COMIC SKATING<br>GEO. MILTON, | SKATORIAL EXERCISES,<br>MISSES ROSE and EMMA AUSTIN<br>and MR. R. G. AUSTIN. | COMIC SKATING<br>CHAS. RENCH. |
|---|---|---|
| THE DUDE ON THE WIRE<br>PRINCE HASSAN.<br>Acrobatic Brothers<br>LIVINGSTONS & GILLETTES. | HORIZONTAL BARS<br>DUNBAR, VERNON,<br>WORLAND and EVANS. | THE<br>ROMAN LADDERS<br>CHERIFFE and BROS. |
| THE<br>PERFORMING STALLIONS | H. COOKE<br>E. COOKE | THE<br>SEA-SAW PONIES |
| Sextuple Equestrian,<br>JAMES LEON. | Quintuple Equestrian,<br>MONS. VAN ZANDT. | |

### THE PERFORMING LIONS
**BY GEO. CONKLIN.**

### Finale

feat "in which she walks head down on the ceiling [was] a marvel of skill, nerve and daring."[2]

They were joined in aerial work by the Maretta Sisters and Dunbar & Vernon. The principal equestrienne was Lizzie Agazzi, who had performed in England and on the Continent for several years—Hagenbeck's in Germany, Cinco Price in Spain, Sanger's and Hengler's in England, and a member of the circus at Covent Garden, London, for three years—before coming to America. Add to this the wire walking horse, the twelve Arabs, roller skaters, bicycle riders, the see-saw ponies, performing horses and elephants, Conklin's den of lions, Vacquero riders and lasso throwers, and you've got yourself a show.

## PROGRAMME—Continued.

### FINALE

#### AFTER THE CIRCUS, SAME TENT,
# MAMMOTH DIME ENTERTAINMENT

Introducing 25 Artists in Latest Songs, Dances, Burlesques, Sketches. Also the Wonderful Aerial Suspension, the Floating Lady and Professor Handy, the Mesmerist.

## IN THE MUSEUM, OUTSIDE TENT

#### Are to be Seen the Most Wonderful of all Curiosities:

The LIVING TWO-HEADED COW, having two heads, eats with two mouths; four eyes, four horns, one body—a perfectly formed and beautiful animal; also, MISS ANNIE HOWARD, Tattooed Lady; COL. STEERE AND WIFE, Smallest Married Couple Living, Weight combined but sixty-five pounds, Ages 29 and 22, Height 30 and 28 inches; MISS ANNIE BELL, the California Giantess—Largest Lady Living; FRANK HOWARD, Tattooed from Head to foot; MISS AGGIE ZOLUTI, the Albino Lady; FATIMA, the Living Half Lady; LIEUT. ALLEN, the Ventriloquist; PROF. CAZANOVIA, the Great Magician; Woods, the Musical Wonder, and others. ADMISSION, 10 CENTS.

After opening in St. Louis, the company went into Indiana and Kentucky. Their arrival at Terre Haute was met with by the "greatest ovation in the annals of amusements ever yet chronicled," the *Journal* proclaimed unashamedly. A vast crowd filled windows, balconies and rooftops with people who had traveled from far and near to view the promised spectacle. The parade was described as being at least a mile long, "a glittering display of beautiful chariots, elegantly trapped horses, gaily caparisoned ponies, and gaudily dressed male and female riders." There were three bands and a calliope, at least ten of the cages were open to the public, and the herd of elephants and camels was led by Samson, "the largest Asiatic elephant in America." The two performances were attended by vast crowds. "Mr. Cole will always find a warm welcome here when he returns," the paper enthused.³

At Evanston, too, the tent was crowded for both performances. "The sight at the show grounds made one think that an army had encamped there," the *Daily Journal* reported, "so numerous were the attaches and so great the signs of preparation." The paper approved of the rapid succession of acts, with no waiting, enlivened by excellent music.[4]

The Louisville stand was said to have played to over 16,000 people on the day. "Mr. Cole has evidently been at work during the winter," the *Courier-Journal* observed, "and his circus is far better than it ever was before." The correspondent was particularly intrigued by the Mexican exhibit, which contained antiquities, idols, jewels, plants, agricultural implements, etc.[5]

Bad weather followed the circus in the early going. At Lexington on May 6 a punishing rainstorm arrived about the time the audience was entering the tent and stubbornly continue throughout the performance. Intruding water pored through the sieve-like canvas, causing the people to sit with their umbrellas full open, doing their best to keep dry. Everything on the lot was afloat. Such conditions did not agree with Samson, who the following day at Richmond knocked his keeper down, for which he got a distasteful threshing.

By June the show was in Ohio and Michigan. While in the latter state it encountered opposition from Forepaugh. Perhaps to avoid an expensive war, Forepaugh not given to being an amiable adversary, Cole extended his route as far north as Machinaw, the topmost tip of the Michigan mitt. Then the rail cars were ferried on a barge four at a time the eight miles across the Straits of Machinac to St. Ignace in the upper peninsula, a process which occupied nearly a full day. Here, in Michigan's northern regions, Cole raised the general admission to $1.00 and sideshow and concert to 25¢.

Samson acted up again on June 23 at Lapeer, still in Michigan. He got away from his handler while in the ring and surrounded by audience. After going for the camels, knocking them in every direction, he threw the leaping board about, leveled the leaping run and made fast tracks for the bandstand, which he soon demolished. The full tiers of a row of seats was his next target. Finally he went outside and made his way to a swamp, in which he was quickly mired, stuck to the extent that it was possible to put chains around him. Through the use of planks and tackle he was pulled out and returned in irons to the show grounds and, as we have seen before, punished for his misdeeds.

It is a miracle that no one was killed in the outburst. Many were frozen to their seats not realizing the extent of danger that was occurring. The side on which the dressing-room stood was in shambles, with quarter-poles, side poles, stringers and jacks broken and lying in a heap. But Cole, soon on the spot, and with the aid of McIntyre, quickly restored order and convinced the audience that the performance should continue. The show went on as if nothing had happened; although one lady came out of the commotion with a broken leg, for which Cole settled with a goodly sum.

From Michigan Cole moved east into New York state and Pennsylvania. August brought heavy rains, hot weather and opposition from the Barnum show, resulting in loss of revenue. Johnstown, Pennsylvania, the bane of all circuses because of the rowdy conduct that traditionally occurred, was surprisingly quiet during its two large houses. Not a stone was thrown. This was attributed to the tough st and taken by the mayor and council against anyone cutting and destroying ropes, canvas or any other property belonging to the circus, or creating a disturbance in the tent or about the grounds, the penalty being a twenty-five dollar fine or thirty days in jail.

After Pennsylvania, the circus went south into West Virginia, Virginia and the Carolinas in August, but encountered only fair business. At Charleston, West Virginia, on the 22$^{nd}$ about ten people showed up for the matinee. With a $75 license levied for each performance, Cole gave them their money back and struck the tents.

There was a serious rail smash-up near Cornwallis, Virginia, in late August. The cause was the narrowness of a tunnel that swept clean a car of nine cross-wise cages, liberating some of the animals and killing others. The engineer, fireman and brakeman, unable to pass through the wreckage, walked over the hill to the end of the cars where flares were placed as warning to a train due within an hour. One of the kangaroos, an anteater and a wild boar were fatalities. A loose kangaroo, a leopard and a hyena caused some fright, but, under the direction of Cole, the circus was able to continue onward some hours later.

By the end of October the show had headed further south into Georgia. At this time the general admission price for adults was raised from 50¢ to 75¢ and children under nine from 25¢ to 50¢. The outfit was set on a lot on Market Street in Augusta on November 5, where it receive a most appropriate observation by the *Chronicle*. "Mr. Cole is a young man, not over thirty-five years of age, and has congregated a host of artists, each one of whom excels in his or her specialty. He is a man of energy, pleasant address, and is well liked by all who are associated with him. Mr. Cole has secured a company of the best men in the show business to assist him. Everything moves along like well oiled machinery. The men are all polite and attentive to the patrons, and everything is done inside and outside of the canvas to please the people who go to the show. Mr. Cole certainly has able and competent assistants."[6] The writer also expressed gratification that only a small portion of the program was devoted to the clowns, because, he judged, such business was boring to everyone but the youngsters.

The Savannah *Morning News* welcomed the show to that city. "The streets represented a lively appearance long before the time the procession was announced to start. Many of those on the streets were strangers, and the time was spent in taking in the sights. When the head of the procession did come into view away out Drayton street, the crowd lined the sidewalk in ranks from the building line to the curb. At the head of Drayton the band, chariots, dromedaries, elephants, lions, buffalo, trick horses, and the two score of wagons and cages on wheels turned into Bay street and moved up to West Broad and thence to the grounds, a great crowd following. After that very few could resist the temptation to go 'just to take the children.'"[7]

It was estimated that a total of 12,000 people attended the two performances at the lot on the west side of Whitaker Street, south of Anderson. "The large canvas-covered amphitheatre was well filled in the afternoon, and at night seats on the ground around the rings were scarce. A long ways farther than a face could be recognized, heads rose in tiers one above the other until in the distance they became an indistinguishable mass. And when something especially funny was done, such a burst of laughter arose that the strong ropes almost shook."[8]

At Macon all available space was taken by the large matinee crowd, leaving no desirable place to stand. The reception was one of enthusiasm: "The performance was given in two rings and on an elevated stage between so that there were from three to five acts going on all the time, in such quick and rapid succession that it made the eyes dance and the head dizzy to keep up with the different features." The writer complimented the gentlemanly behavior of the ushers and other auxiliaries—"no loud talk, no profanity can be heard, everyone seems to know his place."[9]

Dates in Florida and Alabama followed. At Mobile the tents were pitched on a lot near the corner of Government and Ann streets. The order of the mile-long parade that was started from there was headed by the large band chariot drawn by dromedaries. Then came the costumed equestrians and equestriennes, the dragon chariot, guards, knights, warriors, the Roman chariot drawn by four fiery horses, a line of cages, thirteen of which were open, a tableau wagon drawn by five elephants, and the steam calliope brought up the rear.

The *Daily Register* rated the quality of the performances very good, higher than the previous year. But the writer couldn't resist complaining about the concert. "As with all circuses, however, the concert nuisance was imposed upon the spectators. When people go to a circus it is disagreeable to them to be assailed at intervals of about ten minutes by the man with strong lungs, who mounts the rostrum and interrupts the clown's newest joke by shouting out in stentorian tones: 'Everybody stay for the grand concert, in which appears the most stupendous aggregation of minstrelsy ever brought together under a canvas. For the small sum of 10 cents, one dime, you can see it all!'"[10]

Following Mobile, the season ended at Birmingham on December 5, thus completing a typically long tour, one of Cole's trademarks.

Surprising news was revealed to the circus world in August by the *Clipper*. An item stated that "W. W. Cole, James A. Bailey, J. L. Hutchinson and P. T. Barnum concluded arrangements in [New York City] Aug. 11 whereby Mr. Bailey disposed of his third interest in the Barnum, Bailey and Hutchinson Show to Mr. Cole."[11] So Cole, who was doing so well on his own, like those before him, was allured into joining his name with the magical one of Barnum.

Much of what we know comes from a collection of correspondence between James L. Hutchinson and P. T. Barnum. These letters are part of a recent discovery of material by Australian Stuart Hicks.[12] We are grateful to him for sharing them with us.

Bailey was having problems of stress from overwork and did not go on the road with the show this year. Barnum was anxious to have him replaced and Cole was considered the most likely candidate. Secret negotiations between Barnum, Hutchinson and Cole had been in progress from as early as April and perhaps well before that in the off-season. A letter from Barnum dated April 26, 1885, mentioned the preparation of contracts to be signed by the four principals. Yet, in a letter to Hutchinson dated June 29, Barnum told of a conversation with Seth B. Howes in which Howes inquired about what Barnum intended to do if Bailey's health disqualified him from work. "I said," Barnum wrote, "probably take another in his place & asked if *he* wanted to buy in case of an opening."[13] Howes, of course, was not interested. What this suggests, however, is that the Cole's signing was not firmed yet and that Barnum was inclined to switch to Howes if he thought he could make a sharper deal. When Howes was asked who he could recommend, he replied, "Cole, if he would buy, but Cole is worth nearly a million & his mother governs him & might oppose it."[14]

Apparently Bailey was not made aware at this time of a search to replace him. A letter from Barnum to Mrs. Bailey, dated July 5, assured her that the business would not suffer in his absence, that Hutchinson, Young and Fish had things well in hand. "Mr. Bailey need not think of the show for six months to come," he added.[15]

A contract in the Bridgeport public library confirms that the arrangement was completed by the signing on

August 11, 1885. With this Barnum owned three-eighths of the circus, Cole three-eighths, and Hutchinson two-eighths. Cole and Hutchinson were to manage the show just as Bailey and Hutchinson had previously.

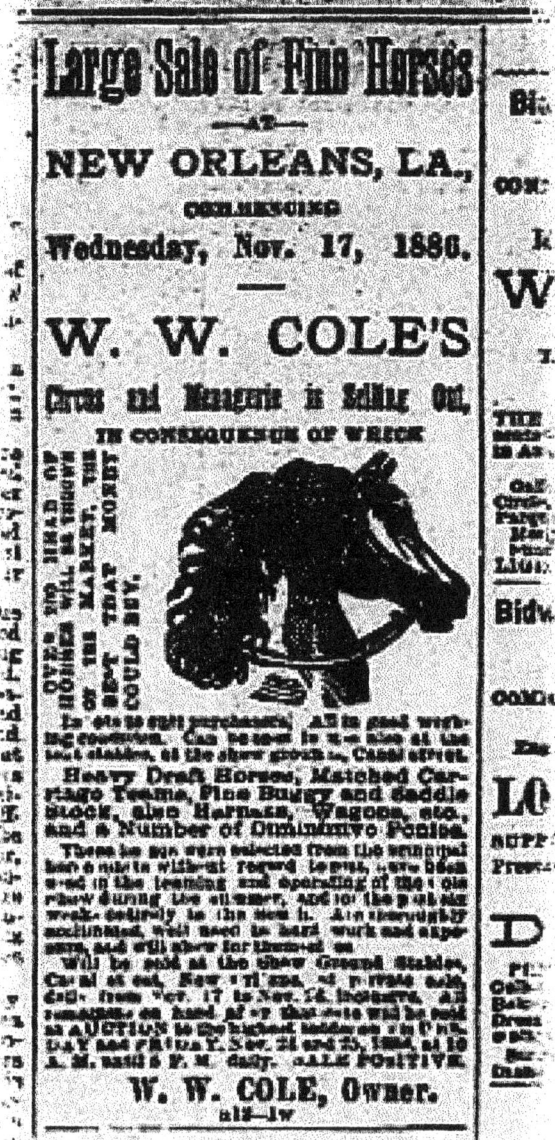

## XXII

If Cole signed on with Barnum and Hutchinson in late summer of 1885 why did he continue with his own circus through another year? Unfortunately, his motive is unknown. A letter in the Hutchinson papers reveals that Barnum, just a month after the contract was signed, suspected that Cole was planning to continue with the W. W. Cole show, thereby profiting from both organizations. Barnum wrote that this was contrary to the terms of the contract, but that he might be agreeable to it if he and Hutchinson shared in the ownership.

An early season item in an 1886 *Clipper*, announcing the Cole show personnel, included Cole as the "sole proprietor and manager." Cole's route book for that year also lists him alone with that title. However, some arrangement could have been made through an "under the table" deal for Cole to share profits with the new partners; but more likely an agreement gave him a year's grace to profitably dispose of his circus hardware and accommodate the employees who had been so faithful to him for years.[1]

Nevertheless, the W. W. Cole show did go on the road for 1886. "60 Minutes of Circus, with 200 Meteoric Performers! 30 Minutes of Theatre, with 50 Eminent Actors! 30 Minutes of Hippodrome Races, with 40 Riders and Drivers! 30 Minutes of Wild West, with Dr. Carver and 100 Indians, Cowboys and Scouts! 30 Minutes for the Museum, with 1,000 Animate and Inanimate Curios! 30 Minutes for the Menagerie, with 500 Varieties of Animals! 3½ Hours of Solid, Unapproachable Entertainment!" So read advertisements that year.

Evidence suggests that Cole's primary presence was with his original organization, while a former employee, John Evans, was sent to represent him on the Barnum show. Notes of daily events in the Barnum route book indicate that Cole visited on two occasions. An entry on Tuesday, June 29, reads, "Mr. W. W. Cole witnesses the evening performance in company with Mr. Hutchinson who has been absent a day or two." There was another on Monday, July 19, "W. W. Cole, Charles Stowe, W. Gardner, L. Fuller, 'Tody' Hamilton and C. Loyd witness the show."[2]

The official program taken from the Cole route book shows that again the action took place in two rings and on a center stage. T. B. McIntyre continued as equestrian manager. The orchestra was under the direction of Prof. Good. Press agent A. E. Richards, a fixture of many years with the company, occupied a tent near the main entrance, where he welcomed the press and his many friends in royal fashion and attended to their pleasures and comforts.

The program commenced with the traditional entrée of richly costumed knights and ladies, caparisoned elephants, dromedaries, camels, ostriches, llamas, horses and ponies, all creating a spectacle of elegance and splendor. The entertainment continued in this order: 1. Performing horses in the two rings, introduced by T. B. McIntyre and Ernest Cooke. 2. Leaping over elephants, camels, etc., in the full arena by the company, but featuring John Worland. 3. Educated elephants, performed by George Conklin, in one ring; canine wonders in the other, performed by Fred Watson; and an intelligent donkey on the center stage accompanied by T. B. McIntyre. 4. A high wire act by Mlle. Pauline in one ring; *la perche equipoise* in the other by Worland and Ledesma; and juggling on the stage by William Dutton. 5. Somersaulting on horseback in each ring by William Dutton and James Leon; the clowns being Billy Rollins and Ernest Cooke. 6. A sole act, described as "the incredible performance of Jack, the only dog that ever turned a somersault in mid-air," handled by Fred Watson. 7. *Haute ecole* and *manège* in the rings by Lottie Watson and Nellie Monroe; and the Livingston's bicycle riding on the stage. 8. A sole act, Fritz, the equestrian riding dog, introduced by Fred Watson. 9. In all performing areas, the Silbons in "statuesque posturing and reproduction of ancient gladiatorial feats and combats." 10. "Zoological eccentricities by the Great Spanish Nondescript," introduced by Ernest Cooke. 11. Aerialists Worland and Ledesma in one ring and the Livingstons on the horizontal bars in the other. 12. Five-horse bareback riding by Leon in one ring, with competition of the same by William O'Dell in the other. 13. An aerial display by the Silbons concluded the first section.

The second half of the program consisted of hippodrome and wild west competitions, judged by John Worland. 14. A jockey race, three times around the track, by William O'Dell, Harry Hodges, Nellie Monroe and Effie Imson. 15. A race between elephants, once around the track, by Charles Prewitt and John Fischer. 16. A pony express demonstration by "California Frank." 17. Camels on a rampage, once around the track. 18. Mexican vaqueros and Texas cowboys on bucking broncos. 19. Rifle shooting by W. F. Carver. 20. A Roman standing race, three times around the track, by William Dutton, Fred Watson and Charles Lowry. 21. A wheelbarrow race by the company. 22. A four-horse Roman chariot race between Fannie Eckles and Frank Williams. 23. A comic race by the clowns. 24. A pony race with monkey riders. 25. And, finally, an Indian attack on the Overland Mail Coach, repulsed by Dr. Carver and a band of cowboys.

As we can see, the program was split between circus acts and a hippodromic and wild west exhibition. The season's headliner was Dr. Carver, the Champion Shot of the World, and his entourage of Indians and cowboys. His wild west show, which constituted the last half of the program, was essentially what he had toured with previously under his own name.

He was described at this time as standing six feet two inches in height, weighing 248 pounds, with long, blond hair framing a handsome face. Although born in Stephenson

County, Illinois, in 1840, he spent a number of years on the frontier, trapping, hunting and trading with the Indians. On contract in the winter of 1874, he shot and killed 5,000 buffalo in western Nebraska.

His performance pleased Cole's spectators by the shooting of glass balls while riding full speed, then dismounting and breaking doubles and singles with grace and rapidity, and finally breaking three balls tossed into the air. "He broke a bushel basket full of balls, aiming from the most difficult positions and frequently changing his rifle from the right to the left shoulder. The secret of his marksmanship seems to be in the possession of a peculiar dexterity of the hand and mind in which the eye, beyond its function of general observation, does not seem to cut much of a figure."[2]

When a reporter inquired about his most memorable shooting, his reply was: "On July 18, 1879, in Brooklyn, N. Y., in a match to shoot 5,500 balls in 500 minutes I broke them in 430 minutes, and had 70 minutes to spare. The next great feat was in London for the championship of the world. I shot for three days against fourteen of the best shots the world could produce, winning the championship of the world, scoring 93 out of 100 and having seven to fall dead out of bounds, which is the greatest pigeon record. The next was a clay pigeon match, and I made 595 out of 600, scoring 300 in succession. In New Orleans in 1884 I killed 1,000 bats in seventy-one minutes, loading my own gun. In New Haven, Jan. 12, 1884, I shot 60,000 balls in the six days, shooting 10,000 each day. The gun weighed ten pounds, and lifting this each shot made 10,000 pounds which I lifted each day with my left arm. It required a pressure of forty-eight pounds to load and unload for each shot, which made a pressure of 480,000 pounds, which is the most wonderful feat of endurance on record."

The reporter then asked what he attributed to his success. He responded with: "Chiefly to my prohibition proclivities. My nerves have never been shattered by either whiskey or tobacco. I have been held up as a shining example by the temperance people all over the world. I was never sick a minute in my life."[3]

The attack on the stage coach by the Indians was considered very realistic. There was much whooping and hollering as nearly 200 shots were fired, some leaving blood on the shirts of victims. The excitement continued through the daring rescue of the passengers by Carver and his cowboys.

The remainder of the company was made up of somewhat mediocre talent. William Dutton was an equestrian and general performer who was a particularly useful addition to many circuses over the years and was well known to the public. But now, at forty-six, his star had lost its glow and his earning power along with it. John Worland, as a leaper, was not on a level with either Batcheler or Gardner and he is not remembered for his work on the high perch. It was probably Joseph Ledesma, who had been with the Barnum show the previous year, that solidified *la perche equipoise* within the Cole program.

Fred and Carlotta Watson were seasoned English performers, he as an acrobat and rider and she as a female Sampson. Fred also had a knack for training animals. His canine, Hero, pleased audiences by dancing, walking on a rope, and characterizing "dudes," prize fighters, clowns and policemen, then topping the act by somersaulting on the back of a speeding horse. Fred also had a school of educated English greyhounds.

An important new feature, and perhaps the most prestigious act of Cole's sixteen seasons of management, was the versatile Silbon family—Charles, Walter, Master Eddie, and sister Kate—English acrobats working in the modern style. They came to the United States in 1882 to join Adam Forepaugh's circus, where they remained for three seasons as the most popular aerialists in the country. Immediately before joining Cole they toured with their own combination for some eighteen months.

Their novel act, devised by Charles, the eldest of the group, was performed on an elaborate arrangement of rigging. Kate and Little Eddie, a lad of some thirteen years, executed a number of fearless acts in the center of the arena, while the brothers carried out thrilling feats on either side. These consisted of Walter taking a flying leap and after a double somersault, a distance of about fifty feet, being caught by Charles swinging on the lowest of the several trapeze bars; and then finishing with a death-defying leap from the top of the tent into the rescuing arms of his partner.

After the tragic death of Jumbo in September, 1885, Samson was legitimately touted as "The Tallest and Heaviest Elephant this Side of the Orient." But the irascible Asian wasted no time in misbehaving. On April 13, at the St. Louis fair grounds quarters, while circus attaches were preparing for the 1886 tour, Samson was reported to have made a "grand kick" for a period of about three hours which resulted in considerable damage to the place. Shumake, the keeper, was injured by receiving numerous blows from the elephant's irate trunk.

The street procession, as described by a pre-opening item in the St. Louis *Post-Dispatch,* was divided into three sections. The first section contained ladies and gentlemen equestrians, knights in armor, the dragon bandwagon, cages, racing chariots, Roman riders, and red tableaux. The second section followed with animal cages, white tableaux drawn by elephants, the snake cage, a golden tableau drawn by twenty horses, Conklin's den of lions, Mexican tableaux, the rhinoceros, wax statuary, and the hippopotamus. And, lastly, the third section highlighted the wild west features led by a cowboy band and followed by Dr. Carver on horseback, the stage coach, twenty Indians and twenty cowboys, twenty Mexican ponies, an elk team, burros, and a calliope.[4]

The St. Louis opening day parade on Monday, May 3, was somewhat impaired by rain, but the weather did not interfere with the performances. The matinee was given to passing the children in free and was so successful that some one thousand of them were turned away. The evening performance, too, entertained the largest opening night audience in years. "Circus parties," blocks of seats sold to organizations at a discount, were in evidence. This is the first time we have heard of such a device being used for arenic entertainments.[5]

"The performance last night was, taken altogether, the best first-night performance which has been given here," so reported the *Post-Dispatch*. "There was scarcely a hitch, and all the important acts went smoothly and with fine effect."[6] The four Silbons, "one of the greatest trapeze acts ever given," got the writer's attention. The audience enjoyed Dr. Carver and his band of cowboys and vaqueros and the attack on the stage coach by a group of Indians which was repulsed by the cowboys.

Early in the season the show went into Missouri and Kansas. The correspondent for the Fort Scott *Weekly Monitor* was aglow with praise, calling Cole's circus the most complete and satisfying exhibition ever to perform in that city.[7] On the 20th the Olathe *Mirror-Gazette* warned its readers that although Cole has always had a good reputation "it is more likely that the usual crowd of harpies will follow them" and suggested that the citizens would do well to see that their houses were securely locked. Following show day, however, the editor conceded that "Cole's circus averaged better than any similar affair we have witnessed in Kansas. The freedom from camp followers and hard characters was especially notable and commendable."[8] At Topeka the *Daily Capital* called the program first-class in every respect. "The riding was very good, the horse exhibition perfect, the dogs clever and amusing, the leaping, tumbling, balancing, posturing, etc., of the most attractive nature, all accompanied by an unusually excellent band."[9] The Lawrence *Tribune* was equally enthusiastic. It noted that the audiences were well pleased because the Cole circus was one of the very best traveling. "Cole comes nearer to showing everything he advertises than any other manager."[10]

The Kansas stands were followed by ones in Nebraska, Iowa, Minnesota and Wisconsin. The Eau Claire, Wisconsin, *Free Press* expressed satisfaction that all the people in management positions were motivated to conduct of good business sense and social courtesy. For the July 1 date the menagerie was seen as first-class and the ring performances superior. There was complaint, however, that a good bit of gambling was indulged in during circus day. One Eau Claire merchant was relieved of $30 within twenty feet and under the watchful eye of a local policeman.[11]

A misfortune occurred the following day at Menomonie. After the circus train had been unloaded and placed on a Chicago, Milwaukee & St. Paul siding, near what was then the Wisconsin Red Pressed Co.'s grounds, a fire from a pile of sawdust ignited by the locomotive at about 11:00 a.m. destroyed two sleepers and a baggage car, a damage estimated at $20,000. Members of the company suffered heavy losses of trunks and money stored inside.[12]

The tour continued through the Dakotas, Idaho, Washington and Oregon. Another misfortune developed at the Portland stand. The show trains arrived too late for the parade, disappointing some 15,000 who had gathered and waited until noon on First, Third and Washington Streets with happy expectations, only to go home disappointed. A railroad accident was responsible for the tardiness. The circus train was delayed through the carelessness of the locomotive engineer who brought it down the incline at Albina much too fast, causing one car to derail and slip halfway into a river. Little damage was done other than the baggage and part of the canvas being water soaked, but precious time was lost.

Once in Portland the tents were erected and the doors opened on time to satisfy the matinee crowd. But the rings and rigging were not ready, so the audience was able to observe the men readying the necessary equipment for the performance. Still, it was impossible to finish everything, which forced the show to continue in a single ring, the stage and hippodrome track.

By evening everything was ready and the tent was packed with people spilling onto the raceway. The next day the *Morning Oregonian* waxed enthusiastic. "The circus—that is to say, the entire performance which takes place under the tent, before the spectators—embraces some of the very finest acts ever performed under canvas, or anywhere else. The Silbon family of gymnasts in swings, leaps, jumps and dives, all on the high trapeze, and in classical posturing, are the most skillful artist the writer has ever seen, and he has seen everything that 'came his way' for thirty years. The Livingston family do an act on the horizontal bar in mid-air as neatly as the best. The dog actually turns a somersault, not one, but a dozen or more, and four other dogs are clever in various tricks. Dutton in one ring and Leon in the other, do a bareback act, each so near like the other that the act may be called twins. Odell in one ring and Dutton in the other do a neat five-horse act. Then there is fine bicycle riding, balancing on the slack-wire, trained horses in numerous antics, three performing elephants, very expert juggling, excellent vaulting, lady equestriennes, whose horses leap hurdles, and pretty high hurdles too, and two first-rate clowns."[13]

Returning east by way of Idaho, the show moved southward into Utah, Colorado and Kansas; then, for October and November, into Arkansas and Texas. A Dallas audience showed preference for the western exhibitions. "Numerous were the new features performed by man and beast, but all were overshadowed by Dr. Carver's exploits at shooting glass balls and afterward in the management of the stage robbing scene."[14] The Galveston *Daily News* was more restrained in its reportage. Although it concurred with the Dallas appraisal of Carver, it called the hippodrome events tiresome, and suggested that "with a little less hippodrome and a little more circus, Mr. Cole might make an improvement of his present attraction."[15]

After eight more dates in Texas, Louisiana and Mississippi, the season ended with five days in New Orleans at the Canal Street lot, November 17 through 21. During the twenty-nine weeks on the road the show had traveled over 13,700 miles, covering twelve states, seven territories, and one province.

A torchlight parade exceeding a mile long announced the arrival of the circus in New Orleans on the night of November 16. Bad weather had threatened a postponement, but the event occurred and was received by expectant throngs along the route. E. D. Colvin, Cole's assistant manager, accompanied by contracting agent Charles Sivalls, preceded the spectacle in an open barouche. "The music for the parade was made by three excellent brass bands, which belong to the show, and a steam calliope, which brought up the rear and tooted taking airs for the small followers. A mile of cages and handsome horses, with elephants and camels harnessed and walking, all to be seen free, was a treat."[16] Continuing bad weather attended the opening performances which affected the turnout but did not diminish the enthusiasm of the press. "Mr. Cole has allowed his show to grow until it is second only to the Barnum show. He puts canvas over several acres of ground. Around the performing rings is a quarter mile race track for hippodrome races and wild west exhibitions. An ordinary small town can turn out and all find room in the circus. A great menagerie and museum attracts the attention of visitors first. Beyond the menagerie tent, which is as large as any ordinary circus, comes the great circus tent. In this are two performing rings or arenas—for sports and horsemanship—between the two is a large platform on which various specialty performers do their acts. Three performances are going on at the same time. It is all the eye can cover and the mind grasp. Circuses in some respects are all alike. Cole's great show is like other circuses, only it is better and bigger. He has fine horses, good riders, agile acrobats, the best dogs ever seen—performed by Fred Watson—and he has the seven Silbons, who, in their classic posturings, groupings, gymnastic and aerial work are a whole show in themselves."[17]

The attendance picked up as the weather became more accommodating. Directly following the final performance on Sunday, the 21st, the entire company took a farewell bow as the band played "Auld Lang Syne," and in this way concluded sixteen years of Cole's independent proprietorship. "His career as a manager has been marked with very flattering success and he retires from the show business with a very handsome fortune."[18]

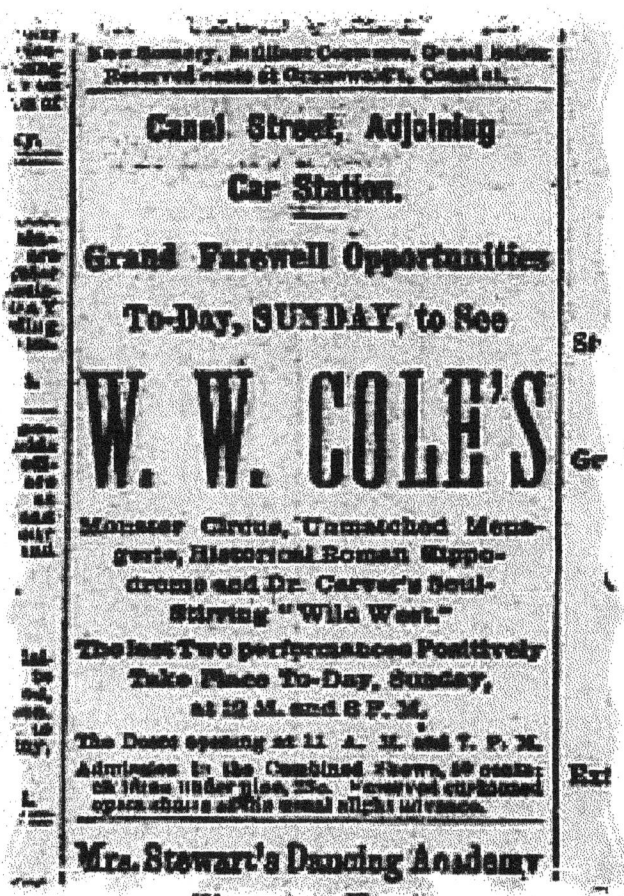

This left only the disposal of the circus property to mark the end. A large ad in the New York *Clipper* of November 20 listed the countless items to be auctioned beginning on the 22$^{nd}$ at the circus grounds—horses and other animals, tents, cages, seats, harness, wardrobe and uniforms, lights, sideshow and cook tent equipment, bedding, wood cuts, etc, but the sale of horses had been in progress since the 17th. With the arena and sideshow canvases quickly packed away, the sale was conducted in the menagerie tent. Parties interested in the bidding included Ephraim and Allen Sells of Sells Bros.' circus; W. E. Franklin of the King, Burke & Co. circus; W. A. Conklin of New York's Central Park Zoo; Thompson & Vanderveer, tent makers from Cincinnati; a representative for Adam Forepaugh; Eugene Robinson, proprietor of a dime museum in New Orleans, and Signor Faranta, owner of a variety theatre there.

The auction, which took place from Monday through Saturday morning, netted Cole somewhat less than $50,000, the animals going for much less than the cost would be to import them. The sale of eighty-one horses came to $7,600; fifteen cages for an average of $125 each; other show property to about $18,000. Signor Faranta bought four of the elephants—Tom, Jennie, Lizzie and Laura. The fifth, Samson, was not sold, there being but one bid for him through a telegram from New York by James L. Hutchinson, which allowed him to be set aside for the Barnum show.[19]

So ended the sixteen year career of W. W. Cole as an independent circus proprietor, a tenure during which there was never a losing season. On the contrary, profitable management allowed expansion from a modest beginning to an organization in a class with the best circuses in America. And, throughout those years, Cole wisely invested his surplus in real estate ventures, which, in the end, made him a millionaire several times over and a phenomenon among circus proprietors.

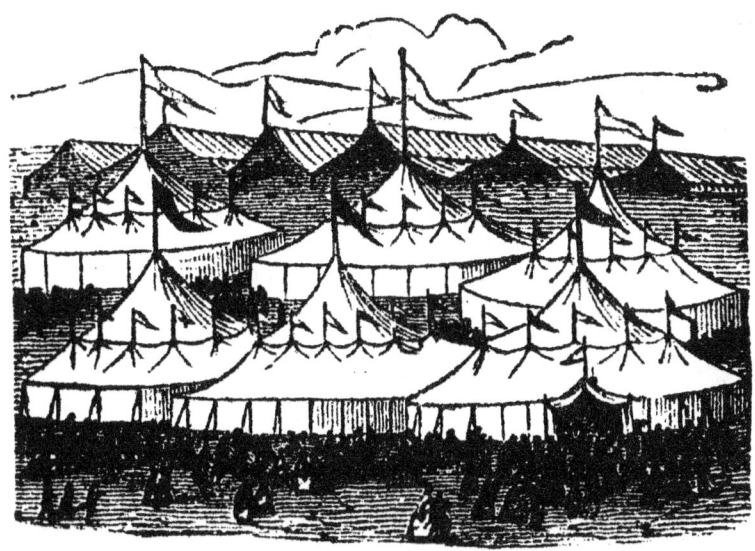

## NOTES

### CHAPTER I

[1] *Billboard*, March 20, 1915.
[2] George Conklin, *The Ways of the Circus*, p. 303.
[3] Charles H. Day, *Ink from a Circus Press Agent*, p. 153.
[4] "As much a sphinx as U. S. Grant to all appearances, Mr. Cole in the company of his intimates is a genial man, and beneath the surface has a keen sense of the humorous and the ridiculous." J. Milton Traber, "W. W. Cole, Showman," p. 20.
[5] Des Moines (IA) *Iowa State Register*, June 6, 1883.
[6] Day, p. 153. "It is no accident nor chance that contributed to the success attained by the original Cole show, for its proprietor, William Washington Cole, was recognized as a master strategist in organizing, routing, and profiting from a circus property." C. G. Sturtevant, "Little Biographies," p. 5.
[7] J. Milton Traber, p. 20.
[8] "The over-advertised was often reproved by the newspapers, but it does not appear from the perspective of a hundred years that buncombe ever caused a show's demise. There were no practitioners of restraint in circus advertising and the largest and the smallest puffed equally their claims." Stuart Thayer, *Mudshows and Railers*, p. 11. Relating to Cole's establishment, the Kansas *Saline County Journal* observed: "One thing which created a bad feeling towards the circus was their

charging twenty-five cents more for their admission tickets than they advertised. It was a downright swindle." The writer may have been referring to reserved seats. But further: "The show of animals was good, although that mule which was striped according to order in imitation of the zebra, was pronounced by some to be a base imitation. The gorilla we did not discover." Published prices were Adults, 50 cents, children, 25. *Saline County Journal*, May 22, 1873, taken from Orin King, "Only Big Show Coming," *Bandwagon*, September/October, 1987.

[9] Sedalia (MO) *Bazoo*, September 20, 1883.

[10] Conklin, p. 306.

[11] "W. W. Cole, whom I will first mention, because of my early acquaintance with him, also because he was the first to give me employment to the tented field, and who now survives nearly all of the old school whom I will mention, was, and still is, a man of remarkable resource, a cool, calculating and keen observer of men, their moods and all financial conditions; a fellow of infinite ability to plan a campaign or solve knotty problems, and one well qualified to pass upon the merits and demerits of almost any business proposition. My early mental studies of Mr. Cole was to confirm the opinion that he was something of a human enigma, in which caution, foresight, and perhaps suspicion, largely predominated. This, coupled with his even tempered self-control, enabled him to take advantage of circumstances and conditions that a more impulsive individual might overlook. His boyhood days, as often described to me by his mother, and himself, must have been fraught with all sorts of obstacles, advances and reverses, but with unfaltering courage and perseverance he always seemed to feel that financial success was in store for him, and I have frequently heard him remark, when disaster seemed inevitable, 'Well, it is all in the business, and I am never alarmed when I can find a reasonable excuse for anything'; and then, continuing, he would say, 'It will probably be all right in the end.' And now, since he has acquired fame, fortune and the highest regard of his fellowmen, with plenty of capital and even bank buildings to his credit, it proves conclusively that it is all right in these days of partial retirement from circus life and incidental cares." Louis E. Cooke, "Some Circus Men I have Met," *The Show World*, December 21, 1907.

[12] Letter from P. T. Barnum to James L. Hutchinson, June 29, 1885, Saxon, *Selected Letters*, pp. 262-263.

## CHAPTER II

[1] James Edwin Cooke, Sr., died in America.

[2] George Cooke was also a principal equestrian; Alfred Cooke was a slack-rope performer; Henry Cooke, an acrobat and tightrope walker; and Thomas Cooke, Jr., the ringmaster.

[3] Charles Durang, , "The Philadelphia Stage from the Year of 1794 to the Year 1855," Vol. IV, Chapter 52, p. 150.

[4] "*Cooke's Equestrian Arena* is so far up town that it derives its principal support from the residents in its immediate vicinity. We hear it is very well patronized since Cooke's 'Card' appeared, in which he denies having stopped a young man's entrance into the boxes, attired in a jacket that had seen service, and whose hands and face were not on familiar terms with soft soap and Manhattan water. It would have evinced more firmness and decision of character than we give Cooke credit for, to have presumed to hint to one of the *elite* to the *market* that he would not be allowed to occupy his seat in the dress circle with a 'long nine' in his mouth, a veal pot pie under his arm, and his pockets redolent of peanuts. Such a *houdashus* 'infringement upon the liberties of an American Citizen' would have called down the virtuous indignation of every denizen of the Five Points...." *Spirit of the Times*, January 21, 1837, p. 386. The company remained at the Bowery for some twenty successive nights to far greater success than they had met up town. "The grand spectacle of *Mazeppa* at this theatre," we learn from the *Spirit of the Times*, "is the most gorgeous and splendid presented in this city since the days of Miss Kelly and Miss Tatnall electrified the town with *Cherry* and *Fair Star*, and *Timour the Tartar*." The popular equestrian dramatization of Lord Byron's tale of *Wild Horse, or Mazeppa, the Child of the Desert* was arranged and produced by George Woolford of the Cooke troupe, incorporating the exceptional stud of horses and utilizing extensive platforms, scenery, and machinery. All this was judged to be in excellent taste, and the combining of Cooke's equestrians with the Bowery Theatre company, creating "the pomp and circumstance of glorious war," was most impressive. There were some twenty or thirty mounted knights in armor, along with a small regiment of infantry, and the necessary accessories of combat, all on Dinneford's stage at one time. The role of Mazeppa was performed by William Sefton (Adah Isaacs Menkin not yet in fleshings), new to the Bowery company with the 1836 season, but who would become admired for what was termed his "Bowery school" of acting. Playing opposite him as Olinska, was his wife,

Miss Waring. Most of the other acting roles were taken by the Bowery regulars, with the Cooke contingent handling the equestrianisms. The grand spectacle, replete with scenic transformations, exotic attired actors, and unsurpassed action of horse and foot, pleased the *Mirror* correspondent, who reacted with: "This piece, it is not too much to say, has been got up with surpassing magnificence. The splendid stud of horses which are introduced on the stage, the beautiful scenery, under careful management, and the general effect of the piece, have been seldom equaled." George C. D. Odell, "Annals of the New York Stage," Vol. IV, p. 164. The audience reception, too, was much improved here. "The house is nightly filled from pit to gallery," was the boast; and, Ireland informs us, to average receipts of $800. To be sure, the prices were more encouraging for mass attendance—boxes 75¢, pit 37½¢, and gallery 25¢.

[5]This prompted a letter from Dinneford to Hamlin, who was in London: "I am almost crazy—I cannot describe the anxiety I have experienced, but thank God tis over and I am under Full sail .... I offered Cooke 5,000 for 24 nights and a ½ ben[efi]t [and] he accepted it—tomorrow night is his benefit—the receipt of his engagement is [sic] about 23,000 dollars, and the most fashionable audiences you ever saw in this country—not a single disturbance since the opening and I am proud to say the Bowery is the handsomest and best conducted theatre in the city." After relating his disgust at the "slippery trick" Cooke played on him by deserting to the National, Dinneford went on: "I do Mazeppa on Thursday with my own company—engaged 14 beautiful horses and good riders [and] practiced the company for combats—dances &c. for the last fortnight and I am of the opinion I shall excel Cooke." Odell, Vol. IV, p. 165, from a letter in the Harvard Collection. The National's press release read: "The manager has much pleasure in announcing to the public that he has made arrangements with Mr. Cooke, the Equestrian, for his entire company to produce at this theatre on Wednesday next (March 29), under the direction of Mr. Woolford, a magnificent and unequaled Legend of Splendor called ST. GEORGE AND THE DRAGON; OR, THE SEVEN CHAMPIONS OF CHRISTENDOM."

[6]Durang termed it a "novelty." Designed much like the old Roman amphitheatres, with an eye to accommodating the greatest number within the available space, the tiers of seating were raised, one after the other, to such a degree that those sitting behind could look down at the feet of those directly in front of them. The structure was built

from designs and drawings of Thomas Barlow, another of Cooke's sons-in-law; but the actual builder was William Hopper. John Foster, described by Durang as an artist of great taste and originality, was the scenic designer. A magnificent chandelier of his work hung from the building's dome, illuminating the entire interior with two thousand gas burners. His allegorical figures made of *papier maché* decorated the auditorium, all in unison with the bas-relief of horses' heads that ornamented the rows of boxes.

[7] Philadelphia (PA) *Public Ledger*, September 1, 1837. The circus was first presented to the public on August 28, 1837. The doors opened at 7:00 p.m.; the performance commenced at 7:30. The boxes, 75¢; pit, 50¢. For children, boxes, 50¢; pit, 25¢. Lessons in the art of riding were given daily by riding master Woolford. A calendar of events taken from the local newspaper illustrates the amazing variety of the company's repertory and confirms its array of talent (a more complete and detailed description of the arenic events was contained in distributed handbills). The first of these appeared on August 12, 1837: "Mr. Cooke begs leave very respectfully to announce to the public of Philadelphia, that his new and splendid CIRCUS, situated in CHESTNUT STREET, between Eighth and Ninth, will very shortly be opened with magnificent Scenes in the Circle, Pageant, Gymnastic Representations and Horsemanship, in all its various departments, by one of the most numerous and talented assemblages of artists ever collected." Philadelphia *Public Ledger,* August 12, 1837.

[8] The circus debut performance opened with a "Chinese Flag Fete," and was followed by such Cooke standards as James Cooke's "The Courier of St. Petersburg," the juvenile company's "Cinderella," and the "Dashing White Sergeant," dancing ponies, "Cupids and Rosebuds," and "The Trained Barbary Courser." Added to the troupe for this occasion were Americans Matthew Buckley (English by birth), John Gossin, and Alexander Rockwell. Immediate competition came from the Holliday Street Theatre where on this Thursday the great Junius Brutus Booth was holding forth in *Julius Caesar*. This was a repeat from two nights earlier when, as the advertisement claimed, the crowds left the theatre from the impossibility of obtaining admission. Then, on January 4, Bacon's American Circus set up shop on Pratt Street. At the outset, the names of John Wells and the Polish Brothers, who had come to America as part of Cooke's company, appeared in the Bacon circus advertisements. Whether a thorn in the side or just a thorn, the rival circus would remain beyond the occupancy of

Cooke's outfit, advertising its "POSITIVELY THE LAST NIGHT" on March 17. Baltimore *American & Commercial Daily Advertiser*, March 17, 1838.

[9] Durang, p. 154.

[10] Joseph Blackburn, *A Clown's Log*, p. 98.

[11] Cooke died in 1866. His ever-bearing wife, Mary Ann, outlasted him by two years.

[12] Among the group were clowns John Wells and Robert "Bobby" Williams. Both became familiar faces within the American circus scene. Wells worked on various shows up to the time of his death in 1852. He raised three daughters, Mary Ann, Amelia, and Louisa, who were also prominent in the circus business as equestriennes. Bobby Williams, too, worked with all the major companies, including Cooke's Royal Circus in 1860, a show under the management of James M. Nixon, who took the title from William Cooke's appearance at Niblo's Garden that year. Billed as the "English Grotesque," Williams was clowning as late as 1868. Equestrian Henry Needham was active into the late 1840s. We will encounter him as ringmaster at Niblo's Garden, equestrian director for Welch's circus in Philadelphia, for Nathan Howes', and for Rockwell & Stone. Clown and scenic specialist Joseph Foster was another member that deserted the Cooke troupe for an American experience. The reader will recall his artistic handiwork in the decoration of the Philadelphia amphitheatre. He was a part of the Noah Ludlow and Sol Smith circus addition to their St. Louis dramatic company in 1840. We also find him with a number of other American circuses throughout the decade. J. H. Amherst, considered to be this country's first literary puffer, became well known for his connection with Welch's Philadelphia circus. Unfortunately, the demand for his services dwindled and he died in abject poverty in 1851 at Philadelphia's Blockley Hospital and was buried by the Actors Order of Friendship.

## CHAPTER III

[1] Rupert Croft-Cooke, *Circus: a World History* p. 97. Recording the Coles' complete activities during these early years is unrealizable. Acquiring biographical specificity of such secondary performers is an impossible quest. I am deeply indebted to Stuart Thayer and his outstanding *Annals of the American Circus* for the spine of what I am able to impart.

[2] Stuart Thayer's collection.

[3] Odell, Vol. IV, p. 333.
[4] New York *Evening Post*, November 11, 1839.
[5] New York *Evening Post*, November 18, 1839.
[6] New York *Evening Post*, November 11, 1839.
[7] "The beautiful amphitheatre of Messrs. Welsh, Bartlett & Co. was filled to overflowing by a highly respectable audience, at an early hour last evening, to witness the first performance of the highly talented equestrian troupe. The riding rope-dancing, vaulting, and other gymnastic feats, were most gracefully executed, and received the unanimous applause of the audience." New York *Evening Post*, November 20, 1839.
[8] Odell, Vol. IV, p. 511.
[9] New York *Evening Post*, December 3, 1840.
[10] New York *Evening Post*, February 1, 1841.
[11] *Ibid*.

## CHAPTER IV

[1] "The fine equestrian company under the management of Mr. S. B. Howes will commence their performances this evening at the Amphitheatre on Haverhill Street," was the announcement in the Boston *Daily Evening Transcript* of November 24. Further, "The company is said to be excellent and their performances very expert and graceful. Those who are fond of witnessing equestrian performances can pass a pleasant evening at the Amphitheatre in rational amusement." Boston *Daily Evening Transcript*, November 24, 1841.
[2] The "American Brothers" was a two-man acrobatic act performed either on the ground or aloft. The "Shipwrecked Sailor" was a scenic riding act which by dumb show portrayed a sailor undergoing a storm at sea, then being marooned on a desert island and, finally, dancing a hornpipe when rescued. The "Flying Indian," a popular scenic riding act, portrayed the various aspects of Indian life, such as hunting, warring, etc. All of these could vary in display from one performer to another.
[3] Although Thayer (p. 288) does not list the Coles for the summer tour, it is quit likely they were a part of it.
[4] New York *Evening Post*, December 12, 1842.
[5] Odell, Vol. IV, p. 613.
[6] "R. Welch respectfully announces to the citizens of New York that he has made arrangements with Mr. E. Simpson, in order to fit up the PARK THEATRE as an elegant OLYMPIC CIRCUS. The decorations of which are completed in the most rich and perfect taste by J.

R. Smith & Speyers and their numerous assistants." New York *Evening Post*, January 5, 1843.

[7] John H. Glenroy, *Ins and Outs of Circus Life*, p. 43.

[8] A sample program included a Polish entrée of twelve riders. This was followed by a comic song. Master John Aymar performed a feat of horsemanship. Ground gymnastics were led by Henry Gardner. W. C. Johnson cavorted in a four-horse act. Henry Gardner returned for a "A life on the Ocean Waves." There was vaulting by the whole company, led by McFarland and Franklin. Next came a show of horsemanship by Wilson Howes. Then an *alemande* on horseback by Mr. and Mrs. Gardner (where was Mary Ann?). William Cole appeared in what was probably his Indian rubber turn. Concluding, there were a Brothers Act, individual riding displays by Seth B. Howes and Henry P. Madigan, and Hiram Franklin on the swinging cord.

[9] New York *Evening Post*, November 22, 1843. "The new equestrian corps of Mr. Rockwell made its first appearance last night to a crowded theatre. Everything went off with great applause. The Burmese Entries is truly a magnificent affair. Messrs. Turner and Stone are highly accomplished equestrians; the dresses and appointments are very superior; there was but one fault, the theatre was too warm, but this was an error on the safe side, and can be easily remedied, and proves that no establishment in the city is better adapted for a winter theatre than Niblo's." New York *Evening Post*, November 23, 1843.

[10] New York *Evening Post*, December 7, 1843.

[11] New York *Herald*, January 5, 1844.

[12] New York *Herald*, January 13, 1844. "Messrs. Rockwell and Stone, the greatest equestrian managers in the country, commence at the Chatham Theatre tomorrow evening [January 29], a series of circus performances of the most splendid description. Their stud of horses and troupe of performers are immensely large and complete in every department. The public may expect to witness a series of the most brilliant entertainments ever offered." New York *Herald*, January 28, 1844. "This is now one of the most beautiful and *recherché* places of amusement in the city. The house has been cleansed, decorated and enlarged, so that visitors can enjoy all the comforts of a home parlor, and at the same time an evening's supply of wit and humor, with the sublime and ludicrous display of the men, women and animal performers. Every family in the city should, to the extent of every member, patronize the enterprise." New York *Herald*, February 4, 1844.

## CHAPTER V

[1] *Billboard*, March 20, 1915.
[2] Letter to Slout from Kenneth R. Cobb of that office dated November 2, 2000.
[3] Advertisement, Portland (ME) *Daily Argus*, September 20, 1848.
[4] *Ibid.*
[5] Again, the advance advertising prepared the citizens for the entrance of the Golden Chariot. "The U. S. Circus, in its progress through the country, will be preceded by the great triumphant GOLDEN CHARIOT! Drawn by 20 cream colored horses, and devoted to the conveyance of a celebrated NEW YORK BRASS BAND. The magnitude and splendor of this immense vehicle baffles description. It is the ONLY ONE of modern times which approaches the achievements of art described in ancient history. Its weight exceeds FIVE TONS, and its elaborate carving and gilding surpasses anything of the kind ever witnessed." Poughkeepsie (NY) *Journal and Poughkeepsie Eagle*, July 14, 1849. The 1848 western unit, which went to winter quarters in Pittsburgh at season's end, was sold to John P. Crane. The show was renamed Crane & Co.'s Great Oriental Circus for 1849.
[6] St. Louis *Missouri Republican*, April 19, 1852. The source is taken from Thayer's *Annals*, p. 483.
[7] New York *Clipper*, December 11, 1897. The 1857 date has been disputed, with one source placing it in 1856 and the *Clipper* obituary for Mary Ann reporting it to be 1858. But, relying on his intimate association with Cole, we are confident that Louis Cooke's listing of 1857 is correct.
[8] Cincinnati *Daily Commercial*, May 15, 1858.

## CHAPTER VI

[1] Thayer, *Annals*, p. 381, from the Burlington (IA) *Hawk-Eye*, September 28, 1854.
[2] Thayer & Dahlinger, *Badger State Showmen*, p. 28.
[3] We make this judgment because we have been unable to find evidence of the Ortons being on the road until 1864. However, Sharpe, in his article on the Ortons, wrote: "The show wintered in Independence, Iowa, following the Rockford closing. Older owned the property in Independence. Older continued with the show for one more year." Adrian D. Sharpe, "The Orton Circus," p. 6. Most of Sharpe's information came from R.Z. Orton's daughter, some of which is erroneous.

[4] Independence (IA) *Bulletin-Journal*, October 22, 1965.

[5] "DeHaven Circus.—By reference to new advertising in this issue De-Haven's Great Union Circus will be found most prominent. The troupe will perform on the 24$^{th}$ inst.; and judging by notices in our State exchanges, we have no hesitancy in saying that the best of satisfaction will be given to those who attend. Among the performers we may mention the names of Mrs. Cole and Miles Orton, both of whom have resided here and are known to be good actors...." Independence (IA) *Civilian*, July 15, 1862. After a date at Dubuque on the 28$^{th}$ of July the Dubuque *Herald* carried a perplexing item: "How little we outsiders know of what wires are pulled and what machinery is moved when the great little puppets of life dance up and down upon the stage.... How our exalted ideas of grace and beauty of Miss Mary Ann Cooke in the Circus Monday ... suddenly became reversed when we were informed that she belonged to the male 'pursuasion.'" Dubuque (IA) *Herald*, July 30, 1862. It had been only two years since young Omar Kingsley, in the guise of a female rider named Ella Zoyara, created a sensation at New York's Niblo's Garden. The deception was soon discovered, but the bogus female idea was imitated by other male riders for at least the next few years. However, the *Herald* writer may simply have been misinformed. With Mary Ann in the troupe, why would another take her name?

[6] New York *Clipper*, September 2, 1865.

[7] St. Joseph (MO) *Morning Herald*, May 18, 1865. And on the 19$^{th}$: "Yesterday was an exceedingly gala day for the juveniles and country folks. Hundreds of the latter came to the city to attend and witness the attractive and interesting performances of the best company now traveling. The riding, vaulting, tumbling, singing and dancing are not to be excelled." The three day stand at St. Joseph was reported to have been profitable. On the 20$^{th}$ the *Herald* concluded the visit with: "The circus was again crowded yesterday to the utmost capacity by our city and country folks to witness the last day's performance. It proved a rich treat and all were satisfied. This company will on their return from Kansas perform here two days more on the 30$^{th}$ and 31$^{st}$ of May. This will afford an opportunity for all those who failed to see it in the past three days." We also learn from the paper that Gilkison's clowning provoked laughter from young and old, that the Misses Ortons were accomplished and charming in their Highland Fling dance, and that strong man Gaffney showed his powerful presence by raising four people in the air at one time and making a circuit of the ring with

them all held aloft.

[8] St. Paul (MN) *Pioneer*, September 30, 1865. The company included Mrs. Miles Orton, Misses Irene and Celeste, Maude Stanley, M'lle Lotina, Master Jesse, Messrs. Miles, Den and Lester Orton, Walter Wentworth, Henry Gardner, M. Hosmer, James Dunbar, George Wescott, Messrs. Sherman, Moore, Case, Masters Leon and R.Z., etc. New York *Clipper*, June 27, 1867.

[9] The advertised roster included clowns Gilkison and Billy Andrews; bareback rider Miles Orton; Den Orton, scenic rider and *la perche*; Mrs. Miles Orton, with her trained horse, Jupiter; Andrew Gaffney, Herculean performer; Master Leon Orton and Master R.Z., and the Misses Irene and Celeste. J. F. Johnson was the advertising agent. We learn of elements in the program through an item in the Lawrence, Kansas, newspaper: "The exhibition of Mr. Gaffney with cannon balls weighing from thirty to fifty-five pounds was a miracle of the capacity of practice and muscle, and Mr. Gaffney may be literally said to 'go it on his muscle.' The Lover's Quarrel was a laughable performance, eliciting unbounded applause. Mr. Orton, in his daring feats of bareback riding, has seldom been equaled. Miss Orton, with her educated pony, Flora Belle, commanded the admiration of her audience. The Indian exhibition was good as a specimen of horsemanship, but we have Delawares and Kaws in Kansas who would beat him on the 'whooping' business. The clowns kept the spectators in a roar of laughter with their inimitable drolleries. On a whole it was a most creditable performance." *Kansas Daily Tribune*, May 19, 1867.

[10] The remaining roster included the Lamont Brothers (Albert, Newton, and William), Harry Hart (clown), Jerry Hopper, Harry Gardner, Julian Harvey, William Holland, N. Rainforth, and Andy Judson.

[11] New York *Clipper*, June 4, 1870. Others in the company were Ira Evans, treasurer; Joseph Garton, band leader; C. A. Wilson, advance agent; John Carroll, Cornell, Cooke, Richards, Gleason; and William Stowe, son of the proprietor.

[12] A report to the *Clipper* asserted that Miles Orton had been shot and killed on November 22; but the rumor was put to rest two weeks later.

## CHAPTER VII

[1] Traber, p. 20.

[2] Carl Landrum, "W. W. Cole's Five-Continent Circus," p. 15. According to Thayer, 40 horses indicates 13 wagons.

3. *Ibid.*
4. *Ibid.*
5. *Ibid.*
6. This represents the roster at season's end. New York *Clipper*, November 11, 1871, p. 255.
7. Detroit *Free Press*, October 31, 1871, p. 1.
8. "THE CIRCUS is the most extensive equestrian aggregation in the world. It contains more and better Performers; the finest number of Performing Horses, Ponies, and Mules; and inside and outside and all around is in every particular ahead of any that ever was and now is exhibiting in this country. The Circus and Menagerie Entertainments are given under TWO BIG TENTS completely separated from each other, constituting two immense Pavilions, lighted with gas and capable of holding 5000 people, who can view the wonders of the Museum and Menagerie, or pass in and behold the wonders of the performances of the CIRCUS. Remember the name 'COLE,' the Magnitude, the Attraction, the Day, the Date and Place. Look at the elegant Pictorial Posters, read the Programmes, Advertisements, and Notices, and fail not to come and see the Biggest Thing on Wheels that ever was or ever will visit this section of the country. AWAIT THE ADVENT OF THE MONARCH."
9. Henry was defined as manager in the *Clipper's* 1872 pre-season listings. "Circuses innumerable have visited Memphis during the past few years, but never has any mammoth menagerie been filled as was that of Cole's Circus last night. To call it a regular jam would be to express the appearance in a very slight degree. Every seat was occupied, standing room was at a premium, and many juveniles encroached even into the ring itself. One of the witty clowns, however, soon caused them to draw their legs out of the circle by telling them somewhat wittily that they could not play there the game of the Muscovy ducks, when placed in a stable, and say to the horses: 'Let us all be friends and not tramp on each others toes.' The boys made the application and the horses had the ring to themselves. The entertainment throughout was really capital, and the liberality of the management highly commendable. One grand important feature of the exhibition was George Bachelor (sic), the great champion leaper of the world, who took a flying leap over sixteen horses and cleared them like a bird. He also, with Professor Star, threw a double somersault, a feat seldom to be seen in one night, under the same canvas, by two performers. M'lle Rosa is a graceful little equestrienne, and succeeded in

eliciting rapturous applause. The talented little ladies who performed on the trapeze literally brought down the house. The classic groupings have seldom been equaled in Memphis. The management is well worthy the study of natural history. The company perform this afternoon and evening." Memphis (TN) *Daily Appeal*, September 17, 1872, p. 4. Aside from those already mentioned, others in the company included O. W. Hyatt, general business agent; J. B. Gaylord, contracting agent; Fred Levens, treasurer; C. A. Wilson, press agent; George Stevens, master of canvas; John Higby, master of horse; C. A. Jones, band leader; F. M. Hosmer, ringmaster. The riders were Miles Orton, Young Leon, William Batchellor, Master Claude, James Martin, George Dunbar, Mlle. Caroline, Miss Rosalie, and Miss Jessie. Gymnasts were some of the above as well as George W. DeForest, Bensley Brothers, William Reynolds, Leo Levere, Babcock Brothers, Fred Castle, Rice, Price, Larkins. The clowns were Billy Andrews and Charles Adams. Taken from the pre-season listing of the New York *Clipper*, April 13, 1872, p. 12.

[10] Detroit *Free Press*, April 7, 1872, p. 1.

[11] Dan Rice may have been the first to use the term for circuses with his Dan Rice's Circus and Great Hippodrome in 1852. He was soon followed by James M. June & Co.'s Hippodrome and Menagerie, 1853; North's Hippodrome, Circus, and Menagerie, 1853; Welch's Parisian Hippodrome, 1853-54; Robinson and Eldred's Combined Circus, Menagerie, and Hippodrome, 1854; and National Circus and Hippodrome (H. C. Lee and John R. Marshall, proprietors), 1855.

[12] New York *Clipper*, March 10, 1866, p. 383, from a letter dated February 15.

[13] Conklin, p. 83. By 1870 the total population of the state was only 818,579, less than 3 people per square mile. Compare that to New York state with its 4.3 million people. Still, there were very few amusements in this raucous and violent region, and enough money from farming and mining to spend on whatever came around. Circuses brought whole families into town from miles away. Many arrived early, a day or two before the show's arrival, and camped out in tents or the covered wagons in which they came, and remained as long as the circus was there.

CHAPTER VIII

[1] An early listing gave the number of 29 cars; by the time the show reached Oakland, California, 27 were advertised.

[2] New York *Clipper*, June 14, 1873, p. 87.

[3] *Saline County Journal*, May 22, 1873, taken from King, *Bandwagon*, September/October, 1987, p. 25.

[4] *Ibid.*

[5] Conklin, p. 79. Conklin is in error in giving the year of joining Cole as 1875.

[6] Riders—Harry Welby Cooke, Young Leon, A. D. Van Zandt, Kate Cooke, Rosina Cooke, Jessie Orton. Clowns—Jimmy Reynolds, William Worrell, John Carroll, Thomas McIntyre. Gymnasts, tumblers, and leapers—Austin Brothers, Van Zandt Brothers, Leon, Gallagher, Dunbar, Long, Rice, Newton, Lamont, Rivers, Gardner. Trapeze—Marietta Sisters, Austin Brothers. Animal man—George Conklin. New York *Clipper* Supplement, April 19, 1873, p. 1.

[7] *Saline County Journal*, May 22, 1873, taken from King, *Bandwagon*, September/October, 1987, p. 25.

[8] Clipping, *Deseret Evening News*, August 1, 1873, n.p.n.

[9] Clipping, *Desert Evening News*, July 23, 1873, n.p.n. Also new to the company was a San Francisco troupe of gymnasts and acrobats.

[10] St. Paul *Dispatch*, August 21, 1873, p. 4. The Pioneer concurred: "The people of this city had an opportunity of witnessing, yesterday, the largest, and in nearly all respects, the best circus and menagerie that has pitched its tents in St. Paul for years. There is no mistake about it, the New York and New Orleans establishment of Cole's is an immense institution. That it proceeds on no small scale is shown by the fact that it came from Omaha on its route from San Francisco to St. Paul, and made but four stops between.... To sum it up, it is one of those fine exhibitions of which a newspaper can conscientiously speak in thorough praise." New York *Clipper*, August 30, 1873, p. 175, from the St. Paul *Pioneer* of August 21.

[11] *Saline County Journal*, May 22, 1873, taken from King, *Bandwagon*, September/October, 1987, p. 25.

[12] Conklin, pp. 165-167. The privileges, as described by Conklin, depended on the skill of a "fixer." The circus advance agent, before leaving town would suggest to the chief of police, the mayor, etc., that they would be contacted by someone concerning the use of "little games of chance" connected with the show. Immediately on circus day the "fixer" went to work on the local authorities. If he was successful in his efforts to pay them off, the place was considered "fixed" or "safe." If the town was not "fixed" the grift went on anyway, but with the swindlers working with greater caution and fully

prepared to abandon their schemes and disappear. During show hours the "fixer" mingled with the crowd to take care of any demonstrative malcontent disturbed by his losses, either through "soft soap" or the return of the money.

[13] Copy of the divorce papers at the Parkinson Library and Research Center, Circus World Museum, Baraboo, Wisconsin. Elizabeth Hayes and Miles Orton were married in 1879 and within the relationship produced two children.

[14] Of Seal, Charles H. Day once wrote: "Wasn't he a slick one. Just the *beau ideal* of the 'King's Jester.'" In addition, there were Gurr & Bastian (Harry Gurr and wife) on the double trapeze; Mlle. Adelaide Restland, the attractive character rider; and gymnasts Holland, Murray, McIntyre, Long, Davis, Hart, and Rice. Artists returning from the previous year were Mlle. Jessie Orton on the slack-wire; Young Leon, bareback rider; William Batcheller, champian leaper, and the Van Zandt Brothers. Jessie Orton and Young Leon were not related to the Orton family. Partially raised in Dubuque, Iowa, they were said to have been sold to Hiram Orton some years earlier "by their unnatural and half-witted father" for the sum of $30. Dubuque *Herald*, June 10, 1875, n.p.n.]

[15] Advertisement, Buffalo (NY) *Daily Courier* Supplement, July 10, 1874, p. 1.

[16] Buffalo (NY) *Daily Courier*, July 13, 1874, p. 2. "... Of the menagerie, it is enough to say,— in view of the fact that Mr. Cole's claims have been before the public for several weeks,— that it is in all respects what he has represented it to be. The collection of animals and birds is unusually good, but the Alaska Sea Lion is after all the centre of attraction.... This Sea Lion is a veritable wonder. He can be seen at San Francisco in all his glory, but everybody hasn't the time to go that far, or to the further Alaska, to see the Sea Lion of the Pacific, and so Mr. Cole has brought them one, and shows the public how he conducts himself in his native haunts." *Ibid.* "W. W. Cole's exhibition attracted two immense assemblages yesterday afternoon and evening, and we verily believe that if the proprietor had remained with us for a week he would have his mammoth pavilions crowded every afternoon and evening. Mr. Cole has met his obligations to the public faithfully, and when next he comes he may be assured of a warm reception." Buffalo *Daily Courier*, July 15, 1874, p. 2.

[17] "Galveston sustained her reputation on the circus question last night, and 'turned out' one of the largest audiences that ever sat under

canvas in this city. From first to last the spectators evinced their appreciation of the performances by their close attention, and between the jokes of the clown a pin could have almost been heard to fall. Twenty cages of animals were arranged around the exhibition tent, noticeable among which was a Malay tapir, two fine lions, and others that have probably never been here before. A den of huge snakes was an especial attraction. Today, at 1 o'clock there will be rope-walking—a public exhibition—and an hour later the regulat afternoon performance will commence." Galveston *Daily News*, October 21, 1874, p. 2.

[18] Quincy (IL) *Daily Herald*, November 5, 1874, p. 4.

## CHAPTER IX

[1] Cole bought an older vehicle later in the season, as referred to in a letter from him to Yankee Robinson. Sent from Logansport, Indiana, and dated July 5, 1875, he wrote: I received yours at New Lisbon also the dragon wagon but I had no car room for it and I had to ship it to Chicago. Not using it between there and here I withheld the money.... I can only go two hundred on it, $200, as it will have to be done up and is more or less used up, that is to say, cracked, tail broke, and somewhat dull looking...." Copy of letter at circus World Museum.

[2] New York *Clipper* Supplement, April 17, 1875. Management roster: W. W. Cole, sole proprietor; Henry Cooke, assistant manager; J. B. Gaylord, general agent, assisted by C. A. Alexander; Fred Quick, press agent; Frank Eckles, program agent; Abe Ogden, chief billposter; Fred Levens, treasurer, assisted by Sam Charles; A. E. Richards, secretary; Pat Harris, museum director; Judd C. Webb, master of canvas, assisted by Archie McArthur; P. H. Johnson, master of horse.

[3] Add to this Mary Ann Cole, William O' Dale, Little Daisy, and Master Walker; Millie Marietta, the Van Zandt Brothers, Newton Rentfroth, James Stowe, Joseph Virella, W. White, C. Fox; and Miss Jessie Richards (nee Orton).

[4] Letters Patent No. 135,486, dated December 31, 1872. Copy on file at the Circus World Museum.

[5] Baltimore *American and Commercial Advertiser*, September 14, 1875.

[6] Reprint of an article in the *Daily Globe* by a Burlington paper, 1875.

[7] The balloon ascension was discontinued somewhere along the route.

[8] New York *Clipper*, May 15, 1875.

[9] *The Citizen*, Beaver Dam (WI), July 1, 1875. The *Argus* agreed with: "The streets were perfectly jammed, and the circus pavilion was

packed full—in fact we don't remember to have ever seen a larger crowd witness an afternoon circus performance. The crowd didn't get cheated either, for a better performance was never given in this section. Many of the performances were new, novel and attractive, and everything attempted was done with accuracy and precision, and to the entire satisfaction of the large audience which greeted the daring artists with hearty applause." Beaver Dam (WI) *Argus*, July 1, 1875. From St. Paul, Minnesota, June 19: "This was the first circus of the season here and, notwithstanding the fact that the weather was threatening all day, a large audience during both the afternoon and evening performances greeted the show. The exhibition throughout is a good one, and gave general satisfaction. Several new features are noticeable. Among the prominent ones are the bounding-jockey act by Van Zandt, and the pedestal somersaulting by the Milton Jaspers, which were enthusiastically received." Correspondent to the New York *Clipper*, July 3, 1875.

[10]New York *Clipper*, July 24, 1875.

[11]Baltimore (MD) *American and Commercial Advertiser*, September 14, 1875.

## CHAPTER X

[1]"... Mr. Cole will put on the road this year the largest and the most complete establishment of the kind in the United States, a Hippodrome, Circus, and Menagerie combined. Heretofore the New York and New Orleans Circus of which Cole was the manager ranked with the best on the road and in many respects far surpassed rival institutions. This year Mr. Cole aims to eclipse all his previous efforts and to present to the public the finest entertainment ever witnessed under canvas...." Quincy (IL) *Daily Herald*, April 16, 1876. Riders for the events: Miss J. Salmonski, Miss Rosina Cooke, Miss Jessie Richards, Miss Lizzie Conklin, William O'Dale, William Ashton, Young Leon, Frank Gardner, Walter Reis. Chariot drivers: Miss Jennie Sawyer, Miss S. Rhinehart, Miss F. Livingston, Miss Mattie Walker. Hurdle races: Miss Jennie Sawyer, Miss Maggie Taylor, Miss Florence Kent, Miss Minnie Curtis.

[2]Memphis (TN) *Daily Appeal*, October 3, 1876.

[3]Quincy (IL) *Daily Herald*, April 30, 1876.

[4]Quincy (IL) *Daily Herald*, April 16, 1876.

[5]T. L. Fitch was assistant manager; Fred Levins, treasurer; Robert Fryer, equestrian manager; W. R. Hayden, general agent; E. A. Alexander,

284

general advertiser; C. Sivalla, contracting agent. At Lexington, Tennessee, William Ashton badly fractured one of his ankles, forcing him to remain in that city. The injury was caused when a ladder he was holding for the Leroy Brothers' gymnastic act fell on him.

[6] New York *Clipper*, August 5, 1876.

[7] Louisville (KY) *Courier-Journal*, September 23, 1876.

[8] Nashville (TN) *Daily American*, October 18, 1876.

[9] Memphis (TN) *Daily Appeal*, October 3, 1876.

[10] On March 17, 1880, the *Ella Hughes* sank and was lost near New Orleans.

[11] Memphis (TN) *Daily Appeal*, January 27, 1877.

## CHAPTER XI

[1] Memphis (TN) *Daily Appeal*, March 14, 1877.

[2] Memphis (TN) *Daily Appeal*, March 18, 1877. "His is a first-class establishment of seven years standing, well known and well liked everywhere—an exhibition that has been the first to add attractions and novelties as fast as they come to light, and to increase in size from year to year. Being a young man he has had something besides temporary remuneration to strive for—a reputation to work up and hold, not for a day, but for all time. While many in his line have succeeded for a time, but eventually fell by the wayside, he has been plodding safely and surely along until no exhibition has a better reputation or more widely known, none more huge in proportions or more magnificent in attractions, than W. W. Cole's Great New York and New Orleans combined shows." *Ibid.*

[3] The troupe included Batcheller, Gardner, Castle, Long, White, Murphy, Holland, Adams, Linn, Hogle, Crossley, Elder, Leonard, Avery, Little, Simpson, Richards, and Gooding.

[4] "In 1877 I saw Cole's circus in Ashtabula, O. William Batcheller did a double somersault over 18 horses, neck to neck. I have seen all the great leapers in the last half century, and never saw one as good as Batcheller.... It was a swell one-ring railroad circus, with one elephant.... Cole's mother and his uncle were taking tickets." Walter L. Main, *Billboard*, November 3, 1934. Writing from Wheeling, West Virginia, "The leaping match between Frank A. Gardner and W. H. Batcheller took place at the afternoon performance before an immense audience. Tom McIntyre, the clown, introduced the contestants, who were received with great applause." New York *Clipper*, September 15, 1877.

⁵Memphis (TN) *Daily Appeal*, April 3, 4, 5, 1877.
⁶Walter L. Main's letter to the *Billboard*, November 3, 1934. Later, Main would have a circus of his own for several years.
⁷Atlanta (GA) *Constitution*, November 13, 1877.
⁸New York *Clipper*, December 22, 1877.
⁹New Orleans (LA) *Times Picayune*, December 16, 1877. "W. W. Cole's really fine circus and menagerie has taken the popular heart at a bound. The great tent was crowded yesterday noon and night, and a crowded tent, such as Cole puts up, means an audience of at least six thousand people. These may be hard times, but every man, woman and child appears to have two or four bits for the circus. They all do it, and all enjoy it." New Orleans (LA) *Times Picayune*, December 11, 1877.
¹⁰Conklin, p. 100.

## CHAPTER XII

¹The couple were married at St. Martin's, Trafalgar Square. They honeymooned for two days at the fashionable Star and Garter Hotel, a few miles from the city. The Captain was quoted as saying, "Our bill was over seventeen pounds, and it was as long as my arm, every incidental being put down. I have it framed at home." While in London they appeared before the Queen and other royalty. Monroe (WI) *Green County Reformer*, June 12, 1879, reprinted from an interview in the St. Louis (MO) *Globe*.
²The size of both of the Bates was, of course, exaggerated in the advertising with such statements as: "Half a ton represents the joint weight of this remarkable pair." "The largest man and largest woman in the world." The claims continued with, "Mr. Bates, the male giant, is eight feet high, lacking one half inch, and his better half, who appears along with him, boasts the same number of feet of womanhood."
³"Reminiscences of a Showman," Newark (NJ) *Evening Star*, June 3, 1915, p. 10.
⁴*Ibid.*
⁵St. Louis (MO) *Republican*, February 24, 1878; New York *Clipper*, March 2, 1878.
⁶Quincy (IL) *Daily Herald*, July 20, 1878.
⁷Detroit (MI) *Free Press*, July 30, 1878.
⁸Topeka (KS) *Daily Blade*, July 14, 1878.
⁹Wamego (KS) *Tribune*, July 13, 1878. It might be useful to some of our readers to learn the process of packing up and leaving for the next

town used by shows at this time. Except for the obvious modern technology, the system appears very similar to that of today. "While the band inside were yet playing, and before spectators had left their seats, a shrill whistle was audible to ears whose owners were not intent upon the performance. Within a short time afterwards, (other matters preventing the notation of time) every yard of the canvas wall that had surrounded the great tent had rustled to the ground. An empty ring was visible through the lattice work formed by the raised seats. The roof of the tent yet rested upon the supporting poles. The army of short-sleeved or no shirted Arabs were now visible, but no order was issued and not a word was uttered. Some caught hold of the long ends of the long pieces of canvas that lay on the ground, and ran back and forth in the process of folding them up. Some caught up in their arms four seat planks at a time and delivered them to others who were waiting below to receive them. The lights from within then revealed the presence of scores of wagons backed up and standing in a great circle around the tent. In each one stood a man ready to receive and stow away canvas or other parts of the great tent as it should be brought to him. When all beneath the roof had been taken away, the roof itself.

"First, all of the supports were taken away except the great main pole in the center and those at the edges. Then the whistle sounded again. Instantly the whole spread of canvas fluttered silently to the earth, like a great white winged sea fowl softly covering her eggs. The center pole, which pierces the canvas, yet stood. Lacings which hold the huge sections of the roof together were quickly drawn out, and the pieces were soon doubled and redoubled into great masses, each of which filled a wagon. The other large tents had been taken down while the spectators were applauding the circus performance. One of these was for the museum of natural curiosities, one for the menagerie, and one served as a green room for the circus tent.

"At the depot there was an exciting scene. It is a railroad show, and the circus, museum, menagerie and annex employ we know not how many. Most of these are platform cars. A long train of them was drawn up on the side track. By the light of flaming naphtha lamps wagon after wagon was drawn up an inclined plane upon the rear car, and then run by hand from car to car. This process was continued until the train was full of wagons. Then another train was loaded in the same manner. Heavy beams at the edges of the cars prevent the wagons from running off. The wheels of the wagons are blocked with pieces of wood which are nailed to the floor of the car. Sheets of thick iron turning vertically on hinges form bridges from car to car for the wheels to pass over. The horses are taken from the wagons when they have drawn them to the foot of the inclined plane. Then a pulley is attached to each wagon, and the strength of one pair of horses is sufficient to send it rapidly up the incline, the pole being guided by the men. While all this work was being done, most of the performers were asleep in their berths. It is in this way that the Circus Arabs gather up their duds and get out of town." *Ibid.*

[10] W. R. Hayden was the general agent; Fred Stevens, treasurer; T. L. Fitch, assistant manager; and Tom B. McIntyre, equestrian director.

[11] St. Paul (MN) *Pioneer Press*, June 11, 1878. "Never before in the history of St. Paul has a more imposing pageant been seen on the streets than the monster procession in the forenoon, comprised as it was of gorgeous chariots, brilliantly costumed equestrians, splendidly caparisoned steeds, beautifully decorated animal vans, and a multitude of other attractions, both novel and elegant. To the residents of St. Paul a very good idea of the magnitude of the parade may be gathered from the fact that the head was passing Wabasha street on seventh, just as the end was leaving the bridge, its length extending entirely around Seven Corners, thus making a length of nearly thirty blocks." *Ibid.*

[12] King, "Only Big Show Coming," Chapter 2, Part Two.

[13] *Ibid.*

[14] Quincy (IL) *Daily Herald*, July 20, 1778. "Quincy people take an interest in Mr. Cole's establishment, which they regard as a Quincy enterprise from the fact that it made its start from this city. They take an interest in Mr. Cole himself, from the fact that he has spent much of his time, has expended large sums of money in this city, and in his intercourse with our people, made himself a favorite." Quincy (IL) *Daily Herald*, July 19, 1878.

[15] Detroit (MI) *Free Press*, July 30, 1878.

## CHAPTER XIII

[1] New Orleans (LA) *Daily Picayune*, November 29, 1879.
[2] *W. W. Cole's Avant Courier*, 1879.
[3] Nashville (TN) *Daily American*, October 31, 1879.
[4] Savannah (GA) *Morning News*, November 12, 1879.
[5] St. Louis (MO) *Post-Dispatch*, April 22, 1879.

[6] Maggie Claire and Harry K. Long from the Cole company were married at Carlisle, Pennsylvania while the show was playing there on September 6.

[7] Champion leaper William Batcheller, who had been with Cole since 1875, was gone. He was with Cooper & Bailey, fresh back from their Australian and South American tour.

[8] Atchison (KS) *Daily Champion*, May 22, 1879.

[9] New York *Clipper*, June 7, 1879.

[10] New York *Clipper*, July 26, 1879.

[11] Indianapolis (IN) *Journal*, July 17, 1879. "... Cole's circus has gained the enviable reputation of being one of the few concerns which exhibit all the features advertised, and which rely on their intrinsic merits and not on the exaggerated advertising of sensations not possible to present—hence it deserves the patronage of those who find pleasure in amusements of that order...." *Ibid.* News from Evansville revealed that the circus had grossed $3,450 for the day.

[12] Wausau (WI) *The Torch of Liberty*, June 26, 1879.

[13] LaCrosse (WI) *Republican and Leader*, June 21, 1879.

[14] Sheboygan (WI) *Times*, July 5, 1879.

[15] Appleton (WI) *The Crescent*, July 5, 1879.

[16] Indianapolis (IN) *Journal*, July 18, 1879.

[17] Louisville (KY) *Courier-Journal*, October 21, 1879.

[18] Nashville (TN) *Daily American*, October 31, 1879. "The street display of Cole's circus and menagerie, upon its entrance into the city, was one of the most imposing of its kind that had been seen here for years, and the sidewalks were densely packed with spectators of all ages, sex and color. The main chariot in front, drawn by a team of camels, and the elephants with their housings produced no little entertainment among the horses in the streets, and even a pair of street-car mules on Church street were nearly panicked at the approach of these queer-looking quadrupeds. The gorilla, the lions, the huge serpents, the grotesque effigies on some of the coaches, the steam calliope, and the cavalcade of knights and ladies contributed in themselves a first-class free entertainment, which the public seemed to appreciate very heartily." *Ibid.*

[19] Savannah *Morning News*, November 12, 1879. The electric light is fully described with: "This light, caused by electricity, requires a twenty horse power engine, a thirty horse power boiler, and twenty thousand yards of insulated telegraph wire. It is a great, bright, dazzling light, yet emits no heat. A newspaper of the finest print can be

read two miles from the jets. Colors appear natural. Blue is blue; green is green, which is not the case with gas light. There are no dangers in its use. It does not vitiate the air, and is perfectly white. A thousand gas jets has the appearance of a few tallow candies burning when placed by the side of this wonderful electric light. The only expense attending it being the original investment of engine, telegraph wire and machine or battery, which amounts to about fifteen thousand dollars. The actual daily cost of the light is merely a trifle. It is the light of the future, and will soon be utilized so as to illuminate cities. It is certainly the greatest discovery of the present century, and has caused more astonishment, excited more admiration, and is the theme of more conversation than any circumstance that has come to the notice of the public within the last decade. It is a most beautiful light, almost indescribable. A grand refulgent brightness. Heaven's own gift to man." Avertisement, Savannah (GA) *Morning News*, November 8, 1879.

[20] New Orleans (LA) *Daily Picayune*, November 25, 1879.

[21] New Orleans (LA) *Daily Picayune*, November 29, 1879.

[22] Leavenworth (KS) *Daily Times*, July 11, 1880. "It is not often that any traveling affair exhibits everything that is 'set forth in the bills.' But Cole's Circus and Menagerie is an exception. It is an honest show. It is fully up to its pretensions. The collection of animals is large and varied and includes the curiosities advertised. The performances in the arena are also according to the promises made to the public. They are all first-class. There is nothing vulgar or objectionable in the entertainment." Salt Lake City (UT) *Desert Evening News*, August 11, 1880.

[23] New Orleans (LA) *Daily Picayune*, November 30, 1879. "Mr. Cole promised a great street parade and he kept his word. The display was as fine as has ever been made here, and was complimented by the thousands who filled the streets on the line of march. The features of the parade were too numerous to mention in detail. Everything had a new look. The wagons, the chariots, the trappings, banners, harness and costumes were bright, and the line was a glittering one. It is but just to say that Mr. Cole excels all other managers in the quantity and quality of his horses. Finer looking horses than those in his procession never passed through the streets of this city. The parade in all particulars was all that was promised and even more." Leavenworth (KS) *Daily Times*, July 11, 1880.

## CHAPTER XIV

[1] Cooke, "Reminscences of a Showman," June 10, 1915.

[2] On the roster were T. Fitch, assistant manager; John D. Evans, treasurer; Tom B. McIntyre, clown and equestrian director; A. M. C. Arthur, trainmaster; E. V. Wicks, boss canvasman; agents J. M. Gaylord, Louis E. Cooke, W. R. Hayden, Charles Sivalls, supported by nineteen billposters; and performers Frank A. Gardner, Pico Adams, William O' Dale, A. Vangand, Fred Barclay, Ella Stokes, Harry K. Long, J. Sours, Burt Richardson, W. W. White, "Hurricane Jim," Tom B. and Mrs. McIntyre, Mike Longmire, the Claire Sisters (Minnie and Maggie), Mlle. Adelaide, Miss Fanny Morgan, the DeComas (3 in number), the Livingston Brothers (4 in number), Dunbar & Reno, John Murtz, Dan Kennedy, George and Mrs. Conklin.

[3] *W. W. Cole's Avant Courier*, 1881, p. 2.

[4] San Francisco (CA) *Daily Alta California*, October 10, 1880.

[5] Evansville (IN) *Daily Journal*, May 2, 1880.

[6] Leavenworth (KS) *Daily Times*, July 11, 1880.

[7] St. Louis (MO) *Post-Dispatch*, April 15, 1880.

[8] Louis B. Cooke, New York *Clipper*, February 15, 1913.

[9] *Ibid.*

[10] St. Louis (MO) *Post-Dispatch*, April 10, 1880.

[11] Loeffler, "Candles, Flares, Gas, Electric, All Used to Light the Circus," p. 31.

[12] Galesburg (IL) *Republican-Register*, May 22, 1880. "The electric light worked to the full satisfaction of everybody, and proved the fact that Mr. Cole has the only genuine electric light, everything being as bright as day." Indianapolis *Daily Sentinel*, May 9, 1880, n.p.n. "The electric lighting is a novelty, emitting a soft and brilliant [glow] like magnified moonlight, and causing the ordinary lamps to look yellow and foggy as if beaming through smoke." Salt Lake City (UT) *Desert Evening News*, August 11, 1880.

[13] St. Louis (MO) *Post-Dispatch*, April 13, 1880.

[14] Indianapolis (IN) *Journal*, May 9, 1880.

[15] Ellingham (IL) *Democrat*, May 12, 1880.

[16] Galesburg (IL) *Republican Register*, May 22, 1880. "If the last two attractions in the circus line drew immense audiences, W. W. Cole certainly outdid all their efforts in his performances yesterday. The procession was one of the best given by any circus; the paraphernalia all new; the wagons freshly painted; the horses in good condition— thus forming one continuous line of glittering splendor. The afternoon

performance found the canvas filled to overflowing, and in the evening hundreds of people were turned away unable to gain admittance. And what is the cause of all this rush? Simply, because Mr. Cole does all he advertises, and more, too." Indianapolis (IN) *Sentinel*, reprinted in the Salt Lake City (UT) *Desert Evening News*, August 9, 1880.

[17] Leavenworth (KS) *Daily Times*, July 11, 1880.

[18] Denver (CO) *Daily News*, July 27, 1880. "The menagerie contains a fine selection of animals. Among the curiosities are a couple of Sea Lions and an Ox of immense size. The Lions are splendid specimens of the 'King of the Forest' and the Royal Bengal Tiger is a splendid animal. The other carriages contain a great variety of wild beasts, including a tough two-horned rhinoceros. Birds of every clime and monkeys of every breed are shown in profusion, the former beautiful as the latter are repulsive." *Ibid*.

[19] Salt Lake City (UT) *Desert Evening News*, August 10, 1880.

[20] Cooke, "Reminiscences of a Showman," Newark *Evening Star*, June 10, 1915.

[21] Los Angeles (CA) *Herald*, September 16, 1880. "An admirable feature of Cole's Circus, which will exhibit in this city this afternoon and evening, is the reserved seat arrangement. Special tickets for these seats are sold just inside the tent door and ushers are assigned to the work of seating the holders. All who avail themselves to those advantages are assured plenty of elbow room, a sightly place of observation, and absolute protection from the rough element which sometimes makes its presence disagreeably prominent at such places." Los Angeles (CA) *Herald*, September 15, 1880.

[22] *Ibid*.

[23] San Francisco (CA) *Sunday Chronicle*, October 10, 1880.

[24] San Francisco (CA) *Daily Alta California*, October 10, 1880.

[25] New Orleans *Daily Picayune*, November 21, 1886.

## CHAPTER XV

[1] The roster for Australia included: Mary Ann Cole, Mrs. Ryland, Miss A. Austin, Mr. and Mrs. Fred Barclay, Mr. and Mrs. Wooda Cook, Mr. and Mrs. George Conklin, Mr. and Mrs. William O'Dale Stevens, Tom McIntyre, Pico Adams, William O'Dale, George Dunbar, John Murtz, Livingston Brothers, James Campbell, Cassnovia, Burt Richardson, Dan Hernandez, Mike Longmire, Count Littlefinger, Count Rosebud, Van Zandt, a troupe of ten war-dancing Indians led by Dick Deadeye. John D. Evans was the treasurer; Frank Lemen, as-

assistant; John Lampright, boss hostler (with 12 men); George Wicks, boss canvasman; Fred Marshall, boss property man; E. Walters, chandelier man; W. Goodloe, electrician; George Conklin, superintendent of animals, with George Prentis and four assistants.

[2] Cooke, "Reminiscences of a Showman," June 10, 1915.
[3] Conklin, p. 101.
[4] New York *Clipper*, January 15, 1881.
[5] Cooke, "Reminiscences of a Showman," June 10, 1915.
[6] *Ibid.*
[7] New York *Clipper*, March 12, 1881.
[8] Cooke, "Reminiscences of a Showman," June 10, 1915.
[9] New York *Clipper*, March 12, 1881.
[10] St Leon, *Circus in Australia*, p. 81.
[11] *Ibid.*
[12] *Ibid.*
[13] *W. W. Cole's Avant Courier* for 1881.
[14] Conklin, p. 110.
[15] *Ibid*, p. 111.
[16] From a Cole interview, New Orleans *Daily Picayune*, November 21, 1886.

## CHAPTER XVI

[1] *W. W. Cole's Avant Courier*, 1881.
[2] Performers were Linda Jeal, Adelaide D'Atalie, Elena Jeal Ryland, Millie Turnour, George and Mrs. Conklin, William O'Dale, Wooda Cook, Fred Barclay, A. D. Van Zandt, William O'Dale Stevens, George Dunbar, John Murtz, Dan Kennedy, Charles Campbell, Livingston Brothers, Pico Adams, Tom McIntyre, and William Organ. Staff members included J. F. Printer, assistant to Conklin; John Lambright, veterinary surgeon and master of horses; Archie McArther, superintendent of transportation; John D. Evans, treasurer; J. B. Gaylord, general agent; W. R. Hayden, railroad contractor; Louis E. Cooke, press agent and superintendent of the advance corps; R. C. Campbell, advertising agent; Charles Sivalls, contracting agent; Alf Riel, chief billposter with 20 assistants.
[3] San Francisco (CA) *Daily Alta California*, May 24, 1881.
[4] Sacramento *Bee*, June 21, 1881. The previous day the paper had described the parade: "First came the new band wagon drawn by 10 camels in gay trappings, then followed a cavalcade of knights and ladies. Next came a Roman chariot drawn by four snow white horses

and driven by a lady attired after the manner of the ancients. Then followed the three monster elephants with a keeper astride the back of each and the baby elephant in tow, securely chains to prevent his cutting up any antics; then followed a long line of wagons in which were the features of the menagerie, conspicuous among them being the open den of lions. The steam calliope brought up the rear screeching out 'My Baby.'"

[5] Los Angeles (CA) *Daily Herald*, June 14, 1881.

[6] Louis E. Cooke, Newark *Evening Star*, June, 10, 1915. The Santa Fe *New Mexican* found the bareback riding to be good and the horses used for it in excellent condition. The eight vaulters were particularly excellent, going over elephants, camels and horses.

[7] New York *Clipper*, July 9, 1881.

[8] Pueblo (CO) *Colorado Chieftain*, June 26, 1881. "The menagerie was all that could be desired. A huge two horned hairy rhinoceros occupied one den, a male and female sea lion another, two cages contained over one hundred and fifty snow white cockatoos, several cages well filled with monkeys of all kinds and ages, from the gray-haired veteran to those of but three and four weeks of age. A marked feature of the menagerie was a white buffalo from Australia, which attracted considerable attention, as did also the kangaroos and ostriches from the South Sea Islands. Lions, tigers, leopards, hyenas, etc., were in abundance. The new departures in the circus were numerous." *Ibid*.

[9] New York *Clipper*, September 10, 1881.

[10] Louis E. Cooke, "Reminiscence of a Showman," June, 10, 1915. Cole's *1882 Courier* listed the following:

|  | No. of stands | No. of days | Attendance |
| --- | --- | --- | --- |
| 1880 American tour | 146 | 166 | 1,228,580 |
| 1880-81 Foreign tour | 48 | 135 | 1,084,973 |
| 1881 American tour | 111 | 130 | 1,040,642 |
| Grand Total | 305 | 431 | 3,353,195 |

True distance traveled, 44,172 miles, at sea 56 days.

Louis E. Cooke, finding enough rejuvenation from the many continuous months on the road, was quietly married to Miss Kittie Bartlett, daughter of a Newark, New Jersey, lumber dealer and a great favorite of Newark society.

## CHAPTER XVII

[1] "The huge elephant Samson is one of the leading attractions, his enormous bulk towering over his fellow mammoths so that they appear insignificant beside him. He is gentle and kindly, as becomes his fifty years, but he will not permit any impertinent liberties. A youth who tried a little impudence with him yesterday afternoon was seized in the vast trunk and lifted so far away that he will be likely to keep out of the reach of elephants hereafter." Buffalo (NY) *Courier*, May 5, 1882, reproduced in the Topeka (KS) *Daily Commonwealth*, July 8, 1882.

[2] Cooke, "Reminiscences of a Showman," June 17, 1915.

[3] *Ibid.*

[4] *Ibid.*

[5] Cleveland (OH) *Plain Dealer*, May 1, 1882. The advertising department consisted of Charles Sivalls, general agent; Louis E. Cooke, advance manager and press agent; R. C. Campbell, contracting agent; agents Henry Berger and M. W. Tobin, in charge of advertising cars No. 1 and No. 2, each with a crew of nine. "Cole believes in the virtue of printer's ink," it was stated in Janesville's *Rock County Recorder*. "He has five crews of men, one following the other, and every available spot in the country is plastered with paper when the last crew go through." Janesville (WI) *Rock County Recorder*, August 11, 1882.

[6] Janesville (WI) *Rock County Recorder*, August 11, 1882.

[7] Grand Rapids (WI) *Reporter*, August 24, 1882. The then Grand Rapids is now Wisconsin Rapids.

[8] Addie was a member of the Austin family of versatile performers, also connected with the D'Atalie troupe of acrobats who made their debut in 1870.

[9] Other ladies listed on the *1882 Courier* were Rosa Fletcher, Lizzette McIntyre, Lellie Fletcher, Alma Curry, Louise Jardine, Helen Gardner, Jessie Richards, Fanny Murray, and the Rodowski Sisters (Lulu, Blanche, Ella).

[10] Buffalo (NY) *Courier*, May 5, 1882, reproduced in the Topeka (KS) *Daily Commonwealth*, July 8, 1882.

[11] Topeka (KS) *Capital*, as related in King, "Only Big Show Coming," Chapter 3, Part One.

[12] Buffalo (NY) *Express*, reproduced in the Topeka (KS) *Daily Commonwealth*, July 15, 1882.

[13]Indianapolis (IN) *Daily Sentinel*, June 13, 1882. "In the ring the twenty leapers did good work, the beautiful lady equestriennes rode bareback steeds, jumped through paper banners, and the clown told funny jokes. The aerial bicycle act on the high wire was good, the shooting of Captain Bogardus and sons was the finest ever seen, the great Russian roller skaters did a splendid act, Miss Deutatie (sic) especially distinguished herself. The $50,000 troupe of performing stallions took the audience by storm." *Ibid.*

[14]Cleveland (OH) *Plain Dealer*, May 2, 1882.

[15]Janesville (WI) *The Daily Recorder*, August 16, 1882. "There was the gilded band chariot drawn by the sedate and hump backed dromedaries of Holy writ; the elephants with their trunks packed for the campaign; the brave man surrounded by a toothless lion, who could scarcely eat raw meat that was dripping with gore; the snake charmer who seemed to delight in having the slimy reptiles thrust their heads in his mouth; the prancing stallions, automatic monstrosities; the steam calliope, the musical (?) notes of which distance lends enchantment, and a long array of possible empty cages, the whole being followed by the proverbial small boy." *Ibid.*

[16]Memphis (TN) *Daily Appeal*, October 3, 1882.

[17]Little Rock (AR) *Daily Arkansas*, November 16, 1882.

[18]New York *Clipper*, December 2, 1882.

[19]Cole now has real estate in Chicago worth $300,000. A notice in the *Clipper* of February, 1883, revealed that he had returned there to look after the investments. New York *Clipper*, July 8, 1882, p. 259; February 17, 1883, p. 782. We have tried to find evidence of Cole's business transactions through the files of R. G. Dun & Co., but none exist. Evidently he never borrowed to finance his real estate deals.

CHAPTER XVIII

[1]Sedalia (MO) *Bazoo*, September 20, 1883. Publicity suggested the show traveled in thirty-six new sixty foot cars. The Mankato, Kansas, *Review* counted only twenty-five being hauled by two locomotives. Cole himself stated there were thirty-one used for transportation.

[2]The Arabs were Abdullah Ben Said, Sheikh Said Ben Ahmed, Hadj Ibrahim, Hadj Shereef, Kassem Ben Ali, Hadj Muhammed Ambak, Hadj Taah Ushen, Hadj Omar, Muhammed Spitish, Abdullah Ben Edar, Yusef Ben Omar, Yaru Ben Suir (wife of the Sheikh). Clipping from the Chicago *Inter-Ocean*, n.d., n.p.n.

³Sedalia (MO) *Bazoo*, September 20, 1883.
⁴Middleton, *Circus Memoirs*, p. 39.
⁵Sedalia (MO) *Bazoo*, September 20, 1883.
⁶St. Paul (MN) *Pioneer-Press*, as reproduced in the Mankato (KS) *Jewel County Monitor*, May 16, 1883. "The show in the tents excelled in novelty and exceeded in excellence all others. The menagerie was exceptionally presentable. The appearance of animals in vans was the theme of constant comment; sea lions in water, serpents in glass, rhinoceroses, aardvarks, armadillos, hippopotamuses, apes, tigers, ocelots, yaks, ostriches, emu, cougars, leopards, white buffalo, and numerous other animals, all excellent specimens, were seen. Elephants from Samson, the largest ever seen here, the baby the tiniest. The wax statuary of noted men (an innovation) all just as advertised. The circus certainly, the crème de la crème, was a most wonderful change from the accepted and usual version of that entertainment." *Ibid*.
⁷Sedalia (MO) *Bazoo*, September 20, 1883. Asked for a brief sketch of his life Cole responded with: "I grew up in a circus. My grandfather was a circus rider, and my mother was owner of a show. I am a New Yorker by birth and 36 years old. My father died in 1856, but my mother is still alive and travels with me generally. Just after my father's death in 1856, I came West, and since then have been constantly with circuses. Twelve years ago I established my first circus, and have had it every year since."
⁸King, "Only Big show Coming," Chapter 5, Part One.
⁹Des Moines (IA) *Iowa State Register*, June 6, 1883.
¹⁰Clipping, Milwaukee (WI) *Sentinel*, June 19, 1883.
¹¹Appleton (WI) *Post*, June 28, 1883. "Upon the whole the parade was excellent, and was witnessed by one of the largest crowds that ever gathered on the avenue. The streets, windows, doors and many of the roofs, were packed, and if we are not called upon to chronicle many cases of pick pockets, it will be surprising." *Ibid*.
¹²Racine (WI) *Daily Journal*, August 31, 1883.
¹³Racine (WI) *Daily Journal*, September 1, 1883.
¹⁴Jamestown (ND) *Morning Alert*, July 11, 1883.
¹⁵King, "Only Big show Coming," Chapter 5, Part One.
¹⁶*Ibid*.
¹⁷*Ibid*.
¹⁸*Ibid*.
¹⁹San Antonio (TX) *Daily Express*, November 25, 1883.

## CHAPTER XIX
[1] New York *Clipper*, May 3, 1884.
[2] *Ibid.*
[3] Topeka (KS) *Daily Commonwealth*, April 13, 1884.
[4] The seven sisters were with Cole the previous year but did not receive advertised billing. "The seven long-haired ladies, whom, let us say, are cultivated and attractive, were one of the principal features in the Annex and drew large crowds." San Antonio (TX) *Daily Express*, November 25, 1883.
[5] King collection, Topeka (KS) *Daily Commonwealth*, April 8, 1884.
[6] New York *Clipper*, February 23, 1884.
[7] King collection, Atchison (KS) *Daily Champion*, April 25, 1884.
[8] St. Louis (MO) *Post-Dispatch*, April 24, 1884.
[9] St. Louis (MO) *Globe Democrat*, as retold in the Lawrence (KS) *Journal*, April 29, 1884.
[10] We are indebted to Orin King and his collection of Kansas circus material for much of what we know about this billing war.
[11] St. Louis (MO) *Post-Dispatch*, September 9, 1881.

## CHAPTER XX
[1] King collection, Topeka (KS) *State Journal*, April 28, 1884.
[2] King collection, Topeka (KS) *Daily Capital*, April 11, 1884.
[3] King collection, Topeka (KS) *State Journal*, April 25, 1884.
[4] King, "Only Big Show Coming," Chapter 6, Part One.
[5] King collection, Topeka (KS) *Daily Commonwealth and Mail*, May 10, 1884. "Previous to Mr. Doris' advent hither a few hot-headed spirits conspired to create a prejudice against him and thus keep people away from his attraction by preaching that W. W. Cole had been the first here; that W. W. Cole is a man worth $8,000,000, therefore could not help having the best show on earth, and that if his was rotten, as those claimed who said it, Mr. Doris' would be worse. But the people came all the same to see for themselves and be convinced." *Daily Commonwealth*, May 9, 1884.
[6] King collection, Lawrence (KS) *Journal*, May 1, 1884.
[7] King collection, Lawrence (KS) *Journal*, May 4, 1884.
[8] King collection, Leavenworth (KS) *Times*, May 4, 1884.
[9] King collection, Leavenworth (KS) *Evening Standard*, May 2, 1884. "The average circus advertiser seems to have a passion for distributing bills which the people do not read. The back alleys of Atchison are already knee deep with Cole and Doris bills; now comes Sells to

cover up all the others. The man who distributes the most bills in a town is not the best advertiser by any means." Atchinson (KS) *Globe*, May 1, 1884.

[10] St. Joseph (MO) *Daily Herald*, May 6, 1884.

[11] *Ibid*.

[12] St. Joseph (MO) *Daily Herald*, May 7, 1884.

[13] St. Joseph (MO) *Daily Herald*, May 8, 1884. "The HERALD does not know that Mr. Cole has started out with the determination to elevate the moral status of the circus in general, but it is evident that if he maintains the policy and methods adopted on this occasion in St. Joseph his brethren of the profession will find that this is a proper course to pursue." *Ibid*.

[14] King collection, Atchinson (KS) *Globe*, May 3, 1884.

[15] Michael D. Sporrer collection, clipping, Spokane *Review*, October 21, 1954.

[16] Michael D. Sporrer collection, Missoula (MT) *Weekly Missoulian*, June 27, 1884, referring to the Butte *Inter Mountian*.

[17] Michael D. Sporrer collection, Missoula *Weekly Missoulian*, July 4, 1884.

[18] Michael D. Sporrer collection, Walla Walla (WA) *Union*, June 28, 1884. "The 'Human Fly' act where Mlle Aimee walked suspended from a temporary ceiling was the greatest novelty. Although much credit is to to the electric battery stationed in the side tent. The Livingston Brothers, gymnasts, did beautiful work on the trapeze and were daring enough to suit the taste of the most critical. Two leapers with a run and spring cleared four camels and four elephants, including 'Samson,' making a double somersault on the fly. The bicycling was too scientifically simple until the rider stood on his head and propelled the instrument. The slack wire performance was one of the best acts and was received with loud applause. The platform bicycling and roller skating was also very fine. The 'Arabs' did some fair tumbling and juggling and their pyramid act 'took the house by storm.'" *Ibid*.

[19] Michael D. Sporrer collection, Ashland (OR) *Tidings*, July 4, 1884.

[20] Michael D. Sporrer collection, Portland *Standard*, as reported by the Ashland *Tidings*, July 4, 1884.

[21] Michael D. Sporrer collection, Vancouver (W.T.) *Independent*, July 31, 1884. The correspondent included this view: "The menagerie is one of the great features of this show, and alone is worth the price of admission. Animals of nearly every clime could here be seen."

[22]Michael D. Sporrer collection, Portland (OR) *Oregonian*, as retold in the Missoula (MT) *Weekly Missoulian*, July 11, 1884.
[23]Conklin, pp. 139-140.
[24]*Ibid*, pp. 141-142.
[25]King collection, Atchinson (KS) *Globe*, May 7, 1884.

CHAPTER XXI
[1]St. Louis (MO) *Post-Dispatch*, April 21, 1885. The personnel included—W. W. Cole, sole proprietor and manager; G. H. McGlasson, treasurer; Henry Cooke, chief door keeper; Ernest Cooke, second door keeper; Frost Lemen, third door keeper and manager of concert; Burt Richardson, fourth door keeper; A. M. Van Zandt, hotel manager and postmaster; T. B. McIntyre, equestrian director; Frank Eckels and J. McEllony, masters of horses; William Kelley and Henry Hodges, masters of canvas; George Conklin, master of animals; William Printer and Jack Shoemake, masters of elephants; Archie McArthur, master of transportation; E. Burk, assistant master of transportation with 23 people; Charles Weller, master of chandeliers. Annex—Dan Green, manager; E. Hathaway, lecturer; Walter Allen, assistant; John Herbert, master of canvas. Cook tent—J. Alderwick, steward with 10 assistants. Advance department—Charles Sivalls, general railroad contracting agent; R. C. Campbell, manager of advance; O. P. Myers, general contracting agent; W. C. Boyd, director of publications; E. H. Madigan, excursion agent; W. R. Peck, special agent with 2 assistants; W. Green, chief bill poster; A. Marrony, assistant bill poster. Bugle Corps—6 people in charge of L. E. Coke. Mobile (AL) *Daily Register*, December 3, 1885.
[2]*Ibid*.
[3]Terre Haute (IN) *Journal*, April 23, 1885, as reprinted in the Evanston (IN) *Daily Journal*, May 1, 1885.
[4]Evanston (IN) *Daily Journal*, May 2, 1885. We learn from the paper that the menagerie was enhanced by a large collection of Mexican flowers and antiquities and a facsimile of the Aztec calendar stone.
[5]Louisville (KY) *Courier-Journal*, May 5, 1885.
[6]Augusta (GA) *Chronicle*, November 6, 1885.
[7]Savannah (GA) *Morning News*, November 10, 1885.
[8]*Ibid*. "Music, costumes of glittering tinsel and gaudily colored silk, acrobats flying through the air, horses rushing around the rings, mountains of elephantine flesh performing tricks, with dozens of other things, made a sort of dizzy effect that will long be a fruitful topic

with the small boy.... The performing horses were well trained, as were the elephant, and the bareback riding of Leon and Van Zandt caused the mouths of many to open in astonishment. The troupe of somersault tumblers, the aerial balancing, the skatorial exercises and Hassan's imitation of a dude on the slack wire were all good features, and if the applause bestowed was any criterion they must each have been greatly enjoy." *Ibid.*

[9] Reprinted in the Jacksonville (FL) *Florida Times-Union*, November 19, 1885.

[10] Mobile (AL) *Daily Register*, December 4, 1885.

[11] New York *Clipper*, August 22, 1885.

[12] Referred to as the Hutchinson Papers, this important cache includes formerly unknown facts about the 1880 Barnum, Bailey and Hutchinson merger, as well as the one between Barnum, Hutchinson and Cole. Hicks and co-researcher Judy Griffin are in the process of writing a book, a major part of which will include astounding revelations from the Hutchinson/Barnum correspondence.

[13] Barnum, *Selected Letters*, pp. 262-263.

[14] *Ibid.*

[15] Barnum, *Selected Letters*, p.264. Merritt Young was treasurer for the show; Benjamin Fish was Barnum's representative, looking after his interests.

## CHAPTER XXII

[1] New York *Clipper*, May 8, 1886. A contract of sale at the Bridgeport Public Library states that Cole agreed to pay $75,000 for Bailey's share, but the final $40,000 was not required due until October of 1886. As the reader may recall, it was suggested that Cole must have paid cash for his real estate investments because he had no financial record with Dun & Co. If this is true, it is possible that Cole needed the extra season to make the final payment. The managerial staff for 1886 was listed in the route book is as follows: W. W. Cole, proprietor and manager; Frank Lemen and E. D. Colvin, assistant managers; G. H. McGlasson, treasurer; J. J. Hickey, assistant treasurer; Henry Cooke, general superintendent; John Worland, judge of hippodrome; A. Van Zandt, layer out and mail agent; J. C. Wooters, special U. S. detective; Frost Lemen, program agent; D. Green, manager of annex; A. McCarthy, master of transportation; F. Eckles, master of stock; William Kelley, master of canvas; George Farrell, assistant master of canvas; Frank Collins, master of property; C. Stout, master of ward-

robe; John Herbert, master of annex canvas; Harry Reagand, *chef d'cuisine*; James Alderwick, steward; C. T. Stivalls, general R.R. and business agent; R. C. Campbell, general agent; W. C. Boyd, contracting agent; C. A. Davis, press agent and head of car #1; E. H. Madigan, head of car #3; W. K. Peck, special agent.

[2]Route book titled *Barnum Budget, or Tent topics of the Season of 1886*, pp. 22, 27.

[2]Dallas (TX) *Morning News*, October 26, 1886.

[3]*Ibid.*

[4]The procession left the grounds at Nineteen and Pine Streets and passed out Pine to Jefferson Avenue, along Jefferson to Chouteau, to Broadway, then to Franklin, out Franklin to Twelfth Street, to Cass Avenue, back to Fourth Street and along Olive for a return to the show lot. "Some of the notes of the steam piano with Cole's circus have fallen into a state of 'innocuous destitude.'" Chippewa (WI) *Herald*, July 2, 1886.

[5]"There were numbers of circus parties which promise to become as popular as theatre parties this week." St. Louis (MO) *Post-Dispatch*, May 4, 1886.

[6]*Ibid.*

[7]Fort Scott (KS) *Weekly Monitor*, May 20, 1886.

[8]King, "Only Big Show Coming," Chapter 8, Part One.

[9]Topeka (KS) *Daily Capital*, May 26, 1886.

[10]Lawrence (KS) *Tribune*, May 28, 1886.

[11]Eau Claire (WI) *Free Press*, July 2, 1886.

[12]Losses to the company included: W. W. Cole, $5,000; E. D. Colvin, $1,000; Ernest Cooke, $1,575; Al Richards and wife, $2,500; T. B. McIntyre, $1,000; John Worland, $2,000; George Conklin, $1,000; Frank Eckles and wife, $500; Dan Green, $350; John Murtz, $600; G. H. McGlasson, $500; Dr. Carver, $1,200; Harry Hodges, $250. New York *Clipper*, July 17, 1886.

[13]Portland (OR) *Morning Oregonian*, August 27, 1886.

[14]Dallas (TX) *Morning News*, October 26, 1886. "The performance had the merit of the absence of the stereotyped routine of circus attractions, and had several points of excellence. The aerobatic feats were novel and remarkable for the grace of the performers, no less than the danger of their exploits, including three flights through the air, covering about half of the shorter diameter of the tent. In the course of one of these flights the human aerolite executed two somersaults. The performance by the dogs was unique and made it difficult to draw the

dividing line between sense and instinct, particularly in the case of the polygamous looking hairy cur which amused itself by throwing somersaults of its own volition—as the mental philosopher would say—and without the customary assistance of being projected by the tail." *Ibid.*

[15] Galveston (TX) *Daily News*, November 6, 1886. "To say that Cole's circus is the best that has ever visited Galveston would be to indulge in an exaggeration, and to say that it is the worst would be unjust to the management. It may be classed as fairly acceptable with some few very excellent features, and many that are, to say the least, tiresome to the audience." *Ibid.*

[16] New Orleans (LA) *Daily Picayune*, November 17, 1886.

[17] New Orleans (LA) *Daily Picayune*, November 18, 1886.

[18] Galveston (TX) *Daily News*, November 6, 1886.

[19] New Orleans (LA) *Daily Picayune*, November 24, 28, 1886. The animal sales was revealed as follows:

Sells Bros.—4 monkeys, $34; 2 anteaters, $12; 2 monkeys, $40; 3 llamas, $288; one white deer at $27.50 and one at $40; ibex, $60; one hyena at $35 and one at $27; jaguar, $205; horned horse, $251.

Signor Faranta—2 white peacocks, $28; white buffalo yak, $200; 3 lions, $1,236; elephant Tom, $3,100; elephant Lizzie, $1,600; elephant Jennie, $1,500; elephant Laura, $950; female hippopotamus, $1,500; 28 wax figures and 12 *papier mache* figures, $60; Mexican curiosities, $450.

Forepaugh's agent—black yak, $30; first choice kangaroo, $91; 3 kangaroos, $320; lioness, $125; lion, $36; leopard, $103.50; white bear, $192; ancelot wild cat, $8; male camel, $171; female camel, $160; elk, $101; 5 African boas from $51 to $13.

S. H. Stevens of the Cincinnati Zoological Gardens—zebra, $275; Bengal tiger, $135. *Ibid.*

W. A. Conklin of the Central Park Zoological Gardens—two-horned rhinoceros; $4,200; Brazilian boa, $9.

# BIBLIOGRAPHY

## BOOKS

Barnum, P. T. (ed. by Arthur Saxon). *Selected Letters of P. T. Barnum*. New York: Columbia University Press, 1983.

Blackburn, Joseph (ed. by William L. Slout). *A Clown's Log*. San Bernardino (CA): An Emeritus Enterprise Book, 1993.

Chipman, Bert J. *Hey, Rube*. Published by the author, 1933.

Conklin, George. *The Ways of the Circus*. New York: Harper & Brothers Publishers, 1921.

Croft-Cooke, Rupert. *Circus: a World History*. New York: Macmillan Publishing Co., Inc., 1977.

Dahlinger, Fred Jr., and Stuart Thayer. *Badger State Showmen*. Madison (WI): Grote Publishing, 1998.

Day, Charles H. (ed. William L. Slout). *Ink from a Circus Press Agent*. San Bernardino (CA): The Borgo Press, 1995.

Glenroy, John H. *Ins and Outs of Circus Life*. Boston: M. M. Wing & Co., 1885.

Hippisley Coxe, Antony. *A Seat at the Circus*. Hamden (CT): Archon Books, 1980.

Leavitt, M. B. *Fifty Years in Theatrical Management*. New York: Broadway Publishing Co., 1912.

Middleton, George (as told to and written by his wife). *Circus Memoirs*. Self-published, 1913.

Odell, George C. D. *Annals of the New York Stage*, Vols. IV-VI. New York: Columbia University Press, 1927-1931.

Smith, Eleanor Furneaux, Lady. *British Circus Life*. London: Harrap, 1948.

St Leon, Mark. *Circus in Australia*. Richmond Victoria (Australia): Greenhouse Publications, 1983.

Thayer, Stuart. *Annals of the American Circus, 1793-1860* (revised to a single volume). Self published, 2000.

_____. *Mudshows and Railers*. Published by the author, 1971.

## ARTICLES

Briarmead, Chess L., "The American Circus," New York *Clipper*, April 17, 1875.

Cockerline, Neil C., "Ethical Considerations for the Conservation of Circus Posters," WAAC Newsletter, Volume 17, Number 2, May 1995.

Cooke, Louis E., "Reminiscences of a Showman," Newark *Evening Star*, June 3, 10, 1915, n.p.n.

_____, "Some Circus Men I Have Met," *The Show World*, December 21, 1907, p. 38.

Dahlinger, Fred, Jr., "The Development of the Railroad Circus," Part Three, *Bandwagon*, March/April, 1984, pp. 28-36.

"Kentucky Giant, The," *The White Tops*, July/August, 1951, pp. 9-10. Reprinted from the *Daily Independent*, Ashland, KY.

King, Orin C., "Only Big Show Coming," Chapter 2, Part One, *Bandwagon*, September/October, 1987, pp. 22-33; Chapter 2, Part Two, November/December, 1987, pp. 52-62; Chapter 3, Part One, January/February, 1988, pp. 34-46; Chapter 5, Part One, pp. 66-76; Chapter 3, Part Three, May/June, 1988, pp. 38-47; Chapter 5, Part One, November/December, 1988, pp 66-76; Chapter 6, Part One, March/April, 1889, pp. 36-46; Chapter 8, Part One, January/February, 1990, pp. 48-59.

Landrum, Carl, "W. W. Cole's Five-Continent Circus," *Bandwagon*, March/April, 1975, pp. 14-17.

Loeffler, Robert J., "Candles, Flares, Gas, Electric, All Used to Light the Circus," *The White Tops*, May/June, 1984, pp. 27-34.

Sampson, J. Lou, "Hiram Orton, Pioneer Showman," *Bandwagon*, April 1950, pp. 3-7.

Sharpe, Adrian D., "The Orton Circus," *Bandwagon*, July/August, 1969, pp.4-8.

Sturtevant, C. G., "Little Biographies of Famous Circus Men," #18, *The White Tops*, October, 1929, pp. 5-6.

Traber, J. Milton, "W. W. Cole, Showman," *Billboard*, January 7, 1911, p. 20.

NEWSPAPERS

Appleton (WI) *Crescent*
Appleton (WI) *Post*
Ashland (OR) *Tidings*
Atchinson (KS) *Daily Champion*
Atchinson (KS) *Globe*
Atlanta (GA) *Constitution*
Augusta (GA) *Chronicle*
Baltimore (MD *American & Commercial Daily Advertiser*
Beaver Dam (WI) *Argus*
Beaver Dam (WI) *Citizen*
*Billboard*
Boston (MA) *Daily Advertiser*
Boston (MA) *Daily Evening Transcript*
Buffalo (NY) *Daily Courier*
Buffalo (NY) *Express*
Butte (MT) *Inter Mountain*
Chippewa (WI) *Herald*
Cincinnati (OH) *Daily Commercial*

*Commercial*
Cleveland (OH) *Plain Dealer*
Dallas (TX) *Morning News*
Denver (CO) *Daily News*
Des Moines (IA) *Iowa State Register*
Detroit (MI) *Free Press*
Dubuque (IA) *Herald*
Eau Claire (WI) *Free Press*
Effingham (IL) *Democrat*
Evansville (IN) *Daily Journal*
Fitchburg (MA) *Sentinel*
Fort Scott (KS) *Weekly Monitor*
Galesburg (IL) *Republican Register*
Galveston (TX) *Daily News*
Grand Rapids (WI) *Reporter*
Independence (IA) *Bulletin-Journal*
Independence (IA) *Civilian*
Indianapolis (IN) *Daily Sentinel*
Indianapolis (IN) *Journal*
Jacksonville (FL) *Florida Times-Union*
Jamestown (ND) *Morning Alert*
Janesville (WI) *Daily Recorder*
Janesville (WI) *Rock County Recorder*
LaCrosse (WI) *Republican and Leader*
Lawrence (KS) *Journal*
Lawrence (KS) *Kansas Daily Tribune*
Leavenworth (KS) *Daily Times*
Leavenworth (KS) *Evening Standard*
Leavenworth (KS) *Times*
Little Rock (AR) *Daily Arkansas*
Los Angeles (CA) *Herald*
Louisville (KY) *Courier-Journal*
Lowell (MA) *Advertiser*
Memphis (TN) *Daily Appeal*
Milwaukee (WI) *Sentinel*
Minneapolis (MN) *Tribune*
Missoula (MT) *Weekly Missoulian*
Mobile (AL) *Daily Register*
Monroe (WI) *Green County Reformer*
Nashville (TN) *Daily American*
Newark (NJ) *Evening Star*
New Orleans (LA) *Times Picayune*
New York (NY) *Clipper*
New York (NY) *Commercial Advertiser*
New York (NY) *Evening Post*
New York (NY) *Herald*
Philadelphia (PA) *Public Ledger*
Portland (ME) *Daily Argus*
Portland (OR) *Oregonian*
Portland (OR) *Standard*
Poughkeepsie (NY) *Journal and Poughkeepsie Eagle*
Pueblo (CO) *Colorado Chieftain*
Quincy (IL) *Daily Herald*
Sacramento (CA) *Bee*
Salt Lake City (UT) *Desert Evening News*
San Antonio (TX) *Daily Express*
San Francisco (CA) *Daily Alta*

*California*
San Francisco (CA) *Sunday Chronicle*
Savannah (GA) *Morning News*
Sedalia (MO) *Bazoo*
Sheboygan (WI) *Times*
Spokane (WA) *Review*
Springfield (MO) *Missouri Weekly Patriot*
St. Joseph (MO) *Morning Herald*
St. Louis (MO) *Missouri Republican*
St. Louis (MO) *Post-Dispatch*
St. Paul (MN) *Dispatch*
St. Paul (MN) *Pioneer*
St. Paul (MN) *Pioneer Press*
*Spirit of the Times*
Terre Haute (IN) *Journal*
Topeka (KS) *Daily Blade*
Topeka (KS) *Daily Capital*
Topeka (KS) *Daily Commonwealth*
Topeka (KS) *Saline County Journal*
Topeka (KS) *State Journal*
Vancouver (WT) *Independent*
Walla Walla (WA) *Union*
Wamego (KS) *Tribune*
Wausau (WI) *Torch of Liberty*

MISCELLANEOUS

*Barnum Budget, or Tent Topic of the Season of 1886* (route book)

Durang, Charles, "The Philadelphia Stage from the Year of 1794 to the Year 1855," Philadelphia *Weekly Dispatch*, 1854-1860. (Microfilm in three parts, beginning with issue of May 7, 1854.)

Robert L. Parlinson Library and Research Center, Circus World Museum, Baraboo, WI.

Stuart Thayer research collection.

*W. W. Cole's Avant Courier*, 1879

*W. W. Cole's Avant Courier*, 1881

# INDEX

Adair, Miss, 46
Adams, Charles H., 133, 279, 285
Adams, George "Grimaldi", 82, 93, 98, 105, 111, 122, 133
Adams, James R. "Pico", 132, 133, 143, 157, 167, 290, 291, 292
Adams, Rosina, See Rosina Cooke
Agazzi, Lizzie, 242
Alderwick, James, 301
Alexander, C. A., 282, 283
Allen, Lieut., 240
Allen, Walter, 299
American Museum, 46, 47, 49, 129
Amherst, J. H., 17, 20, 22, 25, 29, 36, 37, 272
Amphitheatre, 45
Amphitheatre of the Republic, 42-45
Andrews, Billy, 71, 277, 279
Argye, M. R., 71
Arthur, A. M. C., 291
Ashton, William, 111, 283, 284
Astley, Philip, 13
Astley's Amphitheatre, 39
Austin, Addie, 195
Austin, Addie (Adelaide D'Atalie), 195
Austin, Aimee, 212, 221, 241
Austin, Aimie, See Adelaide D'Atalie
Austin Brothers, 280
Avery, 284
Aymar, John, 274
Aymar, Mrs., 48
Babcock Brothers, 279
Babcock, Stephen S., 60
Bacon & Derious Circus, 31
Bacon, Charles, 40, 51, 271
Bacon's American Circus, 271
Bailey, James A., 6, 157, 159, 173, 187, 249, 250
Baldwin, Gov. Henry P., 79
Baldwin, Silas, 58
Barclay, Frederick, 157, 162, 167, 179, 290, 292
Barclay, Mr. and Mrs. Fred, 292
Barker, Ace, 78
Barlow, Thomas, 271
Barnum, Bailey & Hutchinson, 188, 217, 266, 300
Barnum, Hutchinson and Cole, 300
Barnum, P. T., 12, 46, 75, 83, 90, 91, 94, 98, 103, 119, 123, 129, 144, 151, 187, 188, 191, 192, 203, 217, 218, 222, 233, 249, 251, 253, 254, 258, 264, 300
Barnum's Great Roman Hippodrome, 101, 107, 108
Barnum's Greatest Show on Earth & the Great London Circus, 187
Baron Littlefinger, 129
Bartlett, Jonas, 31
Bartlett, Kittie, 293
Batcheller, George H., 82, 121, 279
Batcheller, William H., 78, 99, 101, 104, 105, 121, 123, 131, 135, 258, 281, 284, 288
Batcheller & Doris, 197-198
Bates, Capt. and Mrs. Martin VanBuren, 127, 140, 153, 154, 155, 285
Bates, Capt. Martin VanBuren, 127, 129, 131, 136, 149
Bedouin Arabs, 174, 195, 201, 202, 203, 205, 206, 209, 212, 215, 221, 242, 295, 298
Beecher, Henry Ward, 130
Bell, 99
Bell, Annie, 240
Bensley Brothers, 279
Berger, Henry, 294
Betty, Master William,

18
Bogardus, Capt. A. H., 195, 295
Bogardus, Edward, 195
Bogardus, Eugene, 195
Bogardus, Henry, 195
Bogardus, Peter, 195
Bolivar (elephant), 191
Booth, Junius Brutus, 271
Bowery Amphitheatre, 33, 34, 42, 47, 51, 54
Bowery Circus, 49
Bowery Theatre, 19, 33, 34, 43, 269, 270
Boyd, W. C., 223, 233, 299, 301
Bristol, Prof., 104
Broadway Circus, 31
Buckley, Harry, 60
Buckley, Matthew, 271
Buckleys, 28
Buloid, Master, 55
Burk, E., 299
Cadwallader, George, 31
California Frank, 255
Campbell, Charles, 292
Campbell, James C., 9, 111, 167, 292, 294, 299, 301
Cappolo, Signor, 78
Cardozo, Sig. Peluzio, 143
Caroline, LaPetite, 37
Caroline, Mlle., 279
Carpenter, Mr., 29
Carroll, John, 78, 277, 280

Carver, W. F., Carver, 254, 256, 257, 258, 260, 263, 301
Case, 277
Castello, Dan, 75
Castle, Fred, 279, 284
Cazanovia, Prof., 240, 291
Chang the Chinese giant, 187
Charles F. Brush Company, 140
Charles Reiche & Bros., 189
Charles, Sam, 282
Chatham Theatre, 48-49, 274
Cherry, 269
Christina, Mlle., 87
Claire Sisters, 132, 143, 149, 290
Claire, Maggie, 122, 132, 149, 157, 288
Claude, Master, 279
Coke, L. E., 299
Cole & Company's Circus, 77
Cole & Orton's Circus, 77
Cole, Margaret C., 3
Cole, Mary Ann, 10, 12, 16, 17, 19, 21, 25, 26, 27-73, 78, 91, 92, 151, 284, 291, 296
Cole, William H., 3, 12, 17, 19, 25, 26, 27-59
Cole's Great New York and New Orleans, 93

Collins, Frank, 300
Collins, Mr., 46
Colvin, E. D., 263, 300, 301
Conklin, George, 3, 5, 8, 11, 12, 82, 83, 88, 91, 92, 98, 101, 103, 111, 123, 124, 131, 133, 135, 142, 157, 168, 173, 174, 175, 179, 184, 191, 193, 236, 242, 255, 260, 280, 292, 299, 301
Conklin, Lizzie, 283
Conklin, Mr. and Mrs. George, 290, 291, 292
Conklin, W. A., 266, 302
Constable, George, 67
Cook, Mr. and Mrs. Wooda, 291
Cook, Wooda, 167, 168, 179, 181, 214, 292
Cooke, Alfred, 268
Cooke, Ernest, 201, 202, 219, 255, 299, 301
Cooke, George, 268
Cooke, Harry Welby, 82, 88, 93, 98, 280
Cooke, Henry, 5, 15-26, 82, 88, 93, 133, 268, 278, 282, 284, 299, 300
Cooke, James, 15-26, 268, 271
Cooke, John Henry, 82
Cooke, Kate, 88, 280
Cooke, Louis E., 2, 5, 9,

53, 59, 129, 130, 131, 159, 160, 167, 169, 170, 171, 173, 175, 182, 183, 186, 189, 191, 216, 217, 219, 224, 275, 290, 292, 293, 294
Cooke, Mary Ann, 3, 133
Cooke, Mary Ann (T. T. Cooke's wife), 271
Cooke, Master George, 18
Cooke, Oceana, 15
Cooke, Rosina, 82, 93, 98, 280, 283
Cooke, Thomas Edwin, 12, 14, 13, 133
Cooke, Thomas Jr., 268
Cooke, Thomas Taplin, 13-26, 29, 133, 268
Cooke, William, 14, 19, 21, 272
Cooke's Amphitheatre, Philadelphia, 20
Cooke's Royal Cir, 64
Cooke's Royal Circus, 27, 28, 36, 42, 68, 268
Cooper & Bailey, 119, 140, 142, 157, 165, 172, 173, 187, 288
Cornell, 277
Count Littlefinger, 291
Count Rosebud, 129, 291
Coup, W. C., 75
Crane & Co.'s Great Oriental Circus, 277

Crane, John P., 275
Crossley & Elder, 122, 284
Curry, Alma, 294
Curtis, Minnie, 283
D'Atalie, Adelaide, 167, 168, 179, 181, 195, 204, 205, 212, 221, 241, 291, 292, 294, 298
Dan Rice's Circus and Great Hippodrome, 279
Davidson, James W., 159
Davis, C. A., 281, 300
Day, Charles H., 5, 218
De Granville, Millie, 222
De Ruth, Mons., 143
Deadeye, Dick, 168, 291
DeComas, 153, 155, 162, 168, 179, 290
DeForest, George W., 279
DeHaven's Great Union Circus, 275
Dinneford, William, 19, 269
Doris, John B., 155, 189, 197, 221, 222, 223, 224, 225, 226, 227, 228, 229, 230, 231, 232, 233, 269, 297
Dubsky, Rosina, 195, 241
Ducrow, Andrew, 15
Duke, Mr., 47

Dunbar & Reno, 290
Dunbar & Vernon, 242
Dunbar, George, 143, 157, 167, 168, 179, 181, 195, 214, 279, 280, 291, 292
Dunbar, Hattie, 214
Dunbar, James, 277
Durang, Charles, 17, 22, 25
Dutton, William, 255, 256, 258, 263
Duverna, William, 49
E. F. & J. Mabie's Magnificent Arena and United States Circus, 58
E. M. Miller & Co., 77-78, 97, 109, 110
Eckles, Fannie, 256
Eckles, Frank, 282, 299-301
Elder, 284
*Ella Hughes* (boat), 114, 284
Ellsler Brothers, 47
Enoch C. Yale's circus, 33
Ethardo, 133
Evans, Ira, 277
Evans, John D., 136, 200, 254, 290, 291, 292
"Fair Star", 268
Faranta, Signor, 266, 302
Farrell, George, 300
Fatima, 240

Fejee Mermaid, 46
Fielding & Co., 110
Fischer, John, 255
Fish, Benjamin, 250, 301
Fisher Brothers, 222
Fitch, T. L., 284, 287, 290
Fletcher, Lellie, 294
Fletcher, Rosa, 294
Fogg & Stickney's Amphitheatre, 23
Forepaugh, Adam, 5, 119, 151, 191, 203, 207, 217, 218, 222, 233, 259, 266, 302
Foster, John, 270
Foster, Joseph, 17, 272
Fox, C., 283
Franconi's Hippodrome, 83
Franklin, Hiram, 35, 48, 58, 273
Franklin, W. E., 266
French, James M., 78, 79
Fryer, Robert, 284
Fuller, L., 254
Gaffney, Andrew, 71, 73, 276, 277
Gallagher, 280
Gardner, Camilla, 36, 40, 41, 42, 54
Gardner, Dan, 35, 40, 42, 54
Gardner, Frank, 111, 121, 122, 123, 149, 153, 155, 157, 162, 164, 195, 205, 258, 283, 284, 290

Gardner, Helen, 294
Gardner, Henry, 273, 277
Gardner, Henry and wife, 273
Gardner, Mildred, 195
Gardner, William, 254
Garton, Joseph, 277
Gaylord, J. B., 9, 153, 175, 217, 279, 282, 290, 292
George W. DeHaven's Union Circus, 68
Gilkison, James A., 64, 69, 71, 276, 277
Glenroy, John, 31, 32, 45
Gomez, Signor, 194
Good, Prof., 254
Gooding, 284
Goodloe, W., 292
Gossin, John, 36, 51, 55, 58, 271
Gossin, Mrs., 36, 48, 50
Grant, U. S., 267
Great London show, 222
Great New York and New Orleans Zoological and Equestrian Exposition, 85
Great Olympic Circus, 39
Green, Dan, 299, 301
Green, W., 299
Greer, Major, 115
Griffin, Judy, 300
Guiteau, 205

Gulick, Joe, 136
Gullen, Mrs., 48
Gurr & Bastian (Harry Gurr and wife), 281
H. Buckley & Co.'s Circus, 60
Hamblin, Thomas, 23, 269
Hamilton, Prof., 222
Hamilton, Tody, 254
Handy, Prof., 241
Harris, Pat, 282
Hart, Harry, 277, 281
Harvey, Julian, 64, 277
Hathaway, E., 299
Hayden, W. R., 9, 88, 131, 284, 287, 290, 292
Hayes, Lizzie May, 92, 281
Hayes, Rutherford B., 117
Heigle, Mr., 47
Herbert Brother, 132
Herbert, John, 299, 300
Hernandez, Dan, 291
Hickey, J. J., 300
Hicks, Stuart, 250, 300
Higby, John, 279
Hitchings, Mr., 47
Hodges, Harry, 255, 299, 301
Hogle, 284
Holland, William, 277, 281, 284
Holliday Street Theatre, 271
Hopkins, Mr., 31

311

Hopper, Jerry, 277
Hopper, William, 270
Hosmer, F. M., 277, 279
Howard, Annie, 240
Howard, Frank, 240
Howes & Co., 44
Howes & Mabie's, 42, 46
Howes, J. R., 61
Howes, Master James, 40
Howes, Nathan, 39, 46, 272
Howes, Seth B., 10, 12, 39, 40, 42, 45, 46, 54, 57, 58, 75, 119, 250, 273
Howes, W., 61
Howes, Wilson and wife, 273
Howes' & Co.'s Circus, 28
Howes' Great London, 75, 76, 103, 119
Hurricane Jim, 290
Hutchinson Papers, 300
Hutchinson, J. L., 249, 250, 253, 254, 266
Hyatt, O. W., 279
Hyers Sisters, 130
Imson, Effie, 255
Ingalls, Judge, 128
J. M. June & Co.'s Great Oriental Circus, 58
J. R. Smith & Speyers, 273
James M. June & Co.'s Hippodrome and Menagerie, 279
James, Mrs., 87
Jardine, Louise, 294
Jeal sisters, 179, 182
Jeal, Linda, 167, 292
Jennie (elephant), 266
Jim (elephant), 193
John B. Doris' Great Inter-Ocean, 221
Johnson, J. F., 277
Johnson, Mark, 57
Johnson, Miss, 55
Johnson, Mr., 40
Johnson, P. H., 282
Johnson, W. C., 273
Jones, C. A., 279
Judson, Andy, 277
Julius Caesar, 271
Jumbo (elephant), 188, 191, 192, 193, 259
June, Titus, Angevine & Co., 33, 34, 36, 39, 61
Kelley, George M., 99, 101, 104
Kelley, William, 299, 300
Kellogg-Carey Concert Company, 130
Kennedy, Dan, 143, 167, 214, 290, 292
Kent, Florence, 283
Keyes, Elise, 93
King, Burke & Co., 266
King, Orin, 297
King, Thomas, 100
Kingsley, Omar, 276
Koble, Margaret, 12
L. B. Lent's Mammoth National Circus, 60-61
La Petite Celeste, 46
Lalla Rookh (elephant), 193
Lambright, John, 292
Lamont Brothers, 277, 280
Lampright, John, 291
Landrum, Carl, 77
Lane Brothers, 195
Larkins, 279
LaThorne, Mons., 51
Lathrop, Sam, 42
Laura (elephant), 266
Lawrence sisters, 122
Lawrence, Mr., 161
Ledesma, Joseph, 255, 258
Lee, H. C., 279
Lemen, Frank, 291, 300
Lemen, Frost, 299, 300
Lent, Lewis B., 10, 60, 61, 62
Leon, James, 72, 78, 98, 111, 122, 132, 133, 214, 221, 241, 255, 263, 277, 279, 280, 281, 283, 300
Leonard, 284
Leroy Brothers, 111, 284
LeTort, Mons., 34
Levens, Fred, 136, 279, 283, 284
Levere, Leo, 279
Linn, 284
Lipton, Louis, 100
Little, 284
Livingston Brothers,

149, 157, 167, 214, 255, 262, 290, 291, 292, 298
Livingston, Frank, 194
Livingston, Miss F., 283
Lizzie (elephant), 193, 266
Long, Harry, 122, 280, 281, 284, 288, 290
Longmire, Michael, 200, 290, 291
Lotina, Mlle., 277
Lowry, Charles, 256
Loyal, George, 111
Loyd, C., 254
Ludlow, Noah, 272
Mabie & Co.'s United States Circus, 59, 67
Mabie, Edmund F., 39, 46
Mabie, Jeremiah, 39, 46
Macarte Brothers, 222
Macarte, Marie, 28, 42, 51
Madigan family, 28, 51
Madigan, E. H., , 223, 299, 301
Madigan, Henry P., 28, 274
Main, Walter L., 123, 285
Manifold, Prof., 78
Maori War Dancers, 174, 178, 195
Marietta Sisters, 73, 78, 242, 280
Marietta, Millie, 282
Marks, Hiram, 73, 98, 101
Marks, Minnie, 73, 98, 105, 106
Marks, Sallie, 222
Marquez, Signor, 132
Marrony, A., 299
Marshall, Fred, 292
Marshall, Humphrey, 127
Marshall, John R., 279
Martin & Sons, 81
Martin, James, 279
Martino, Mons., 67, 130
May, John, 58
*Mazeppa*, 269, 270
McArthur, Archie, 282, 292, 299
McCarthy, A., 300
McEllony, J., 299
McFarland, James, 40, 41, 100, 274
McFarland, Thomas, 35, 55, 58
McFlinn, Sam, 78
McGlasson, G. H., 299, 300, 301
McIntyre, Lizzette, 294
McIntyre, Mr. and Mrs. Tom, 290
McIntyre, Tom, 121, 122, 131, 135, 136, 143, 157, 167, 181, 214, 246, 254, 255, 280, 281, 284, 287, 290, 291, 292, 299, 301
Menkin, Adah Isaacs, 269
Metzler, J. S., 153
Middleton, George, 203
Military Garden, Brooklyn, 29
Mill, Joe, 55
Milton Jaspers, 98, 104, 105, 283
Minnich, Daniel, 55
Monroe, Nellie, 255
Montgomery Queen circus, 131
Moore Family, 222, 277
Morgan, Fanny, 290
Morgan, Frank, 122
Motty, Herr Otto, 34
Munson, Lem, 73, 78
Murray, 281, 284
Murray, Fanny, 294
Murtz, John, 157, 168, 179, 181, 194, 214, 290, 291, 292, 301
Myers, August, 68
Myers, O. P., 299
Nathan Howes & Co., 51
Nathans & Co., 211
National Circus, Philadelphia, 57
National Theatre, N. Y., 19
Needham, Henry, 17, 47, 50, 55, 272
Nestor & Venoa, 204, 205
Newton, 280
Niblo's Garden, 29, 47, 48, 272, 274, 276
Nixon, James M., 51, 272

North, Levi J., 34, 48, 49
North's Hippodrome, Circus, and Menagerie, 279
O'Brien, John V., 88, 189
O'Dale, William, 111, 121, 133, 143, 157, 165, 167, 179, 282, 283, 290, 291, 292
O'Dell, William, 58, 255, 263
Odell, George, 19, 44, 46, 51
Ogden, Abe, 282
Older & Co., 58
Older, Pardon A., 66, 67, 275
Olympic Circus, 58, 273
Organ, William, 144, 155, 164, 292
Orton & Older's Great Southern Circus, 64, 66
Orton Bros.' Circus, 3
Orton, Caroline, 72
Orton, Celeste, 64, 277
Orton, Dennis, 64, 69, 72, 277
Orton, Hattie, 64
Orton, Hiram, 64, 69, 281
Orton, Irene, 64, 72, 277
Orton, Jessie, 279
Orton, Lester, 64, 277
Orton, Miles, 64, 65, 67, 68, 69, 72, 77, 78, 91, 279, 281

Orton, R. Z., 64, 72, 275, 277
Orton's Badger Circus, 65
Orton's Great Southern Circus, 66
Osborn, Thomas, 65
P. T. Barnum's Great Roman Hippodrome, 83
Palmo's Opera, 51
Park Theatre, 44, 273
Passage, George, 60
Patterson, Johnny, 222
Pauline, Mlle., 255
Peale's Museum, 30, 32
Peck, W. K., 299, 301
Pelham, Master, 44
Pelham, Richard, 35, 41, 44
Pentland, Joe, 58
Pepin & Breschard, 99
Perry, Mr., 41
Polish Brothers, 20, 271
Powell, Lee, 78
Prentis, George, 292
Prewitt, Charles, 255
Price, 48, 279
Price, David C., 101
Printer, J. F., 292
Printer, William, 299
Quaglieni, Signor, 133
Quick, Fred, 282
Quirk, Patrick, 121
Rainforth, N., 277
Reagand, Harry, 301
Reiche, Charles, 193
Reis, Walter, 283

Reno, 157
Reno Brothers, 132
Rentfroth, Newton, 282
Restland, Adelaide, 281
Reynolds, Jimmy, 280
Reynolds, William, 279
Rhinehart, Miss S., 283
Rice, 279, 280, 281
Rice, Dan, 51, 211
Richards, Albert, 78, 122, 165, 254, 277, 282, 284, 301
Richards, Jessie Orton, 72, 78, 104, 106, 111, 122, 280, 281, 282, 283, 294
Richardson, Burt, 167, 214, 290, 291, 299
Riel, Alf, 9, 292
Rivers, 280
Rivers, Richard, 58
Robinson and Eldred's Combined Circus, Menagerie, and Hippodrome, 279
Robinson, Eugene, 266
Robinson, James, 203, 204, 205, 206, 212, 214
Robinson, John, 128, 157
Robinson, Yankee, 67, 109, 282
Rockwell & Stone, 10, 45, 47, 48, 50, 272, 274
Rockwell, Alexander, 47, 50, 58, 271, 274

Rockwell. Henry, 47
Rodowski Sisters, 294
Rollins, Billy, 255
Rosalie, Miss, 279
Ross, Charley, 98
Runnells, Burnell, 58
Russian roller skaters, 204
Ryland, Elena Jeal, 167, 291, 292
Sackett & Covel, 51-53
Salbini Troupe, 222
Salomonski, Mlle. Johanna, 122, 283
Samson (elephant), 189, 190, 191, 193, 194, 197, 199, 211, 216, 236, 237, 243, 245, 246, 259, 266, 294, 296, 298
Sands, Lent & Co., 54
Sawyer, Jennie, 283
Schroff, Paul, 78
Seal, David A., 93, 94
Sebastian, Romeo, 131, 133, 135
Sefton, William, 269
Sells Bros., 157, 229, 231, 232, 266, 297, 302
Sells, Allen, 266
Sells, Ephraim, 266
Sergeant, George, 58
Seth B. Howes & Co., 33
Sherman, 277
Sherwood, Charles, 58
Sherwood, Virginia, 58

Shindle, John, 33
Showles, Willie, 222
Shumake, Jack, 191, 259, 299
Siegrist Brothers, 222
Silbon family, 255, 259, 260, 262, 264
Silbon, Charles, 259
Silbon, Eddie, 259
Silbon, Kate, 259
Silbon, Walter, 259
Simpson, Edmund, 44, 273, 284
Sivalls, Charles, 175, 263, 284, 290, 292, 294, 299, 301
Smith, Sol, 272
Smith, William, 55
Snow Brothers, 122
Sours, J., 290
St Leon circus, 173
St Leon, Gus, 173
St Leon, Mark, 171, 172
Stanley, Maude, 277
Steere, Col. and Mrs., 240
Stevens, Fred, 287
Stevens, George, 279
Stevens, Master, 38
Stevens, Mr. and Mrs. William O'Dale, 291
Stevens, S. H., 302
Stevens, William O'Dale, 167, 182, 292
Stickney, Rosaline, 133
Stickney, S. P., 133
Stokes, Ella, 155, 222, 290

Stokes, Emma, 155
Stokes, Kate, 155
Stokes, Spencer Q., 155
Stone, 274
Stone, Eaton, 49
Stone, Oscar, 50
Stout, C., 300
Stowe & Orton, 72-77
Stowe, Charles, 254
Stowe, James, 282
Stowe, John, 72, 77
Stowe, William, 277
Stowe's Silver Cornet Band, 97
Sutherland Sisters, 216, 297
Swan, Anna Hannon, 128, 129
Sweet, George, 38, 58
Sweet, Isaac, 51
Swiss Brothers, 35, 36, 37
Taylor, Maggie, 283
Thayer, Stuart, 59, 67, 100, 272
Thompson & Vanderveer, 266
Thorpe, Mary Ann, 13
Tilden, Samuel J., 117
Tilton, Theodore, 130
*Timour the Tartar*, 269
Tinkham, Joseph, 65, 67
Tobin, M. W., 294
Tom (elephant), 193, 266
Tom Thumb, 187
Tourniaire, Benoit, 133
Tourniaire, Ferdinand,

133
Tourniaire, François, 133
Tourniaire, Louise, 133
Tourniaire, Theodore, 133
Traber, J. Milton, 77
Tryon, John, 10, 47, 51, 54
Tubbs, Charles, 64, 67, 69
Tufts, Thomas, 42
Turner, Nap B., 35, 38, 40, 51, 274
Turner, T. V., 35
Turnour, Millie, 167, 292
Vacquero riders, 242
Van Amburgh, Isaac, 57, 191
Van Zandt Brothers, 73, 78, 90, 280, 281, 282
Van Zandt, Anson, 98, 104, 105, 122, 214, 241, 280, 283, 291, 292, 299, 300
Vangand, A., 290
Vauxhall Garden, 17
Victory Circus, 51
Virella, Joseph, 282
W. C. Coup's New Monster Shows, 157
W. W. Cole's Colossal Circus and Animal Show, 77
Walker, Master, 282
Walker, Mattie, 283
Walters, E., 292

Wambold, Carlotta, 142
Waring, Miss, 270
Watson, Carlotta, 258
Watson, Fred, 255, 256, 258, 264
Watson, Lottie, 255
Webb, Judd C., 282
Welch & Bartlett, 34
Welch, Bartlett & Co., 31 Welsh, Bartlett & Co., 272
Welch's Olympic Circus, 44
Welch's Parisian Hippodrome, 279
Welch's Philadelphia circus, 272
Welch, Rufus, 11, 31, 44, 273
Weller, Charles, 299
Wells, Amelia, 272
Wells, John, 17, 19, 21, 271, 272
Wells, Louisa, 272
Wells, Mary Ann, 272
Wemyss, Francis C., 20, 23, 25
Wentworth, Walter, 277
Wenzel, Capt. William, 114
Wescott, George, 277
White, Mr., 47
White, W., 282, 284, 290
Whitlock, William, 35
Wicks, E. V., 290
Wicks, George, 292
Willhelm, A. B., 110

Williams, Bobby, 17, 19, 22, 29, 50, 272
Williams, Frank, 256
Wilson, C. A., 277, 279
Wires, R. S., 224
Woolford, George, 17, 19, 25, 269, 270, 271
Woolford, Mrs., 19
Wooters, J. C., 300
Worland, John, 255, 258, 300, 301
Worrell, William, 281
Yale & Co., 33
Yale, Howes & Co., 33
Young, 250
Young, Brigham, 88
Young, D., 40, 42
Young, Merritt, 300
Zingra, 93, 103
Zoluti, Aggie, 240
Zoyara, Ella, 276

www.ingramcontent.com/pod-product-compliance
Lightning Source LLC
Chambersburg PA
CBHW032039090426
42744CB00004B/63